PLANTATION TO NATION: CARIBBEAN MUSEUMS AND NATIONAL IDENTITY

EDITED BY
ALISSANDRA CUMMINS,
KEVIN FARMER,
AND
ROSLYN RUSSELL

PLANTATION TO NATION: CARIBBEAN MUSEUMS AND NATIONAL IDENTITY

EDITED BY
ALISSANDRA CUMMINS,
KEVIN FARMER,
AND
ROSLYN RUSSELL

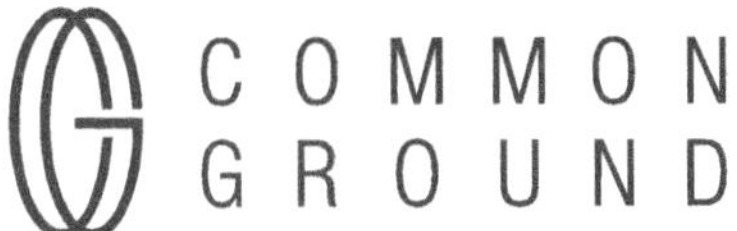

First published in Champaign, Illinois in 2013 by
Common Ground Publishing LLC as part of the
Inclusive Museum book series

Library of Congress Cataloging-in-Publication Data

Plantation to nation: Caribbean museums and national identity / edited by Alissandra Cummins, Kevin Farmer, and Roslyn Russell.

p. cm. — (Inclusive museum series)

Includes bibliographical references and index.

ISBN 978-1-61229-073-7 (pbk: alk. paper) — ISBN 978-1-61229-074-4 (pdf)

1. Museums—Caribbean Area—History. 2. Museums—Social aspects—Caribbean Area. 3. Museum techniques—Caribbean Area. 4. National characteristics, Caribbean. I. Cummins, Alissandra. II. Farmer, Kevin. III. Russell, Roslyn.

AM29.P53 2012
069.09729-^23

2012029201

Front cover top image photo credit: Governor Robinson going to church in Bridgetown, c. 1745, artist unknown, Collection: Barbados Museum & Historical Society

Front cover bottom image photo credit: Young Cubana in Old Havana, 2012, by Alissandra Cummins

Table of Contents

Acknowledgements

First and foremost, we wish to acknowledge the scholarship and commitment of key historians and museum persons who were critical sources of support for the preparation of this book, including Senator Sir Trevor Carmichael and Professor Sir Woodville Marshall for their leadership and commitment to improving museum standards in the Caribbean, Mr. Michael Rutherford, Dr. Debbie McCollin, Prof. Isabel Rigol and Dr. Lovell Francis for discussions on Caribbean identity and the need to preserve our heritage, our museums and our collections. Prof. Michel-Rolph Trouillot was a major source of inspiration for the interrogation of the underlying principles and ideologies which had guided the development of our region's museums. His recent death represents an unimaginable loss for the region.

We would also like to thank the staff of the Barbados Museum & Historical Society, most particularly Mrs. Angela Boyce, Ms. Harriet Pierce, Mr. Kerron Hamblin who provided excellent assistance in assembling both information and images for various authors, and Ms. Kaye Hall for her wonderful technical and administrative support, as well as the Common Ground publishing team, who were not only invaluable in the planning, organisation and publication of *Plantation to Nation: Caribbean Museums and National Identity,* but facilitated all our requirements and made the process as smooth as possible.

Of course, none of this could have happened without the enthusiasm, dedication and hard work of our colleagues and the contributors, most of whose chapters were specifically written for this book, but also for their help in identifying other writers and other untapped sources of information for the book. Each author has been invited to participate based on the extensive knowledge and expertise they bring to issues concerning the history and development of museums and museology throughout the region, and all of whom were immediately responsive and committed to the cause. Moreover, their commitment to honouring the memories and perspectives of individuals with respect to the museological praxis, its issues and paradigms, its challenges and revelations, constitutes the book's main strength and significance.

Thanks also must go to the institutions and individuals who provided additional information for the chapters whenever this was requested. We also wish to acknowledge the University of the West Indies Press and Duke University Press who were generous in their permissions to republish two key articles in the book. Finally we offer our deepest gratitude to our families, as it is important to recognise that, without their unstinting support, preparations for this book would have been virtually impossible.

Alissandra Cummins, Kevin Farmer, and Roslyn Russell
Bridgetown and Canberra November 2013

Foreword

The Empire Survey of Museums in the British Empire, conducted between 1931 and 1936, was undertaken during a period of administrative restructuring that embodied the British vision for the entire colonial empire. The Survey gathered evidence of the need for technical services that provided justification for the deployment of professional curators to colonial museums abroad. It also provided, for the first time in the history of the museum, a detailed inventory of museum institutions at a specific point in time, not just in the West Indies but worldwide. Broadly speaking, the thrust of imperial history in Britain at the time was to focus on the development and achievements of the British Empire and, as Godfrey, Lord Elton described it in 1945, her 'civilising mission'.[1] Viewed in that context, West Indian history is part of a complex historical narrative in which competing values are always jostling for attention. The colonial museum was therefore not simply a means of representing local history or identity; in essence it was concerned with minimalizing (if not masking) those complexities. This had the effect of reducing West Indian history (and other territorial histories) almost to irrelevance, or to a caricature of British (and of course European) history. Ultimately, the West Indian museum at this time functioned almost as a form of collective amnesia.

Plantation to Nation seeks to explore, explain and engage in discussion on the evolution of museums of the Caribbean. This publication first reviews the construction of traditional images and myths of 'national' identity promoted within the West Indian museum a century ago; it then highlights some of the important factors that began to erode these established ideas of identity and contributed to a widening historical consciousness. The authors examine which history - or more to the point, whose history - informed the content and collections of the West Indian museums of the period, and they interrogate some of the assumptions that underline the process of history-making in the museum context.

As Chris Healy has argued, the museum 'installed the nation-state as *the* object of collective identification',[2] performing an essential act of nation creation to which all viewers were expected to subscribe. These selective displays of objects gave authority and legitimacy, in the eyes of both governments and audiences, to the ideas and notions presented as 'authentic'. The importance of these exhibits as displays of power and influence, and their subsequent impact on different sectors of society, should not be underestimated in situations where it became essential to find ways to draw all British subjects together. The results recorded by the Empire Survey Report

[1] Lord Elton, *Imperial Commonwealth*, London, Collins, 1945.

[2] C. Healy, 'Histories and Collecting: Museums, Objects and Memories,' in K. Darian-Smith & P. Hamilton (eds.), *Memory and History in Twentieth Century Australia*, Melbourne, 1994, p. 38.

and Directory of Museums in the West Indies were especially revealing. Specifically the report noted that:

> However difficult the situation may be in Canada, South Africa, or Australia, the island museums suffer from similar disadvantages plus that of almost insufferable isolation ...These particulars, with the information now available, permit us to make a comparison of the cultural efforts these various islands or isolated colonies are making.[3] ...The islands of the British Empire present one of the most difficult problems in the realm of cultural services, and the hope is that in at least one area efforts will be made to evolve the ideal museum and art gallery policy for an island colony.[4]

The Survey Commissioners also acknowledged that historical and possibly 'psychological' reasons might be responsible for the particular circumstances of West Indian museums. Their remoteness, seclusion and insularity were perceived as stumbling blocks, especially when viewed through a prism of Eurocentrism. For the colonial observer and colonial elites, the history of the islands began with their colonization. Implicit in such a rule was the binary perspective that 'colony' equaled 'civilization'. Such a view of island history placed all other histories 'beyond the boundary' and outside the mainstream. Therefore island history could only exist as part of imperial history, not as it is taught today, but as it was perceived over 100 years ago, as dominant and omnipotent.

In reality, such thinking was moribund. The succeeding decades bore witness to a growing self-awareness and burgeoning independence movement that over time engaged that colonial mindset, replacing it with a Caribbean sense of self that the Commissioners would be hard pressed to identify with today. Caribbean identity is both pre- and post-Columbian in its genesis, an identity born of displacement, appropriation and struggle, nurtured to an adulthood that was steeped in survival. The ability to view and interpret such a past is seen in its museums, collections and interpretations. Given the essentially fragmentary nature of Caribbean culture and identity, the term 'intangible heritage', rather than solely the permanence of objects, perhaps best elides with the region's notions of valid expressions of Caribbean history, identity and culture. Contemporary Caribbean curatorship now requires that museums contend directly with how to represent the silences, absences and dislocations which so frequently prescribe both the historical and modern day experiences. Stuart Hall has spoken of the need for museums

> to understand their collections and their practices as what I can only call 'temporary stabilisations'. What they are - and they must be

[3] Henry A. Miers, and S. F. Markham. Compilers. 'Introduction' to *Reports on the Museums of Ceylon, British Malaya, the West Indies, etc. to the Carnegie Corporation of New York,* The Museums Association, London, 1933, p.7.

[4] Museums Association Report, p.8.

> specific things or they have no interest - is as much defined by what they are not. Their identities are determined by their constitutive outside; they are defined by what they lack and by their other ... It has to be aware that it is a narrative, a selection, whose purpose is not just to disturb the viewer but to itself be disturbed by what it cannot be, by its necessary exclusions ... it has to turn its criteria of selectivity inside out so that the viewer becomes [aware] of both the frame and what is framed (Hall, 1990).[5]

This publication presents for the first time an anthology that aspires, in its pan-Caribbean focus, to chronicle, through case studies and discussions of what is past, a developing museum identity, shedding its imperial antecedents as its audiences demand change and strive to give voice to fledgling Caribbean identities. In fact the Island museum is no longer a point of derision: instead it may be a point of departure from which to describe and ascribe to the ethos of Caribbean museum praxis. Its nexus being the acceptance of duality and change, whether in the past or present, pre-Columbian/post-Columbian, pre-emancipation/post-emancipation, pre or post-independence, or tangible/intangible. This duality is now the basis of the Caribbean museum, the space not so much contested but engaged to allow for the voices from past and present to be heard at one and the same time.

The UN Declarations of Barbados 1994 and Mauritius 2004 have emphasized the need to address the location and challenges of Small Island Development States (SIDS) in the contemporary world. Reviews and discussions are already underway for the Barbados+20 deliberations. These will be debated and discussed by the international community in the context of progress made in the achievement of the UN Millennium Development Goals. A new set of Sustainable Development Goals (SDGs) promise to shape the agenda and priorities in 2015. SDGs will be significant for SIDS, which are most under threat by the impacts of climate change. In this context what are the roles and relevance of museums? *Plantation to Nation* is a seminal volume that makes a timely contribution to the contemporary and contextual museological discourse.

Common Ground and its President Professor Dr. Bill Cope are delighted to present the book *Plantation to Nation* to its readers. It is an important publication that promotes cross cultural understanding in a rapidly changing world. We sincerely appreciate the editors Alissandra Cummins, Kevin Farmer and Roslyn Russell for their attention and perseverance to ensure contributions that mark a turning point in Caribbean and, indeed, SIDS scholarship.

---

[5] S. Hall, 1990, 'Cultural identity and diaspora', in J. Rutherford (ed.), *Identity: Community, Culture, Difference.* London, Lawrence and Wishart.

We are also grateful to Jamie Burns, Brian Kornell, and Ian Nelk, former and current Managing Editors of Common Ground Publishing for making the publication possible.

Professor Amareswar Galla, PhD
Editor, Inclusive Museum Series, Common Ground Publishing, Champaign, IL
Executive Director, International Institute for the Inclusive Museum,
Copenhagen & Hyderabad

List of Illustrations

Introduction

Haitian anthropologist Michel-Rolph Trouillot, in his discussion on how the current global Westernized hegemony treats specific historical events, events chosen for their relevance to the text of Western dominance, has addressed absences (or silences) as 'inherent in the creation of sources, the first moment of historical production' (Trouillot, 1995, p. 51). People and places that are designated 'Third World' often find their history has (or has been) 'disappeared'. He references complex historiographical occurrences of this process of historical production, whereby black and poor societies were not just physically ostracized, but in a sense mentally too as they basically 'disappeared' from the historical text. He states: 'History reveals itself only through the production of specific narratives. What matters most are the process and conditions of such narratives ... Only through that overlap can we discover the differential exercise of power that makes some narratives possible and silences others.[6]

This book is the first to focus on the growth and development of Caribbean museums and museology, to address museums across the region regardless of nation or language, and to allow for much-needed discourse on their evolution, particularly in relation to the growing field of museum and

---

[6] Michel-Rolph Trouillot, *Silencing the Past: Power and the Production of History* (Boston: Beacon Press, 1995), p. 25.

heritage studies. Its publication was originally intended to celebrate 20 years of the Museums Association of the Caribbean in 2009. This for various reasons did not eventuate, although a very successful conference was held in Barbados that year to mark the occasion.

Plantation to Nation: Caribbean Museums and National Identity addresses the challenges faced by museums in the Caribbean region, both historically and in the contemporary setting. To date the region's museums have largely been sidelined in the growing field of new museology, especially where this explores the legacies of colonial museum frameworks and the subjugation of local cultures and identities to broader colonialist discourses over the previous two centuries.

The growth in the sheer numbers of museums in the region in the post-independence era, and the expansion of the field of museum studies (as part of heritage studies) which has gained ground within the curricula of regional universities also point to the need for a more intensive examination of Caribbean museums in the early decades of the twenty-first century. Outside the museums, there is a growing interest within communities in expressing elements of their heritage. Some museums in the region have become focal points for such communal expressions of heritage; and others have positioned themselves to take a leadership position in articulating local identities.

The editors, and the contributors whose chapters are included in this book, also view it as a significant contribution to broadening the focus on Small Island Developing States (SIDS), and to identifying those factors that particularly affect SIDS communities. We believe that, by generating new knowledge and consolidating both historical and current museum developments in the Caribbean in book form, this volume will be of interest to all museum professionals across the world, but in particular those in the 52 Small Island Developing States.

The book contains sixteen chapters that make reference, to a greater or lesser degree, to museum developments in nineteen countries: in alphabetical order, Antigua and Barbuda, The Bahamas, Barbados, Belize, Bermuda, Cuba, Curaçao, Dominica, Dominican Republic, Guyana, Haiti, Jamaica, Martinique, Nevis, Saint Lucia, St Vincent and the Grenadines, Suriname, Trinidad & Tobago, and Turks and Caicos Islands.

The majority of these nation states are islands, with the exceptions of Belize, Guyana and Suriname that border the Caribbean Sea, and also share similar histories of colonialism with Caribbean island nations. Bermuda is included, although it is not categorized as a Caribbean nation, as it is a collection of tropical islands in the Atlantic Ocean which has also experienced aspects of the same history as its Caribbean counterparts. It is still in fact a self-governing British Crown Colony.

This book is organised according to the themes of 'Plantation' and 'Nation'. 'Plantation' in this context stands for the colonialist period and the museum institutions and practices that had their genesis in that era of Caribbean history, and the ways in which these are being interrogated and reinvigorated by the application of new museology. The term 'Nation', as employed in this book, embodies all attempts by museums in the Caribbean to articulate and assert the identities of national cultures in the post-independence period; and to redefine the idea of the 'museum' and its operations to better express the historical complexity, richness and diversity of these Caribbean identities.

Museums and collections that had their origins in the colonialist era, and were founded and assembled in line with the prevailing motivations that governed collecting in the nineteenth and early twentieth centuries - scientific curiosity, administrative control of populations, potential for economic exploitation, and antiquarianism - existed and still exist in a number of Caribbean island nation states, as they do elsewhere in the world. Coupled with this tendency in the Caribbean context is the legacy of slavery which, even now, is in danger of being submerged and obscured in museums and heritage sites by narratives that occlude or diminish the histories of the enslaved.

The first chapters of this book, dealing essentially with the 'prehistory' and history of Caribbean museums, consider museums and collections that arose from this colonialist legacy, and assess how far they have travelled from the museum ideology that formed them to a museographical praxis that acts to transcend and transform this legacy. In the course of examining this transition, contributors analyse the complications that arise when memories conflict and historical realities are challenged by nostalgia for the past on the part of some groups, and a strong desire to excavate submerged memories and narratives by others.

Alissandra Cummins in **'Natural History = National History: Early Origins and Organizing Principles of Museums in the English-Speaking Caribbean'** investigates the ways in which local histories were established, organized and presented within early regional museums, modeled upon the Imperial Institute. Established to satisfy the demands for scientific observation, documentation and presentation of the accumulating knowledge emanating from nineteenth-century tropical environments, it was designed and driven largely by the imperial government's determined pursuit, control and exploitation of the region's natural (including human) resources to improve the economy of the Empire. This then becomes the context for understanding the ways in which the 'past' was made, authenticated and disseminated, and the types of historical narratives that were constructed in this process. She establishes the influential role of the region's governors seeking 'accommodation' of newly emancipated populations within the context of colonial society, and that it is the very long 'memory' of these 'scientific' considerations which influenced the region's collecting, exhibiting and interpretation of new knowledge until well past the political independence of regional nation states.

In **'Haiti, museums and public collections: their history and development after 1804',** Marie-Lucie Vendryes examines the glaring lack of preservation and enhancement of public collections in Haitian museums subsequent to the achievement of the first major regional independence movement, following the Haitian Revolution whose symbolism for the region cannot be overstated. The reasons: the suppression - or lack - of legal instruments that regulate these memorials and heritage, the difficulty of sustaining the museums, and the absence of a reflection on the choice of a memorial and ethics in preservation. Finally Vendryes examines the international context that has undermined Haiti and makes it susceptible to the abuse of illicit exploitation of its cultural property. This chapter aims to provide a profile of a public institution, the Museum of the Haitian National Pantheon (MUPANAH), to examine the deficiency in its collections, and to try to identify the causes of its deterioration. At a fundamental level this chapter questions why Haiti is so poor in museums when it is so rich in heritage, clearly paralleling the social context.

José Linares, as both the premier museographer and museum architect in Cuba, draws on decades of invaluable experience with the redesign and development of several of the island's major museum institutions to discuss **'The History and Evolution of Cuban Museums'.** He opines that the museum phenomenon in this part of the world still needs a particular study and a preliminary analysis of its historical, political and social nature. This is why any analysis of these institutions must take into account these multiple perspectives.

Linares' examination of the process of restructuring Cuba's museums - mostly in historic buildings of high heritage value - in the post-revolution context, takes as its point of departure the multiple influences endemic in a society such as Cuba's, where for geographical, historical and cultural reasons European, American and Caribbean cultures and histories have coincided. He insists that it cannot be analysed synchronically with the European evolution of museums nor with North America, although resonances with the latter's developmental process might be demonstrated. Rather he concludes that it is the conditions deriving from both indigenous and immigrant populations, as a result of territorial domination and occupation processes, and the origin of its occupants which may hold the key. Linares' approach in addressing the issue of museological development is through the lens of architectural intervention and lighting as important elements in Cuban museum design, aimed at more effective object-subject communication. Above all, Linares asserts that it is Cuba's specific political and cultural evolution which makes it a phenomenon in the process of identity affirmation, and its consolidation and formation as a nation.

Two chapters trace the evolution of Caribbean museums through the differing though related trajectories of natural history collections and a national art museum. In **'The natural history collections of the University of the West Indies (UWI)'** Mike G. Rutherford traces the story of the natural history resources identifying their principal collectors from their colonialist origins to the present, and contextualizes their connection to and current use, alongside academically generated collections, in educating present and future generations of Caribbean students through the production of seminal publications and, more recently, websites with online accessible databases. He essentially establishes for the first time the bases for the development of the university-based natural history and fossil collections in the Anglophone Caribbean.

Veerle Poupeye, in her chapter, **'The National Gallery of Jamaica: A Critical History'**, examines the history of the National Gallery of Jamaica, established in 1974 as the first national art gallery in the Anglophone Caribbean. Through the development of its collections and through its permanent and temporary exhibitions, education programmes and publications, this institution has articulated a Jamaican art history. Poupeye goes on to describe how these activities have been received by the key stakeholders within the Jamaican artistic community, generating a dialogue which has often been contentious. Special attention is also paid to how the Gallery has engaged, or failed to engage, with local and overseas audiences, and whether it has succeeded in asserting its relevance and utility to Jamaican society as a whole. These developments are examined against the backdrop of the socio-political and economic development of post-colonial Jamaica, the continuing debates about Jamaican culture and its representation, and developments in local cultural policy as well as global and regional museum practice.

Two authors use the context of an historic fort for their examination of the evolution of museum institutions in Bermuda and Suriname. The acknowledgement and interpretation of the colonial fortification as the dominant artefact within a continuing discourse on national identity is a critical aspect which continues to affect many Caribbean museums. Edward Harris relates three decades of museum development in his chapter, **'The Creation of the National Museum of Bermuda, 1974-2011'**, beginning when a small group of determined volunteers established the maritime museum in the nine-acre fort in the old Royal Naval Dockyard. In 1980, the first professional staff member was appointed and the Bermuda Maritime Museum was reorganized to be independent of government charity. Starting in 1981, the Museum began its major research programmes in history and archaeology (both land and marine) and in the later 1980s it established an annual journal for the dissemination of such work. Major buildings restoration has taken place over the last three decades, with the Commissioner's House being opened in May 2000. With a range of exhibitions and community heritage involvement, the Bermuda Maritime Museum has become, *de facto,* the national museum of Bermuda, exemplifying similar museum evolutionary processes elsewhere in the region.

Hilde Neus similarly describes the creation of a modern museum in an historic fort in **'Recapturing History: Suriname Museum in Fort Zeelandia'**. The Suriname Museum Foundation, host of the largest artefact and antiquarian books collection in Suriname and housed in the historic building of Fort Zeelandia (1652), has lived through a precarious history of developments in the last fifteen years, in different respects. The chapter examines the tumultuous events of the museum's development and establishment which, because of a *coup d'état,* was forced to move in 1981 to its storage facilities and had to make do with declining funds and reduced space for exhibitions. It survived through these difficult years. The museum in Fort Zeelandia was reopened in 1995 and a number of exhibitions have been organized, sometimes with aid from abroad (mainly from the Netherlands), sometimes by using its own resources. A productive educational programme, set up in 2000, has been very successful, with the yearly number of school children visiting the museum rising from 750 to almost 7000. The museum also aims to make its collection accessible to a larger audience by publishing books in the series 'Libri Musei Surinamensis'. However, despite these successes, the fortunes of the museum remain uncertain; once again its tenuous hold on the Fort may be threatened as the building's value as a symbol of power is harnessed once again under a new dispensation.

The plantation, and the system of slavery that underpinned and sustained it, is the context for two chapters on museological strategies in Martinique and Suriname and Curaçao. Christine Chivallon, in **'Museography and Places of Remembrance of Slavery in Martinique or the Gaps in a Memory Difficult to Express'** brings a museological focus to actions now being conducted in Martinique to manage the island's cultural heritage, and calls attention to the ways in which slavery has been reworked. She identifies two strategies for handling this past that relate to socio-racial hierarchies: one seeks to make slavery visible, whereas the other effaces its historical reality. The analysis of these different strategies reveals the inadequacy of the language of museum science, which copies the European model with its 'chronological snare'; and shows how the 'places of memory' of a colonial nostalgia are capable of simultaneously constructing themselves in these attempts to recover the memory of the period of slavery.

Valika Smeulders, in **'New perspectives in heritage presentations in Suriname and Curaçao: From Dutch colonial museums to diversifying representations of enslavement'**, describes how the first museums in Suriname and Curaçao presented local heritage from a colonial perspective. From the 1990s onwards, however, with ongoing decolonization of Caribbean museums and the global 'de-silencing' of slavery history, she establishes that the number of representations of slavery is growing. The previously underrepresented social history of transatlantic slavery seems to conquer museum walls, while simultaneously occupying specific new alternative and commercially driven heritage sites.

Using Curaçao and Suriname as case studies, this chapter discusses five types of slavery representations in and beyond the classic museum setting: in seats of colonial rule, plantations, sites of resistance, pilgrim products and replicas. These representations attract distinctive audiences, mostly because of selective marketing channels. Thus, in current slavery representations, traditional museum audience boundaries and subject specific boundaries including education, income and age, national identities, ethnic distinctions and racial identification are either bridged, or reconfirmed.

The latter part of the book largely examines new directions that have informed museum developments in the Caribbean since independence from colonial rule. The independence experiment in the Caribbean emerged full-fledged from the 1960s, continued evolving into the 1980s and has apparently reached a plateau as we enter the second decade of the twenty-first century. This experiment has resulted in the creation of independent multiparty democratic states with varying demographics comprising persons of African, European and Asian descent, with some countries - notably Dominica, St Vincent, Belize and Guyana - nurturing vibrant if diminutive descendant communities of the indigenous people of the region. Culturally diverse, the region shares a common pre- and post-colonization history, though nuanced by the peculiar local histories and geographies of the individual countries.

Emerging Anglophone Caribbean nation-states turned their attention to the creation of a national identity that went beyond designing a flag, singing a national anthem and reciting a national pledge. The role of identity creation became the core mandate of cultural institutions, many of which were museums and heritage institutions. Kevin Farmer, in **'New Museums on the Block',** examines the post-independence landscape for Caribbean museums, and the contested representations that can result when majority populations assert their own culture as the basis for national identity. The duality of contested identities between state sanctioned and marginalized groupings is the focus of this chapter.

Roslyn Russell looks at new museums and displays in Barbados over the last decade in **'Framing identity, encouraging diversity - recent museum developments in Barbados',** at a time when government policy has enabled significant investment in museum and heritage development. Private institutions have also developed museums and heritage sites interpreting aspects of Barbados's history and celebrating its social diversity. The chapter explores the themes of the role of museums, galleries and heritage institutions in building national identity; the role played by museums and heritage sites in building audiences both within the Barbadian community and among tourists visiting the island; and the ways in which Barbados's museums and heritage sites - including the World Heritage-listed Historic Bridgetown and its Garrison - reflect its rich history and cultural diversity. Telling the story of Barbadian identity in museums also means exploring the ways in which this has intersected with broader historical themes that have worldwide relevance: slavery and its abolition; immigration and emigration; the advances in democratisation of parliamentary institutions; and the rediscovery and restatement of diasporic identities.

Luisa De Peña Díaz, in **'The Memorial Museum of the Dominican Resistance: Its composition and role in society',** traces the evolution of this new museum in Santo Domingo, and its mission to convey the compelling story of human rights violations and the ultimate triumph of democratic values. The museum's narrative begins in 1916 and ends in 1978, including the precedents and consequences of the dictatorship that lasted from 1930 to 1961, and revealing the circumstances that led to a dictatorship and its social consequences.

The Memorial Museum of the Dominican Resistance was born almost two decades ago as an initiative by the victims' families with the objective of conserving its assets and memories. Since then, the museum has become known today as an institution of excellence for rescuing the memory of recent history, for teaching about democratic values and human rights, and for providing an Investigation Center to increase awareness of those values and rights. The museum's collections include a great variety of documents, photographs, audio-visual productions, and victims' personal items, all of them used to inform present and future generations of Dominicans, and the rest of the world, of the need to consolidate a society based on the culture of peace, tolerance, non-discrimination, truth, justice and respect for human rights.

Rebecca Tortello's chapter, **'"Children Get Your Culture" - Museums, Individualism and Nationalism in Jamaica',** uses a cross-section of children's museum experiences to consider the role of culture in education policy and practice in Jamaica. The discussion is primarily based on the reactions of schoolchildren (a significant Jamaican museum-going audience) to their museum experiences, and it is specifically guided by a theoretical examination of the roles museums, as informal education institutions, play as educators, culture brokers, citizenship awareness and community makers.

By considering the role of museums in Jamaica's education policy and practice, this chapter expands critical literature on museum education. It both adds a developing country's perspective, and explores how museums stimulate individualism and creativity. It therefore addresses issues related to the resilience of culture and pedagogical skills related to the rise of intellectual capital. Tortello concludes that museums, as they exist in Jamaica and, by extension, in other developing countries, whether geared at child audiences or not, can provide unique opportunities for the growth of progressive education and the stimulation of critical thinking, creativity, and the appreciation of self and others - tenets of global citizenship.

Nigel Sadler's chapter, **'Outreach or out of reach? Seeking new audiences: The Turks and Caicos National Museum Children's Club'** describes an innovative outreach programme designed for the islands' young audience, a Children's Club. Museums have been moving towards more audience inspired projects leading to the development of a wide variety of outreach programmes, activities and exhibitions. In 2002 the Turks and Caicos National Museum started an outreach programme to bring in new local audiences, who had in the past valued the museum and its work, but had rarely participated. At the heart of this development was the Children's Club. The club was formed to attract children to utilise the museum resources and to offer a facility where they could learn about their heritage and environmental issues in a fun way and in a form that did not exist in the formal education process. This chapter discusses how the Children's Club was formed, operated and the activities it held, and how it fitted into the more general museum outreach programmes on offer.

For young nation states like Saint Lucia the development of a national identity is essential if they are to survive in the present environment of globalization. The development of a national identity depends to a great extent on the history and heritage of the nation. Winston Phulgence, in **'Museums and the Challenge for Heritage Organizations in Saint Lucia',** examines the ways history and heritage may be used in the public education process in order to create a distinct national identity. Museums must play an important role in this process. They protect and preserve heritage and artefacts and, through displays, make them accessible to the wider public and create awareness in ways that written history cannot. Heritage organizations started work in Saint Lucia as early as the 1950s. In the 1970s small museums displayed some of the archaeological heritage of the island. Despite these early attempts, after 30 years of independence there is still no national museum on Saint Lucia. This chapter documents persistent attempts to set up museums on the island, with a focus on a small museum created by the Archaeological and Historical Society during the 1970s. Another attempt by the Saint Lucia National Trust in the 1980s is also explored, along with the challenges that heritage organizations have faced in establishing museums in Saint Lucia in both the pre and post-Independence periods.

In complete contrast to the decades long struggle for control of St. Lucia's heritage collections is the scenario outlined in our final chapter, with the opening in 1992 of a museum in Nassau, the Junkanoo Expo, to display costumes from the annual parade. The museum provided the first public exhibition context for costumes outside of the performance frame of the parade. In her essay **'Destroying While Preserving Junkanoo: The Junkanoo Museum in the Bahamas',** Krista Thompson raises a number of critical questions. Was the museum, in its efforts to display costumes that were typically discarded after the festivities, interceding in the cycle of costume creation and destruction? Was the museum inherently unsuitable for the display of the traditionally temporal arts of Junkanoo?

Ultimately, the final word goes to Thompson, who questions the relevance of the existing museum model for Caribbean societies, and suggests the consideration of new museological approaches which resonate with traditional sensibilities in the modern Caribbean context. Barbadian novelist George Lamming has opined that "this thing we call the Caribbean is an unfinished project and where we are now, it seems to me, is still at the 'scaffolding' of that project. No one has any idea what it will be in another fifty or a hundred years."[7] The editors are convinced that this publication may help reveal the stages through which the Caribbean 'project' must, can and ultimately will, progress.

[7] *The Barbados Advocate*, 8 April 2012, p. 13.

Chapter 1

Natural History = National History:

Early Origins and Organizing Principles of Museums in the English-speaking Caribbean

Alissandra Cummins

The eighteenth- and nineteenth-century British model of the museum was transported and applied, not merely to the West Indies but to Canada, Australia and New Zealand and the Pacific Islands; to Asia, and African territories (most particularly South Africa and the former Rhodesia, now Zimbabwe) - in other words, throughout the British Empire. This model, embodying the eighteenth-century Enlightenment concern with scientific observation, documentation and presentation of the accumulating knowledge emanating from nineteenth-century tropical environments, was designed largely to improve the Empire's economy, and to encourage emigration to these regions by highlighting the natural assets that might be exploited on its behalf. This model of the museum never accommodated notions of a 'national' history as having any validity.

The overriding concern with assembling new knowledge was directly related to the imperial government's need to control and exploit these new natural resources - including human resources. This led to the employment of methods of categorization and classification within both the early written and later the exhibited histories of the region. A final factor was the very long 'memory' of these 'scientific' considerations: this influenced the collecting, exhibiting and interpretation of new knowledge until well past the mid-twentieth century, when newly independent nations began to assemble and present their own authoritative narratives in modern museum institutions as part of the process of identity construction.

The Civilizing Mission

Within less than a decade of Emancipation and the end of Apprenticeship during the 1830s and 1840s, throughout the British Empire the rise of an active British humanitarian movement sought to improve the conditions of indigenous people, although such efforts were not necessarily extended so generously to recently emancipated populations. Nevertheless, there was a critical need to establish a new mechanism to accommodate differing working and social conditions, requirements and status, which would transform the lives of colonial citizens and inhabitants from then on. The movement achieved many successes, including the abolition of slavery in British colonies. In Britain, the Cape, the Caribbean and Australasia there were vocal, powerful people, both inside and outside government, who urged recognition that terrible injustices, against the non-European peoples whose lands they now inhabited, had been carried out in the name of the British Crown. Somewhere between these two perspectives, the energies, interests and zeal of colonial administrators who, in the absence of formal policy, effectively 'ran the British Empire', applied their own theories and designs,[8] and created a context within which the utilization of museums as a tool to address these realities rapidly evolved.

Arriving in 1839 in the recently-emancipated Atlantic territories as Bermuda's newly-appointed Governor (later Governor of Barbados and the Windward Islands), with a mandate to improve the deplorable condition of the colony's agriculture, Lieutenant Colonel (later Sir William) Reid found that the project required meticulous identification, categorization, promotion and transportation of colonial products to supply the needs both of the Empire's population and of its trading partners.[9] The necessary institutional bases from which to collate and compile the data were required, so he created these with legislation to establish a public library and museum in the colony, predicated

[8] In her article "Sir William Reid, F.R.S., 1791-1858: Governor of Bermuda, Barbados and Malta," *Notes and Records of the Royal Society,* Vol. 40, #2, 1986, pp. 169-193. Olwyn Blouet has noted that 'Helen Taft Manning has argued that for the period 1830-1850 that no one man or group of men "ran the British Empire" and has suggested that attention be directed to colonial governors who: "applied their own theories of government ... were too far away and too much the source of all the information reaching England to make any effective supervision of their actions or policies possible". It therefore mattered who was appointed to governorships. The backgrounds, interests, skills and general characteristics of governors were important variables in colonial policy.' p. 170

[9] Richard Drayton, *Nature's Government: Science, Imperial Britain, and the 'Improvement' of the World,* New Haven and London, 2000, p. 62.

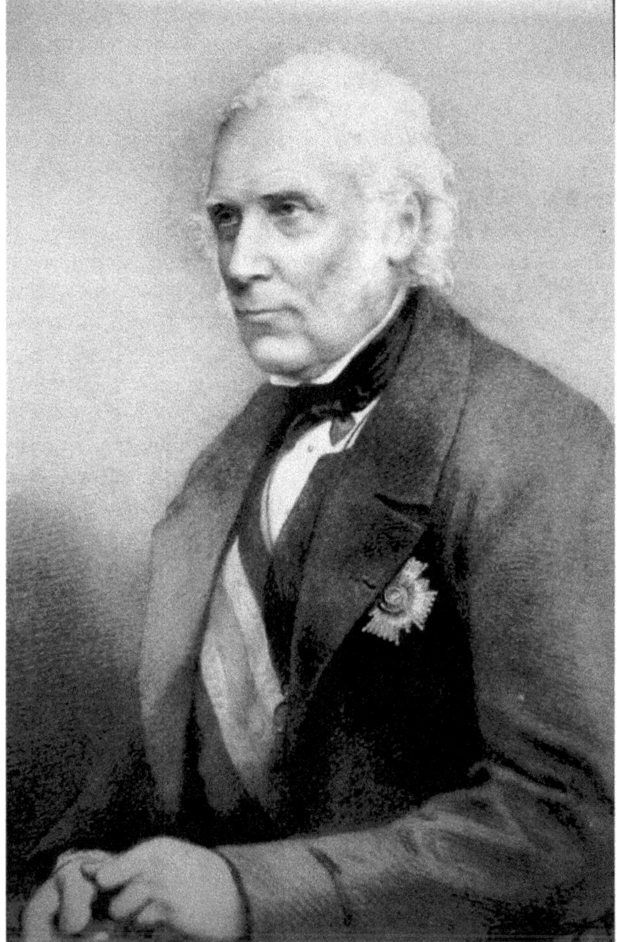

Lieut. Colonel (later Sir) William Reid, the 'Good Governor'
(Courtesy of The Bermudian)

on the imperial government's desire to ensure control over a properly subjugated territory.[10] Remembered as Bermuda's 'Good Governor', Reid, a product of the Scottish Enlightenment who shared the Enlightenment conviction of the inevitability and desirability of material progress and improvement, epitomized the 'improving' British imperialism that emerged at the end of the eighteenth century, a new species of governance based on 'the idea that colonization was an

[10] See Alissandra Cummins, 'The "Caribbeanization" of the West Indies: the Museum's Role in the Development of National Identity', in *Museums and the Making of "Ourselves": the Role of Objects in National Identity,* Flora Kaplan (ed.), London and New York, 1994, p. 194. See also Cummins, 'Confronting Colonialism: the First 60 Years at the BMHS', *Journal of the Barbados Museum & Historical Society,* Vol. XLII, 1994-1995, p. 2.

enterprise of amelioration' and a firm 'faith in its capacity and right to increase the happiness of barbarians'.[11] His primary motivation was the 'securing of the loyal support of the people ... through their own self-interest, by enabling them to prosper under British rule'. By 1846, when he was appointed Governor of Barbados and the Windward Islands, Reid had initiated the promulgation of similar bills to develop these institutions in Barbados, Grenada and Saint Lucia in the late 1840s.[12]

Richard Drayton has noted that 'Agriculture was the cause which tended to precede other kinds of cultural initiative. The improvement of agriculture was the most important stimulus for the empire's gentlemen when they came to constitute ... learned societies.'[13] Scientific research into the region's agriculture was clearly oriented by international interests, whereby these resources were identified for economic exploitation for the empire's benefit.[14] Agricultural societies were created within the region to respond to these requirements; their activities spawned major elements of early museums in assembling the research resources required. Reid extended his philanthropic efforts at comprehensive social improvement through public libraries and museums as principal vehicles for educational reform. He recognized that access to ideas and information was important for development, and also viewed education as helping to ease the transition from a slave society to a free society. He hoped that 'instruction would soften the 'distinctions' within society. Others of the region's earliest museums, first established within a decade of Emancipation, provided little reflection of this transformation in the colony's social landscape, and were driven instead by the need of both mercantilist and planter interests to establish new generators of prosperity and wealth after the social and economic structure founded on slave labour had been dismantled.

Reid's first colonial appointment as Governor of Bermuda (1839-1846) enabled him to initiate 'progressive' policies in agriculture, public works and

---

[11] Drayton, *Nature's Government,* pp. 92-93.

[12] I have noted the development of similar legislation in 'Caribbeanization', p. 194. Essentially the legislation enacted called for 'a public library [to] be established and kept in ... the city of Bridgetown ... and that a public museum be in like manner established and maintained in the same place', specifying the designation as 'The Barbados Library and Museum', 'containing a collection of books of reference and practical works, with a museum of natural and scientific subjects, and productions of art, would be beneficial to the community...', 'and providing for its free use by all residents in Barbados, whether civil, military or naval. The governing body of this institution was to consist of 'five fit and proper' persons nominated by the Governor.

[13] Drayton, *Nature's Government,* pp. 63-64. Amongst those listed were the Society for the Encouragement of Natural History and Useful Arts of Barbados (1784) and the Physico-Medical Society of Grenada (1791).

[14] Essentially, the Society of Arts' initiatives in which scientific agriculture served the mercantile interests of empire through the planting of commodities traditionally purchased through Dutch, French, and Spanish intermediaries from Asia and Africa. The Society's encouragement of the establishment of botanical gardens in the West Indies logically extended a century later into the creation of agricultural and scientific societies.

education, which then were incorporated in the foundation for the region's first libraries and museums. He then reinforced this connection when he moved to Barbados (1846-1848).[15] Reid was a popular governor and he had his admirers in the Colonial Office as well. James Stephen, the Permanent Undersecretary of State for the Colonies, called Reid 'one of the ablest men in the colonial service', and was particularly impressed by his 'extensive knowledge ... unbounded curiosity ... and mental activity'. Within a few months of his return to London from Barbados he was named a Vice President of the Royal Society,[16] and his reputation for effective management and organization was partly responsible for his appointment as chairman of the executive committee of the Great Exhibition early in 1850. What has not been recognized or acknowledged to date is the way in which he then applied the knowledge gained by his experiences in the West Indies to his next mandate, as executive manager of the Great Exhibition of 1851. The exhibition opened to huge success on 1 May 1851, largely as a result of Reid's excellent management, and his 'tranquil energy and determination'.[17] Reid was from the start an energetic and innovative administrator. As Olwyn Blouet has suggested, 'For Reid the diffusion of useful knowledge throughout the colonies was an essential ingredient of imperial policy as he saw it.'[18]

West Indian collections and museums were thus created by commercial (and at the same time political) leaders as early promotional campaigns designed to attract new audiences within the colonies, as well as new clients and investors from the metropole. It was an advantageous marriage between private enterprise and imperial interests, where the major beneficiaries were, intentionally, the white minority, whether local or foreign, as these private Agricultural Societies, established on exclusive membership structures, sought to shore up a way of life widely regarded as under threat.

Many early regional institutions were founded on the basis of donated natural history and geological collections assembled in the preparation of systematic surveys of the islands. Duplicate specimen collections assembled variously for the Royal Botanic Gardens Kew, and to a lesser extent the British Museum, also provided the impetus for developing or expanding local collections. Between the 1840s and 1870s private arts and scientific societies rapidly proliferated throughout the region. An exchange of correspondence in 1859 between Richard Hill and Charles Darwin about indigenous bees in

---

15 Reid was later made governor of Malta (1851-1858) where he similarly established the island's first major museum. In other words he served sixteen years as a governor and museum developer. His enlightened policies even found their way into an article that appeared in Charles Dicken's 'Household Words'.

16 Reid was elected a Fellow of the Royal Society in 1839 based on his scientific research.

17 The first world's fair in history, a display of science, technology and the arts that clearly demonstrated Britain's industrial lead at the mid-century, the Great Exhibition involved over 70 countries and territories creating exhibits at the Crystal Palace. As the initial global exposition the Great Exhibition set the standard for the rest that followed. Much of the success of this model can be ascribed to Reid's capacities, vision and experience. He was knighted in September 1851 as a result of his many contributions.

18 Blouet 1986, p. 171.

Jamaica, revealed the existence of a similar entity in Spanish Town. Hill observed "We have a log in the Museum of our Society of Arts containing a living hive at work, and if I do not possess myself of what you desire early, I shall be able from this stock to get for you Specimens..." In British Guiana (now Guyana) the collections of the Royal Agricultural and Commercial Society (RACS, 1844) and the Natural History Society of British Guiana (1861) were utilized to establish a local exhibition to bring to light 'these hidden sources of wealth and stimulants to industry'. The exhibition organisers had a larger goal:

> ... but because the interest it excites can be evanescent, we desire to connect with it the project of a permanent local museum, to which not merely strangers can have recourse for a general view of what our country offers to the research of scientific and intelligent curiosity but where the resident may at his leisure, review and extend his store of knowledge and by experiment and induction contribute to those of mankind at large.[19]

Fire threatened this ambitious endeavour in 1864, however, by 1867 shares were on sale at £10 each to assist with establishing the British Guiana Museum Company Limited. This initiative received great public support and by 13 February 1868 the doors had opened on the newly constructed 'permanent home of science, art and industry', [20] which later became the Guyana National Museum.[21]

Thus, in common with many similar institutions throughout Britain's colonies, early museums in the region primarily collected and displayed natural history and 'curiosities'. Donald Fleming has posited that:

> The study of natural history] was a fundamental part of the quest for a *national identity* [my emphasis] in societies where the cultural differentiation from Britain was insecure and the sense of the land correspondingly important for self-awareness.[22]

Stimulated no doubt by the 1890 Trinidad and Tobago Exhibition of Agriculture, Floriculture, Horticulture, Manufactures, Science and Art, The Trinidad Society of Arts and Sciences, (established in 1870), joined the Trinidad Field Naturalists Club in 1892 spearheading the creation of the Royal Victoria Institute (originally named the Victoria Institute), modeled along the lines of the Victoria and Albert Museum.[23] It was built as a Science and Art Museum to commemorate the Diamond Jubilee of Queen Victoria. The building, still in its original form, was

---

[19] Opening address of the Lieut. Governor in the *Proceedings of the Natural History Society of British Guiana,* Georgetown, British Guiana, 1863, nn.

[20] *The Colonist* newspaper, 13 February 1868, cited in Arlene Munro, 'A short history of the National Museum', *Stabroek News,* February 2004, nn.

[21] See Caribbeanization, pp. 196-197.

[22] D. Fleming, 'Science in Australia, Canada, and the United States: Some Comparative Remarks', *Actes du Dixième Congrès International d'Histoire des Sciences,* Paris, 1962, pp. 179-81. Quoted in Sheets-Pyenson, *Cathedrals of Science,* p. 15.

[23] See Cummins, 'Caribbeanization', p. 198.

designed in the German Renaissance style by architect Daniel Mienerts Hahn who worked in the Department of Public Works. It opened on 17 September 1902, when the public could see microscopic exhibits for the first time. In a 1908 address by the Institute's President Prof. J Carmody, while the focus was very much on the modernist objective of technical and vocational education, he reminded that "There was another question which they had not lost sight of, and that was the establishment of a commercial museum, that persons coming to the Colony could see what articles were produced here, and what they could introduce with success".[24] Governor Sir Alfred Moloney later responded that he himself was "perfectly in sympathy with the desire to see a museum added to that institution, and, so far as he could afford, he would be delighted to give his support by contributing himself, or from the funds of the Colony".[25]

The General Agricultural Society in Jamaica was one of the founding agencies of the Royal Society of Arts and Agriculture (1864).[26] This society 'for the augmentation of the sources of public industry and the extension of the arts and manufactures of the colony' was supported by voluntary subscriptions. Specimens collected between 1860 to 1866 by the Sawkins and Brown Geological Survey[27] were combined with the newly established Public Library (opened in 1874), and eventually became the nucleus of the Institute of Jamaica (IOJ) in 1879.[28] The Institute of Jamaica was constituted to:

> Maintain a library, reading room, and museum, to provide for the reading of papers, the delivery of lectures, and the holding of examinations on subjects connected with literature, science and art, to award premiums for the application of scientific and artistic methods to local industries, and to provide for the holding of exhibitions illustrating Jamaican industries.[29]

J.A. Froude later recorded his 1886 visit to the Institute in more casual terms:

> [The senior aide-de-camp]... drove me one morning into Kingston. ...There were libraries, museums, public offices, and such like to be seen, besides the town itself... We saw the museum and public library. There were the usual specimens of island antiquities—of local fish, birds, insects, reptiles, plants, geological formations, and such like. In the library were old editions of curious books at [sic] the West Indies, some of them unique, ready to yield ampler pictures of the romance of the old life there than we at present possess. I had but leisure to glance at title-pages and engravings. The most noticeable relic preserved there, if it be only genuine, is the identical bauble which Cromwell ordered to

---

[24] Victoria Institute, *Industrial Trinidad*, p. 512.

[25] *Industrial Trinidad*, p. 514.

[26] See further details in *'Museums of Jamaica'* by Frederick Le Mercier du Quesnay, 1965.

[27] See Francis Bather, Special Report on the Institute of Jamaica for the Encouragement of Literature, Sciences, and Arts, May, 1934 (NLJ MS73), p. 1.

[28] See Cummins, 'Caribbeanization', p. 197.

[29] Bather, p. 2.

> be taken away from the Speaker's table in the House of Commons. Explanations are given of the manner in which it came to Jamaica. The evidence, so far as I could understand it, did not appear conclusive.[30]

However, unlike his critical assessment of museum institutions in Australasia, only the latter artefact appeared to have excited his interest. Those examining these institutions in later years would take special pains to 'emphasize the conjunction of practical and economic aims with [the] scientific and artistic in the history of the successive bodies and their establishing Laws'. These entities were all part of a 'collecting' economy with extensive links to mother institutions in Britain (and sister institutions in the United States and elsewhere) that existed within a system of international trade in objects and specimens. This resulted in the ongoing export of objects, where, as the original research and collecting organizations of the region, they essentially controlled or coordinated the manner and means of illustrating the natural history and indigenous and later enslaved, peoples of these territories, essentially placing these at an equivalent level.

The General Agricultural Society in Barbados, like others in the West Indies, established a committee 'for the purpose of devising how Barbados might contribute to the exhibition of industry of all nations in London'.[31] In British Guiana the committee of correspondence of the RACS responded to the news of the Paris exhibition of 1855, and others subsequently planned for Dublin and New York, by proposing to raise local interest through holding exhibitions and collecting contributions to support these activities. The Society later recommended to the Governor and the Courts of Policy of the colony that it was

> highly desirable to make a renewed effort for the establishment of a museum in Georgetown and in connection with that object and also with reference to the probable holding of a Great Exhibition in London in the year 1861...that it is very important to hold an exhibition...[32]

West Indian communities expedited initiatives that extended well beyond a simple display of samples, and were inspired to create large-scale national exhibitions, for example in British Guiana (1855) and Trinidad (1858).[33]

---

[30] James Anthony Froude, *The English in the West Indies, or, The Bow of Ulysses,* London, 1888, ps. 190 and 192.

[31] *Barbados Globe,* 4 October 1850.

[32] *Report of the Committee of Correspondence of the Royal Agricultural and Commercial Society,* 1857-1861, Georgetown, British Guiana, 1861.

[33] These activities reached their zenith in 1891 when Jamaica 'welcomed the world' to its own Great Exhibition, Trinidad and Tobago having hosted a more modest national endeavour the year before in 1890.

The 'Sinews of Commerce'[34]

Displays at the Colonial and Indian Exhibition of 1886 illustrating the vast wealth in natural products, and the commercial, industrial, artistic and educational achievements of the various colonies and of India, excited great interest throughout the British Empire. His Royal Highness the Prince of Wales suggested that a permanent institution...designed to afford a thorough and living representation of the progress made in the development of their resources',[35] and elaborated on a scale commensurate with the importance of their relations to the prosperity of the Empire, might constitute a fitting 'national memorial commemorative of the fiftieth year of the reign of Her Majesty, an epoch within which some of our most important and thriving Colonies passed from insignificance and even comparative barbarism to exalted positions in the commercial and civilized world.[36]

His suggestion prompted the establishment of an Imperial Institute designed not only to illustrate the industrial and commercial resources of Britain's colonies and India but also

> to diffuse a knowledge of their condition and continued progress throughout the United Kingdom,[and] also to afford to all classes of Her Majesty's subjects opportunities of becoming acquainted with the development, during the Queen's reign, and with the further extension from time to time, of the resources, natural, industrial, and commercial, of the United Kingdom itself, and, by actively promoting technical and higher commercial education, to advance the industrial and commercial prosperity of the country.[37]

---

[34] The Colonies, and the Indian Empire, cannot fail to be greatly benefited by being thoroughly represented in a well-selected and carefully organised assemblage of illustrations of the sources of prosperity which constitute the sinews of their commerce, the continuous exploration and cultivation of which are vital to the maintenance of the influence of each section of the Empire upon industrial and social progress.., *Imperial Institute,* p. 44.

[35] *The Imperial Institute of the United Kingdom, the colonies, and India,* published by the Imperial Institute, London, 1892, p. 13.

[36] Ibid., For the West Indies, the experience which had been developing over the decades following the Great Exhibition meant that the Colonial and Indian Exhibition allowed them far more favourable and meaningful representation in terms of exhibits than the preceding international exhibitions. J.A. Froude in his *The English in the West Indies* (1888) reported that 'The West Indians who had come over for the Colonial Exhibition were most of them already gone. They, along with the rest, had taken back with them a consciousness that their visit had not been wholly in vain, and that the interest of the old country in her distant possessions seemed quickening into life once more. The commissioners from all our dependencies had been feted in the great towns, and the people had come to Kensington in millions to admire the productions which bore witness to the boundless resources of British territory ... The Exhibition had served the purpose which it was intended for. The conference of delegates grew out of it which has discussed in the happiest temper the elements of our future relations.' [pp. 13-16]

[37] Ibid, p. 14.

There could be no more suitable memorial than an Institute that could represent the Arts, Manufactures, and Commerce of the Empire. Such an institution would illustrate the progress already made during Her Majesty's reign in the Colonial and Indian Dominions, while 'it would record year by year the development of the Empire in the Arts of Civilization'.[38] It was believed that these exhibits would be deeply interesting to Her Majesty's subjects, both within and beyond Great Britain. They were expected to help 'stimulate Emigration to those British territories where it is required, to expand the Trade between the different British Communities, and to draw closer the bonds which unite the Empire. It would be at once a Museum, an Exhibition, and the proper locality for the discussion of Colonial and Indian subjects'.[39]

By the time this formal exchange of communication was in train, financial arrangements were already being made by several of the colonies for establishing the collections to be displayed, and providing for their guardianship and annual maintenance.[40] By early 1887 the objectives of the Institute were being publicly disseminated by the extensive distribution, throughout the British Empire, of brief summaries of its main objectives, and also an address delivered at the Royal Institute on 22 April 1887 by Sir Frederick Abel, the President of the Institute,[41] before His Royal Highness the Prince of Wales and a 'numerous' audience on 'The Work of the Imperial Institute'. He indicated that the Institute's approach was to 'combine in some harmonious form a broader and more enduring representation of your Majesty's Colonies and India as well as of the United Kingdom'. His hope was 'that this Institute may hereafter not only exhibit the material resources of the Empire', but would also 'promote the commercial and industrial prosperity of all parts of your Majesty's dominions, and that the scientific and technical education which the requirements of modern industry render necessary may, through its means, receive fresh development'.[42]

---

[38] Letter of H.R.H. the Prince of Wales, to the then Lord Mayor, Sir John Staples, K.C.M.G, 13th of September, 1886, quoted in *Imperial Institute,* p. 14.

[39] Ibid, p. 14.

[40] Records indicate that 'Satisfactory communications had already by this date been received from India, several of the Canadian provinces, New South Wales, Victoria, Queensland, Tasmania, Cape Colony, Natal, the West India Settlements, and the East African Protectorates, as to their willingness to prepare and maintain adequate collections of their commercial and economic products. The arrangements for providing and maintaining collections illustrating the resources of the Indian Empire were already in operation.'

[41] Abel was not only the Institute's president but was also chair of the Organising Committee appointed to advise upon the form and constitution of the memorial of the fiftieth anniversary of Queen Victoria's accession to the throne.

[42] Address presented to Her Majesty Queen Victoria by the President of the Organising Committee of the Imperial Institute, in *Imperial Institute*, p. 20. He continued: This foundation," or "corner-stone" - as our Transatlantic brethren prefer to name it - is a huge block of granite from Cape Colony, and stands on a pedestal of Indian bricks. The ceremony was attended by every auspicious omen, and in the interest it excited it was considered second only to that memorable ceremonial on Jubilee day, which closely preceded it.

Abel went further, asserting that the Great Exhibition of 1851 'gave a vast impulse to commercial activity, and set an example which has been often, followed in the countries both of the old and of the new worlds'.[43] The creation of an Imperial Institute was therefore seen as a fitting development and completion of the work of that 'great and bold' enterprise whose financial success was expected to be emulated.[44]

In response Queen Victoria replied:

> I concur with you in thinking that the counsels and exertions of my beloved husband initiated a movement which gave increased vigour to commercial activity, and produced marked and lasting improvements in industrial efforts. One indirect result of that movement has been to bring more before the minds of men the vast and varied resources of the Empire, over which Providence has willed that I should reign during 50 prosperous years. I believe and hope that the Imperial Institute will play a useful part in combining those resources for the common advantage of all my subjects, and in conducing towards the welding of the Colonies, India and the Mother Country into one harmonious and united community.[45]

The Institute did accept the proposition that the memorial should not 'be merely personal in its character', but should tend 'to serve the interests of the entire Empire', and to 'promote a feeling of unity among the whole of Her Majesty's subjects'.[46] On 12 May 1888 Her Majesty granted a Charter of Incorporation to the 'Imperial Institute of the United Kingdom, the Colonies and India, and the Isles of the British Seas',[47] providing, amongst other things, for such a governing body as, in their opinion, would best represent Her Majesty's subjects in the United Kingdom, the Colonies and India, and the commercial and industrial interests of the Empire. Here, therefore, by the end of the nineteenth century was the culmination of Britain's organizing principle, gathering together in one place for the convenience of the Empire and its subjects all the resources necessary to control, celebrate and communicate the importance and value of the British Empire.

---

[43] Ibid, p. 20. The connection in fact went much further than mere emulation of the Great Exhibition. The Organising Committee directed its attention to the property at South Kensington belonging to the Commissioners of the Exhibition of 1851, and a representation was submitted by the Committee to the Prince of Wales to the effect that the Imperial Institute might reasonably advance a claim for the grant of the same site on which the Exhibition had been held, from the land purchased with the surplus proceeds of the first International Exhibition that had been entrusted to the Royal Commissioners of that Exhibition "for application in the interests of Institutions and undertakings designed for the promotion of Science and Art".

[44] Ibid. p. 20.

[45] Ibid., p. 21.

[46] Ibid.

[47] Ibid., p. 22.

No time was wasted. Assistant Secretary of the Institute, Sir Somers Vine, was dispatched in late 1888 on a mission to the principal colonies where the authorities and commercial bodies in these colonies were acquainted with the objects of the Imperial Institute; their interest therein was demonstrated by promises of practical co-operation from all quarters.[48] In Jamaica the effect was almost immediate. Local newspapers reported that

> in the early days of September 1889 a body of gentlemen representative of the wealth and intelligence of Jamaica gathered in the rooms of the Chamber of Agriculture and Commerce, Duke Street, to meet Sir Somers Vine ... the representative of His Royal Highness the Prince of Wales who had been on a special mission to all the colonies on behalf of the Imperial Institute; the great memorial of the completion of fifty years of Her Majesty's reign, —which was then beginning 'to assume form' at South Kensington, London.[49]

Following Sir Somers' delivery of an 'interesting and powerful address on the object and scope of the Imperial Institute', Governor Sir Henry Blake responded that in fact the Institute of Jamaica had been 'brooding, and was near to hatching, a scheme to get up an Exhibition of our own. He did not see why this could not be done and the exhibits sent afterwards to the Imperial Institute.'[50] The credit for the initial idea for such a venture went to William Fawcett,[51] Chairman of the Board of Governors of the Institute, although the Exhibition itself was the dream of native Jamaican A. G Sinclair, one of the compilers of the annual *Handbook of Jamaica.*[52]

Fawcett proposed to the Board the 'holding a local exhibition in Jamaica in accordance with Section 8 of the Law of the Institute of Jamaica'. He pointed out that 'Exhibitions in which the Institute had taken part hitherto had been foreign.' At the first public meeting on the plan Sir Henry indicated that 'it would be beneficial to the people of the island if an Exhibition could be arranged of our natural products that we import from other countries'. He declared that 'an

---

[48] For much of 1889-1890 Vine was engaged in visiting India and the Straits Settlements, the Australasian colonies, the provinces of Canada, and most of the West Indian and African colonies.

[49] *The Daily Gleaner,* Jamaica Exhibition 1891: History of the Undertaking', 28 January 1891, p. 5.

[50] Ibid.

[51] Fawcett was also Director of Public Gardens and Plantations. This was clearly the driving force behind his interest in such a project.

[52] Rebecca Tortello has reported in her article 'The Great Exhibition of 1891: Jamaica on Show", http://jamaica-gleaner.com/pages/history/storyoo18.html, accessed 30 June 2012, 'Sinclair had been inspired by the 1851 Great Exhibition at London's Crystal Palace. He had tried in vain for many years to drum up support for his ambitious project. When Sir Henry Blake arrived as Jamaica's new Governor in March 1889 Sinclair managed to persuade William Fawcett, director of gardens and plantations and chairman of the Institute of Jamaica (IOJ) to help him present his cause to Governor Blake". Also see K. Booth, 'When Jamaica Welcomed the World: The Great Exhibition of 1891'. *Jamaica Journal,* (1985, August-October) 18, 3, 39-51.

Exhibition of the resources of a country, is not only the best advertisement for business purposes but is the most valuable industrial education for the people.'[53]

The Governor nominated the Institute's Board as an initial organizing committee to 'prepare a plan of operations for the holding of an Exhibition of Jamaica and other products and a loan Exhibition of Works of Art and of Curiosities on a scale commensurate with the great interest and importance of the subject'.[54] The intention of the Jamaica exhibition was clear. Following years of economic recession, 'the years of past gloom in the island ... the tide of prosperity had set in and that here was a splendid opportunity for the people to show that the days of depression were over.'[55] It was intended to be a great opportunity for the people from all the towns and villages to show off their products and to be a great leveler, inviting 'cordial cooperation between all classes of the community', to 'work hard and energetically to grasp success'. At an organizing committee meeting Captain Park moved a resolution that 'the other West Indian Colonies be invited to send to the Exhibition such exhibits as will clearly indicate the great resources of these colonies' and 'special exhibits be invited from England and other countries from which we trade.'[56]

The newspaper records how the project grew from this exhibition idea as it took hold of people's imaginations, and developed into an undertaking very unlike the modest island exhibition first conceived on the model of those executed by Guiana and Trinidad almost 50 years earlier. Instead the view was expressed that 'We must not be satisfied with a mere exhibition of local products, and a few pictures and curiosities. A more comprehensive collection of objects than could be obtained within the island or even within the West Indies should be considered, with an animated public 'liberally subscribing to the Guarantee Fund ... within a month of the public meeting the undertaking was lifted out of the level of a local show into the higher plane of an International Exhibition.'[57] Within months the public subscription stood at more than 5000 pounds sterling. An Act for the planning and development of the Jamaica Exhibition was passed shortly afterwards by the Legislative Council.[58]

---

[53] *The Daily Gleaner,* 28 January 1891, p. 5. Exhibits were to include 'our products and manufactures and invite the countries from which we import food stuffs or machinery to send exhibits for our information.'

[54] The intention was then to hold a public meeting to lay out the main points of this scheme and then invite 'gentlemen of prominence and influence in the several parishes of the Island ... to join the Committee and assist him with their advice and experience'. *Daily Gleaner,* p. 5.

[55] Ibid.

[56] Ibid.

[57] Ibid. Similarly, local coloured business man George Steibel stepped up and loaned 5000 pounds towards the building. The Hon. Col. C. J. Ward and Mr. Louis Verley also lent similar sums to secure the building where the Colonial Bank would not.

[58] The Act provided that 'the management and control of the exhibition should be vested in commissioners who should be appointed by the Governor, and who should possess the following, among other powers; — "The Jamaica Exhibition Commissioners shall have full Power to hold an Exhibition of the products of Industry, Agriculture and the Fine Arts, and of the other productions of this Island and other Countries, to be opened

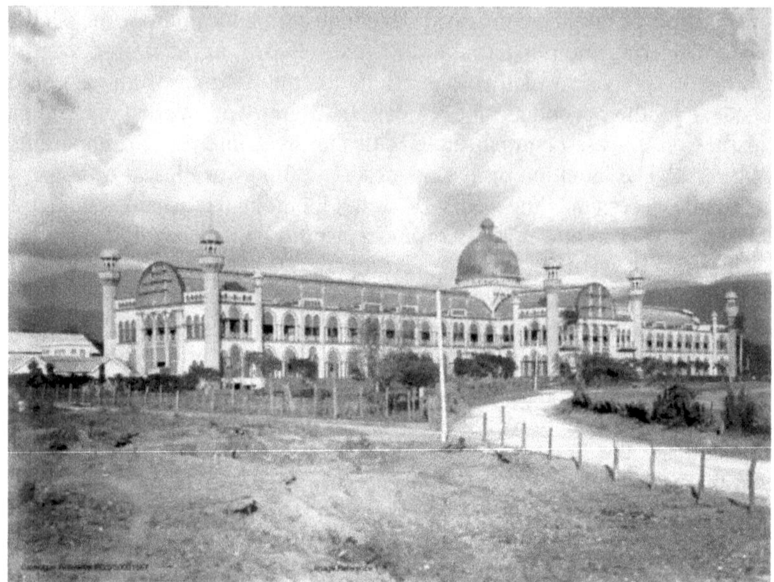

Jamaica Exhibition building, James Johnson, 1891
(Photo Credit: Royal Geographical Society)

By April 1890 the Prince of Wales had agreed to serve as patron of the event, and the Kingston Racecourse (now the site of National Heroes Park) was designated as the most appropriate location for the construction of the exhibition hall. Despite predictions to the contrary this exhibition, billed as 'the most extraordinary commercial event in the history of the Gulf of Mexico and the West Indies', opened on time on 27 January 1891 with Prince George (the future King George V) in attendance representing the royal family.[59] Over 300,000 people, both foreign and local, had visited the event by the time it closed in May 1891. At the formal opening of the Jamaica Exhibition Governor Sir Henry Blake made clear the nature of the exhibition:

> The spontaneous and liberal manner in which funds for carrying out the enterprise were guaranteed by the people of the colony and those interested in its welfare and... the ready response with which the invitation to take part in the Exhibition was met by the Mother Country, by the sister colonies—notably by Canada—and by many Foreign states led to the enlargement of the original scheme and has resulted in an Exhibition on a larger scale, and of a more general and comprehensive character than that at first contemplated by its ori-

---

in the year 1890 or in the year 1891 within this Island, and to manage and conduct the same.."

[59] Major exhibits were included from Britain, America, Canada, and Europe, as well as all West Indian territories. See Booth, 'When Jamaica Welcomed the World: The Great Exhibition of 1891'.

> ginators...Every effort has been made to render the Jamaican Exhibits a complete and representative collection of the agricultural, mineral and industrial products of the Island.

His concluding hope was that 'Your Royal Highness may be introducing an era of renewed and increased prosperity for... Jamaica'.[60] Nevertheless, the Lord Bishop of Jamaica may have uttered the definitive words in his prayer at the Exhibition's opening:

> May it be fruitful in blessing to all classes of people in this Island and be the means of stimulating and directing their industry; and their advancement in all valuable knowledge, in all useful arts, and in all lawful commerce. And we pray that these and the like interchanges of intercourse and of commodities amongst the nations of the earth, may prove to be for their mutual benefit in the increase of material comforts, and also be the means of extending goodwill amongst men; so that instead of glorying in their power, to excel in the triumphs of war, they may cultivate a friendly rivalry in the arts of peace.[61]

Organizing Principles

The symbiotic relationship between the Imperial Institute and the colonies was perpetuated in the establishment of the governing body, when colonial authorities and the Indian government were asked in 1890 to nominate representatives to serve on it. Governors were appointed by their colonial governments to represent the colonies.[62] The charter by which the Organising Committee was made the temporary governing body sets out in considerable detail the purposes and objects of the Institute:

> I. The formation and exhibition of collections representing the important raw materials and manufactured products of the Empire and of other countries, so maintained as to illustrate the development of agricultural, commercial and industrial progress in the Empire, and the comparative advances made in other countries;
>
> II. The establishment or promotion of commercial museums, sample-rooms and intelligence offices, in London and other parts of the Empire;
>
> III. The collection and dissemination of such information relating to trades and industries, to emigration, and to the other purposes of the charter as may be of use to the subjects of the Empire;

---

[60] *The Daily Gleaner,* 28 January 1891, p. 5.

[61] Ibid.

[62] For the West Indies these included British Guiana, Trinidad, and Tobago - Sir Arthur Hamilton Gordon, G.C.M.G.; Jamaica, British Honduras, and Bahamas - Charles Washington Eves, Esq., C.M.G.; The Leeward Islands, the Windward Islands, and Barbados - Sir Rawson William Rawson, K.C.M.G., C.B.

IV. The advancement of trades and handicrafts by exhibitions of special branches of industry and commerce, and of the work of artisans and of apprentices;

V. The promotion of technical and commercial education, and of the industrial arts and sciences;

VI. The furtherance of systematic colonisation;

VII. The promotion of conferences and lectures in connection with the general work of the Institute, and the facilitating of commercial and friendly intercourse among the inhabitants of the different parts of the British Empire;

VIII. The doing of anything incidental or conducive to carrying into effect all or any of the foregoing purposes. [63]

The trajectory of development extending from the international exhibition, to the development, management and interpretation of collections in colonial museums (both at home and abroad) that followed the model of the Imperial Institute is thus well illustrated. The Institute was given responsibility for promoting the cultivation of a better knowledge of the geography, natural history, and resources of the colonies, and for the advancement of the interests of the colonists in Britain. Representative collections of the natural products of the colonies and India, carefully identified along with the more elaborate collections in the Institute itself, were to be distributed to provincial centres 'in order that the provinces be kept thoroughly conversant with the current information from the Colonies and India, the interests of the commercial man, the manufacturer, and the intending emigrant'.[64]

The collections of natural products of the colonies and India, maintained by regular additions and renewals at the central establishment of the Institute, were predicted to be of great value to students in the immediately adjacent educational institutions, and were also expected to serve the purposes of provincial industrial colleges by the distribution of thoroughly descriptive reference catalogues and specimens.

Supplies of natural products from the colonies, India, or from other countries that were either new or had been 'but imperfectly studied', were to be maintained so that material might be readily provided to scientists or manufacturers, either for scientific investigation or for purposes of technical experiment and commercial utilization. The existence of those collections and of all information relating to them, as well as of a library of technology, inventions, commerce and applied geography, in immediate proximity to the government museums of science and inventions, art, and natural history, to the Normal

[63] *Imperial Institute,* p. 44-45.
[64] *Imperial Institute,* p. 44.

School of Science, and to the Central Technical Institute, was expected to contribute substantially to the improvement of commercial education.[65]

Of the special functions to be fulfilled by the Institute, none would be more important than those most immediately connected with the great commercial work of the City of London and with that of the provincial centres of commerce alike. The provision, in central and readily accessible positions, of commercial museums or collections of natural or import products, and of export products of different nations, combined with comprehensive sample-rooms and facilities for the business of inspection or of commercial, chemical or physical examination, was a work to which the Institute could lend most important aid. The Imperial Institute, as a thoroughly modern agency of empire, was especially well positioned to embed its activities and interests in the expressed goals and objectives of British commerce. This was the driving force behind its existence.

Colonialism as a project of imperial control infused the established canon for western approaches to museum creation, collection and display in order to rationalize the emerging natural diversity of the New World, and to prescribe a more 'scientific' way of seeing or observing artefacts or specimens from foreign territories. The eighteenth-century European Enlightenment had created a society that was curious about the world, while at the same time preoccupied with the concept of nation.[66] The need for a single public culture - the creation of an authentic identity - is fundamental to our understanding of nationalism, the nation-state and the role of the national museum in this context. Benedict Anderson has identified the museum as one of the three institutions of power that 'profoundly shaped the way in which the colonial state imagined its dominion'.[67]

Cultural anthropologist Sharon MacDonald has suggested that the fascination with collecting that emerged in the fifteenth century was a way of 'maintaining some degree of control over the natural world and taking its measure'. She points out that 'the growth of taxonomic knowledge ... and ambitions of a science of order' [in the seventeenth century] gave rise to the importance of *observation;* every other sense was made subservient to sight.[68] While both these observations were made in relation to earlier periods, two key concepts emerge that are applicable in this particular context. The act of

---

[65] *Imperial Institute,* pp. 45-46.

[66] The British Museum, that opened its doors in 1759, was established as a result of a bequest by Sir Hans Sloane of his prolific collections from Jamaica and elsewhere in the West Indies, and exemplified both the quest for knowledge which lay at the heart of the European Enlightenment, and at the same time the wealth and privilege of the collector. See for example O. Impey and A. McGregor, eds, *The Origins of Museums: The Cabinet of Curiosities in Sixteenth and Seventeenth Century Europe* (Oxford, 1985); E.P. Alexander, *Museums in Motion: An Introduction to the History and Functions of Museums* (Nashville, 1979).

[67] Benedict Anderson, *Imagined Communities: Reflections on the Origin and Spread of Nationalism,* revised edition London: Verso. 1991, pp. 163-85.

[68] Sharon MacDonald, *The Politics of Display: Museums, Science, Culture,* Routledge London, 1998.

collecting was in itself a form of control over an unknown world; and the methods used to present such items, including indigenous human remains and artefacts which were simply regarded as another form as natural history, within a museological context operated within a taxonomic, almost Linnaean structure. This bestowed on an observer the privilege of rationalizing the relationship between himself and what he observed as the 'natural' order of things, and thus claiming the right to be the owner or master of all he surveyed. Museums as the context for arranging and displaying such forms of documentation and interpretation thus became a way of reinforcing the 'idea' of national identity, through an acculturation process enabling association with imperial claims to universal ownership of the world.

In order to understand this construct as a critical element in the true origins of nascent museums and collections in the English-speaking Caribbean, it is necessary to establish an even earlier origin for the assembly, study and comprehension of new knowledge emanating from the region. During the fifteen months that he was in Jamaica between 1687 and 1689, the physician Hans Sloane (later Sir Hans) undertook in-depth observations of the local fauna and flora, the customs of the local inhabitants, and natural phenomena such as earthquakes. In the relatively short time in which Sloane remained on the island, he gave his deep curiosity about natural history full rein, making extensive notes, and eventually compiling a massive collection of some 800 specimens representing the first plant specimens to be brought back to England from that region.[69] The specimens were mounted in seven bound volumes that have been preserved intact, are still today consulted and remain an invaluable resource for both scientific and historical research. He then began to work on the information he had gathered in Jamaica and in 1696 published a list of the plants he had collected, the *Catalogus Plantarum* (often referred to as the Catalogue).

In 1707 Sloane published the first volume of his *A Voyage to the Islands of Madera, Barbados, Nieves, S. Christophers and Jamaica, with the Natural History of the Herbs and Trees, Four-footed Beasts, Fishes, Birds, Insects, Reptiles, &c. Of the last of those ISLANDS;* referred to in short as the 'Natural History' or 'History'. Even the naming of this and similar publications that emerged from naturalists' pens during the seventeenth and eighteenth centuries essentially categorized these countries as meriting significance only as part of the evolutionary development of an empire, and demonstrated by their very names that any intellectual capital which might be generated was purely incidental to the overall project of empire.[70] Over the next 50 years Sloane's

[69] Sir Hans also acquired the collections of several other important figures in botany at the time, including Leonard Plukenet, James Petiver and Mark Catesby. These collections were rich in plants from newly explored lands and contained many species new to science.

[70] Sloane's second volume did not appear until 1725. This work contains careful and very readable descriptions of not only the plants and animals he encountered, but also of how natural resources were used by the islands' inhabitants. His collections from Jamaica were organized in a series of 'Chapters' that approximate the Natural History, mimicking the production of a history of a place.

collection grew enormously to fill a large part of his house, and he was obliged to employ a full-time curator. Corridors and rooms were filled from top to bottom with plants, animals, gemstones, coins, antiquities and many more objects.[71]

Sloane's 'Museum' became a major attraction of its time and was visited by a stream of distinguished visitors from Britain and abroad. One in particular, the great Swedish botanist Carolus (Carl) Linnaeus, used Sloane's text and drawings as the basis for descriptions of new species in his major work, *Species Plantarum.* Interaction with Sloane's collection helped Linnaeus to develop the organizing principles for his classificatory systems for botanical specimens that he later extended to the kingdoms of animals and minerals.[72]

This last may have seemed somewhat odd, but the theory of evolution was still a long way off. Linnaeus was only attempting a convenient way of categorizing the elements of the natural world. Nevertheless his work eventually evolved into the more ambitious concept of "race" as applied to humans, including mythological creatures. Within *Homo sapiens* he proposed five taxa of a lower (unnamed) rank. These categories were *Africanus, Americanus, Asiaticus, Europeanus,* and *Monstrosus.* They were based on place of origin at first, and later on skin colour.[73] It was these principles that essentially guided the observation and organization of any human remains or material culture representing aboriginal peoples, and eventually African peoples in Europe's and, by extension, colonial museums. These principles gained in popular currency in

---

[71] Before his death Sloane recognized the importance of his collection and offered this vast resource to the nation for the sum of £20,000, a large sum in those days but probably far less than its real worth. After his death, money raised by a lottery was used to purchase the collection and so was created the British Museum at Bloomsbury and later its offspring, the British Museum (Natural History), at South Kensington.

[72] Linnaeus's main contribution to taxonomy was to establish conventions for the naming of living organisms that became universally accepted in the scientific world. In addition Linnaeus developed, during the great eighteenth-century expansion of natural history knowledge, what became known as *Linnaean taxonomy;* the system of scientific classification now widely used in the biological sciences. The Linnaean system classified nature within a hierarchy. His groupings were based upon shared physical characteristics. Only his groupings for animals remain to this day, and the groupings themselves have been significantly changed since Linnaeus' conception, as have the principles behind them. Nevertheless, Linnaeus is credited with establishing the idea of a hierarchical structure of classification based upon observable characteristics. Extract from online resource accessed 24 March 2010.

[73] Linnaeus defined each race as having certain characteristics that he considered endemic to individuals belonging to it. Native Americans were choleric, red, straightforward, eager and combative; Africans were phlegmatic, black, slow, relaxed and negligent; Asians were melancholic, yellow, inflexible, severe and avaricious; and Europeans were sanguine and pale, muscular, swift, clever and inventive. The 'monstrous' humans included such entities as the 'agile and fainthearted' dwarf of the Alps, the Patagonian giant, and the monorchid Hottentot.

the display of non-European persons in Caribbean museums from the later nineteenth century.[74]

The importance of Sloane's ideas and the centrality of these collections to the birth and spread of the museum idea, and the treatment of indigenous and non-European human beings both within and outside the museum context, could ultimately thus be said to have inculcated these notions in the British national pysche as it was extended throughout the British Empire.

The Human Zoo

Another factor encouraging the development of regional museums was the rising interest in archaeological and anthropological research, fuelled in part by the development of these new sciences. For the antecedents of the region's museums, growing interest and curiosity about the origins of human settlement in the region could now be shored up by examining the physical evidence of the earliest Amerindian inhabitants, principally pottery sherds and shell adzes which began to find their place in both private and later public collections. James Anthony Froude effusively described one such collection when he visited Sir Graham Briggs at his Farley Hill estate in Barbados in the 1880s:

> Passing through a hall, among a litter of Carib curiosities, we entered the drawing-room, a magnificent saloon extending with various compartments over the greater part of the ground-floor story. It was filled with rare and curious things, gathered in the days when sugar was a horn of plenty, and selected with the finest taste; pictures, engravings, gems, antiquarian relics, books, maps, and manuscripts. There had been fine culture in the West Indies when all these treasures were collected. The English settlers there, like the English in Ireland, had the tastes of a grand race, ... It was a palace with which Aladdin himself might have been satisfied, one of those which had stirred the envying admiration of foreign travelers in the last century, one of many then, now probably the last surviving representative of Anglo-West Indian civilisation.[75]

Froude has described the genesis of what became the nascent historical evidence in such an antiquarian collection - the assemblage of 'Carib curiosities' representing the native (uncivilized) Indians, and the pictures, engravings, books, maps and manuscripts which demonstrated the 'fine culture of (civilized)' citizens of these colonies. The conjunction of these evidences with the natural history specimens, which had so engaged the collecting endeavours of the previous two centuries in the region, became the basis of the 'national' (insofar as colonial society might be considered such) histories which informed nineteenth and early twentieth-century museum development in the West Indies.

---

[74] Many of these curatorial practices continued in the region's museums well into the twentieth century as well.

[75] Froude, *The English in the West Indies,* p. 106.

The ongoing progress of the global phenomenon of world exhibitions or fairs now joined with growing public interest in exotic cultures and peoples. In the context of this development, 'Human Zoos' (also called ethnological expositions or Negro Villages) were nineteenth and twentieth-century public exhibits of humans, usually in a so-called 'natural' or 'primitive' state. The displays often emphasized the cultural differences between European and non-European peoples. Ethnographic 'zoos' were often predicated on unilinealism, scientific racism and social Darwinism. A number of them placed indigenous people (particularly Africans) on a spectrum somewhere between the great apes and humans of European descent.

In the 1870s exhibitions of exotic peoples became popular in various countries. 'Human Zoos' could be found in Paris, Hamburg, Antwerp, Barcelona, London, Milan, New York, and Warsaw, with 200,000 to 300,000 visitors attending each exhibition. In 1883 native people of Suriname were displayed in the International Colonial and Export Exhibition in Amsterdam, held behind the Rijksmuseum; and the 1889 Universal Exposition in Paris displayed 400 indigenous people as a major attraction. West Indian archaeology rose to new levels with the opening of the World's Columbian Exposition held in Chicago in 1893. The World's Fair, commemorating the 400 anniversary of Columbus' arrival in the New World, popularized West Indian culture for an American audience.[76] Importations by Frederick Ober and P.T. Barnum of 'live' aboriginal Indians[77] from Dominica and St. Vincent fuelled the frenzy of popular interest in West Indian archaeology and ethnology, and proved a successful investment for these shrewd showmen. Both Amerindian culture and people were appropriated by the non-indigenous population for 'scientific' as well as for entertainment purposes.

During the 1904 World's Fair in St. Louis, Missouri, following the Spanish-American War, newly acquired U.S. territories such as Guam, the Philippines, and Puerto Rico, were put on 'display' with some of the native inhabitants. According to Essayist and Indigenist Political Commentator Rev. Sequoyah Ade:

> In what was enthusiastically termed a "parade of evolutionary progress," visitors could inspect the "primitives" that represented the counterbalance to "Civilisation"... Pygmies from New Guinea and Africa, who were later displayed in the Primate section of the Bronx Zoo, were paraded next to American Indians such as Apache warrior Geronimo, who sold his autograph... The purpose was to highlight both the "civilising" influence of American rule and the economic potential of the island chain's natural resources on the heels of the Philippine-America War... As one pleased visitor commented, the human zoo

---

[76] See 'Caribbeanization', p. 199.

[77] For a detailed analysis of this question see Deborah Willis and Carla Williams 'The Black Female Body in Photographs from World's Fairs and Expositions' in 'Race, Photography, and American Culture', *Exposure,* volume 33,1/2, Daytona Beach, Florida, 2000.

> exhibit displayed "the race narrative of odd peoples who mark time while the world advances, and of savages made, by American methods, into civilized workers".[78]

The 1900 World's Fair presented the famous diorama 'Living in Madagascar', while the Colonial Exhibitions in Marseilles (1906 and 1922) and in Paris (1907 and 1931) also displayed humans in cages, often nude or semi-nude.[79]

The movement of objects (and bodies) from these exotic cultures reinforced the specific relationship between master and subaltern histories and cultures. These global expositions (and the museums that emanated from them) were more often seen as places of 'curiosity' - considered as sites of peculiarity and promotion rather than as serving a higher purpose such as education. Jesse Fewkes observed that 'Archaeology is thus able to illuminate obscure chapters overlooked or unrecorded by the historian and ethnologist. It offers the only exact data by which the manners and customs of the aborigines before the advent of Columbus can be interpreted.'[80]

Amerindian artefacts were from the first collected mainly to demonstrate the complete inferiority of indigenous cultures to European civilisation. Amerindians were treated as 'living fossils' and displayed in the nineteenth-century manner of taxonomic classification identical to that of flora and fauna, their artefacts relegated to the ranks of stuffed birds, animals and other curiosities, and divorced from the indigenous people who had created them. As for the more recent arrivals from West Africa and their descendants, they were largely silent and usually absent from the stages of human history as played out in early museums in the West Indies. The movement of objects reflective of the character and distinct features of these exotic cultures was predicated largely on the need to reinforce the specific relationship between master and subaltern histories/cultures, with these global expositions expressly designed for the purpose of exhibiting these resources for international rather than for local audiences.

Towards the end of the nineteenth century Benjamin Kidd gave emphasis to this position, stating that 'The last thing our civilization is willing to permanently tolerate is the wasting of the resources of the richest regions of the earth through the lack of the elementary qualities of social efficiency in the races possessing

---

[78] Rev. S Ade, 'The Passions of Suzie Wong Revisited' in *Aboriginal Intelligence*, 4 January, 2004.

[79] In 1906, socialite and amateur anthropologist Madison Grant, head of the New York Zoological Society, had Congolese pygmy Ota Benga put on display at the Bronx Zoo in New York City alongside apes and other animals. At the behest of Grant, a prominent eugenicist, the zoo director William Hornaday displayed Ota Benga in a cage with the chimpanzees, then with an orangutan named Dohong, and a parrot, and labelled him *The Missing Link,* suggesting that in evolutionary terms Africans like Ota Benga were closer to apes than were Europeans. It triggered protests from the city's clergymen, but the public reportedly flocked to see it.

[80] Jesse W. Fewkes, 'The Aborigines of Puerto Rico and Neighbouring Islands' in *25th Annual Report of the Bureau of American Ethnology*, Washington D.C., Bureau of American Ethnology, 1907, p. 17.

them.'[81] In other words, inhabitants of the tropics had no right to their own resources, which needed to be 'developed' firstly for the benefit of the British ruling class, and afterwards for the colony as an extension of empire.

By the end of the nineteenth century museums everywhere across the British Empire were seen as institutions (or extensions) of power, and instruments of education, enlightenment and social salvation. They took their place, alongside libraries, churches and schools, as a means of providing a sound intellectual and moral culture to the working classes. At the same time, these museums were seen as a vital part of the colonial culture, as they could order and make 'comprehensible the newness of the 'natural world'.'[82] The early museums were thus established primarily for enlightening the general public about the wonders of the nineteenth-century industrial world, and for reaffirming the colonies' place within British and imperial progress and history. Museums of natural history, science and art continued to grow and flourish up to the outbreak of World War I. However, none of these institutions held a significant historical collection representing the human development of their respective countries.

By the early twentieth century museums in the region (even those which functioned as national institutions) could not achieve the desired professional standards, as most of them were still being run almost voluntarily. In Trinidad, for example, a Scottish doctor observed:

> There have been repeated half-hearted attempts to found a museum in Trinidad, but they have all been doomed to failure, as it is nobody's business to run them. Everyone seems to expect a museum to run itself without money or staff. The Victoria Institute in Port of Spain is the only attempt at a museum in Trinidad. It has some quite good things in it, but there is no resident curator, no one with that magic touch which animates a museum and brings its stuffed carcasses to life. Trinidad has the money, and should provide a first-class curator with an adequate salary so that he could spend his life in it without fear of the sack or worry about the wherewithal with which to live.[83]

For colonial institutions in the Caribbean, natural history continued to be equated with national history in the first half of the twentieth century. The tide began to change, as in so much else, in the tumultuous years of the 1930s. On 29 January 1936 at the Institute of Jamaica's (IOJ) annual general meeting the Chairman of the Board, Herbert de Lisser, gave a detailed account of the organization's activities, which was seeking to improve its accommodation from the very neglected and almost derelict building in which the Institute was housed (it had barely survived two hurricanes). The IOJ was seeking to acquire and

---

[81] Benjamin Kidd, *The Control of the Tropics,* 1898, nn.

[82] C. Healy, *From the Ruins of Colonialism: History as Social Memory,* Melbourne, 1997, p. 85. Here the author is speaking of the experience of Australia but these observations are equally applicable to the trajectory of West Indian museum development.

[83] Vincent D. Tothill, *Trinidad's Doctor's Office: The Amusing Diary of a Scottish Physician in Trinidad in the 1920s,* Paria Publishing Company Ltd, Trinidad, 1939 (2009 edition), p. 203.

accommodate a major library of 2000 books with the financial support of the Carnegie Institute. It also wished to recruit a young man to function as an Assistant Secretary for at least two years, after which he might be retained to support (and eventually replace) the venerable Frank Cundall as the Institute's Secretary. He had held the post for almost 20 years.

Over the years, the Chair reported, both he and the Board had been assiduous in seeking the support of various governors and a variety of entities, including the Legislative Council and Colonial Development and Welfare Office, as well as the Senate, but all to no avail.[84] All parties remained unmoved. Nevertheless, the recruitment exercise was undertaken by the Museum Association's Frank Markham back in London. However, rather than the sympathetic support and approval for their noble efforts that the Chair might have expected, the Board soon found itself defending its activities against determined challenges.[85]

Member Basil O. Parks set the tone when he characterized the Institute as an 'inert and passive body' and noted further that 'the remarkable thing about it is that the Governors freely and frankly admit it through a public statement made by their Chairman that they are passive and inert'.[86] *The Daily Gleaner* provided extensive coverage in the days following, noting that:

> Members of the Jamaica Institute met for their annual meeting yesterday afternoon, and for two hours conducted a criticism of the Board of Governors, finally passing many resolutions asking for greater attention to the development of literature, science and art. The Chairman of the Board found it necessary at times to plead for a maintenance of dignity in the discussion so that the proceedings should not resolve themselves into 'a speaking meeting'.

Parks, assisted by 'one of our young barristers', Mr. S. R. Braithwaite, and four young solicitors - Messrs. H. O. A. Dayes, Douglas Judah, N. N. Nethersole and W. E. Foster Davis - 'led the attack upon the Board of Governors who defended themselves through their Chairman'.

This cohort of young challengers was most probably inspired by the published statements of Marcus Mosiah Garvey who, two years before in August 1934 during his address to the 17th session of the Convention of Negro Peoples of the World, had admonished his followers on the importance of living 'artistic lives', stating that "One's civilization is not complete without it [Art]."[87] While claiming proudly that ‘we were [Egyptians] the 'first' of the artistic peoples',

---

[84] Even the normally funded updating of the popular handbook *Jamaica in 1928* first compiled by the Secretary Frank Cundall and published in 1895, by then in its 10th edition, the Government declined to fund its republication on this occasion.

[85] *The Daily Gleaner,* 'A Lively Meeting of Jamaica Institute: For Two Hours Coterie of Young Members Criticize the Board of Management', 30 January 1936, p. 6.

[86] *The Daily Gleaner,* 'Annual Meeting of the Institute of Jamaica, Lively Indeed', 31 January 1936, p. 16.

[87] *The Daily Gleaner,* 'Holding of the Convention of Negro Peoples: Mr. Garvey Speaks of Art and Urges Hearers to live Artistic Lives', 17 August 1934, p. 27.

Garvey had nevertheless been critical of the lack of recognition of the importance of art in the development of the African peoples, and lamented the lack of effort to identify and develop black artists who might equal a Michelangelo in stature. He gave an extensive presentation on the importance of artistic education for the young, if they were to have a hope of developing viable careers in this field. He ended by saying 'No home is complete without a picture on the wall. Why don't you produce it?'[88] Garvey rejected the hanging of cheap 'reproductions of other races' and advocated the display of images of Toussaint L'Ouverture, the 'greatest soldier of the world for the past 300 years', whom he was sure that children would emulate. He trusted that they would 'legislate intelligently' on that subject. Clearly inspired, the quartet of IOJ Members called for sweeping changes to be made in the permanent exhibitions of the Institute.

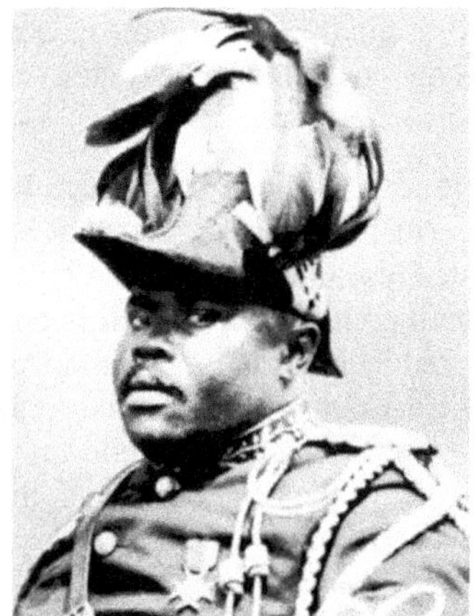

Marcus Mosiah Garvey (web download June 2012)

The general meeting of the Institute provided a broad canvas on which to paint the image of a new Jamaica. The cohort had come well prepared and their resolutions were swiftly passed, though amended from their original form on the advice of the Chairman, who made it clear that 'exception could be taken to certain phraseology'.[89] Each of the resolutions was the subject of considerable debate among the members of the meeting who finally resolved that it deplored the fact that:

> ...the Institute has acquired no significant example of original or creative Art and that unjustifiable preponderance of attention has been given to matters of alleged local, historical interest [and] urge[d]... the gradual establishment of a permanent gallery of contemporary Art, the holding of exhibitions of works of Art.

---

[88] Ibid.

[89] Thirty-one members of the Institute were reported to be present, including prominent artist Edna Manley, who later led the cause for a National Gallery.

> ...the Institute have failed to recognize that it is essential to the promotion of the objects of the Institute, that regular lectures on Literature, Science and Art should be organized and maintained and... that such lectures should be provided for in future.[90]

> ...the Institute is prevented from properly and effectively carrying out the objects for which [it was] created, and that its efficiency is sensibly impaired and its growth and development seriously hampered by the lack of space and want of funds that the Government be asked to increase the vote; so that (*inter alia*) there maybe increased accommodation and house space.

Eventually the meeting agreed on a way forward: that a committee be appointed to 'Confer with the Board of Governors with a view to bringing about the aims of the members as expressed at the meeting'.[91] However, one particular barrier had been breached. Fierce debate ensued, primarily in a 'war of words' in Letters to the Editor in the newspapers.

> ...Now the Institute has made the West India Library and picture gallery, and it is ridiculous to suggest that such a work is not of true historical interest. This collection of books, papers and pictures may not appeal to the "intelligentsia" here, but it is one of the best in existence, and is so considered by historians, and all interested ... [in] Imperial and Colonial history, in England, the United States and elsewhere. It is a pity that in their laudable zeal to extend the activities of the Institute, members should show their ignorance of the value of a possession, which is the envy of other West Indian Islands, and is respected everywhere—outside Jamaica.[92]

The Board of Governors reacted swiftly to this outpouring of criticism. The Director of Education, the Hon B.H. Easter, in a speech at the Institute in 1938 marking the prizegiving for a major art exhibition, said that, in his opinion, 'the exhibition, although he was not qualified to speak on its artistic side, had been an epoch-making event in their history'. Although it had not been the first exhibition to have been held in Jamaica, this 'particular exhibition had marked a renaissance of art and craftsmanship ... It had provided an opening for a large number of people who had never had such an opportunity before'.[93]

---

[90] A further resolution called for the provision of pensions for at least the Institute's senior officers.

[91] This Committee included: Prominent lawyer (later Jamaica's Chief Minister 1955-1959, and Premier during Federation 1959-1962) Mr. Norman W. Manley; (influential artist and proponent of the National Gallery) Mrs. Edna Manley; and two of the Institute's key critics Mr. Braithwaite, and Mr. Parks.

[92] Letter to the Editor by Agnes M. Butterfield, Congreve Park, Spanish Town, *The Daily Gleaner*, 30 January 1936.

[93] *The Daily Gleaner*, 'Art Exhibition Described as Epoch-Making Event', 17 May 1938, p. 7.

During the Jamaica Arts Society's annual dinner Dr. W. E. McCulloch's speech toasting the health of the Society departed from the customary. In responding to the criticisms, he was reported to have:

> ... struck out at the many self-made experts and authorities which he said this island produced in quite goodly numbers. He went on to assert that art was not confined to any particular branch of work; all workers were artists in so far as they did their work competently and with a definite technique. He advised all those who would be artists to get themselves trained and disciplined "in this, the most undisciplined country in the world" and went further to note that "He saw there was going to be an African art exhibition. He thought they were laying too much stress upon the African side of it, African art was very primitive; not primitive in the sense of European art".[94]

As he might have expected in this 'new' Jamaica his pronouncements did not go unchallenged.

In proposing the toast to the guest of honour, Mr. Philip Sherlock, retiring head of Wolmer's Boy's School and the Institute's newly appointed curator and Secretary elect, Mr. Leacroft Robinson referred to Sherlock as:

> ...having an almost inexhaustible store of folk-tales and proverbs. Philip Sherlock had "succeeded in teaching things Jamaican which were deserving of appreciation; things about which they had a right to be proud." And further that "He represented a new age; he fostered an awakening in Jamaica and helped to bring about a renaissance"... in going to the Institute of Jamaica he would spend his time in the education of the whole of Jamaica ... They honoured him that night because he had succeeded, perhaps more than anyone else, in teaching Jamaicans to appreciate their own.[95]

While Sherlock graciously accepted this tribute, he took the opportunity to address earlier statements and made it clear that:

> He did not agree with Dr. McCulloch that they were too apt to emphasise [sic] the importance of Africa. He thought as a people whenever they mentioned Africa it had been with a sense of shame and a feeling of reproach. But if they were going to build up a sense of manhood and self-respect; they must look back to the past which had been theirs. And he did feel that places like Nigeria and The Gold Coast had something to give them because there was a strong spiritual link between Jamaica and those parts: by mixing African and European

---

94 *The Daily Gleaner*, 'Arts Society Honours Mr. Philip Sherlock', 12 December 1938, p. 5.

95 Ibid.

culture it will help them to build up a civilization that was entirely their own.[96]

The 1930s therefore constituted a watershed in this pre-independence society's reaching for a distinctive identity. Similar sentiments developed and expanded throughout the region in the decades to come.

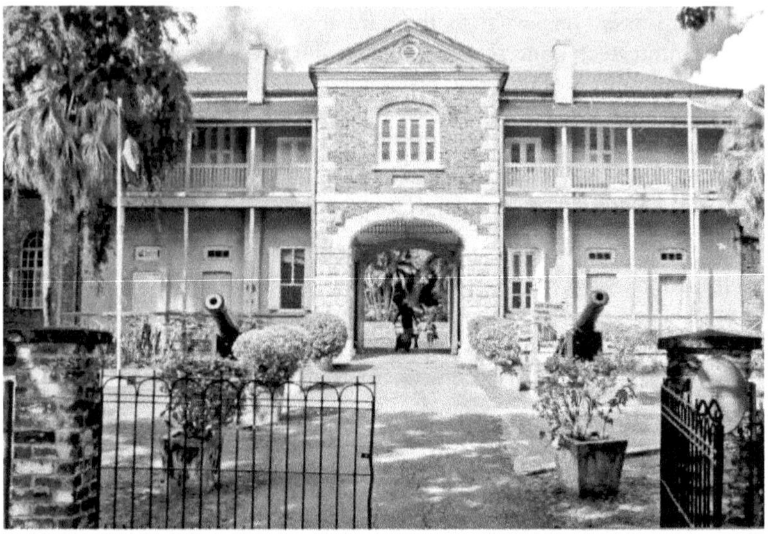

Front Facade, Barbados Museum & Historical Society
(Photo Credit: William St. J. Cummins)

World War II stimulated nationalist sentiments that had already begun to develop by the 1930s. Wartime inflation and restrictions exacerbated Caribbean grievances. West Indians had largely supported the British war effort, but expected major concessions in return. However, the war had also released a group of people in the form of servicemen and women who returned to their countries and their region confident in their skills to meet the challenges of their new lives, and who joined the wave of increased political and economic consciousness and anti-imperialism. For many West Indians, the experience of war had drawn them closer together as a people, and the emergence of their world from the toils of war offered unprecedented opportunities for a better life.[97] At the same time the decolonization movement began to build momentum

---

[96] Ibid.

[97] The growing awareness of a regional identity occurred amongst persons of different islands who met in increasing numbers overseas, mainly in the universities, in the United Kingdom, Canada, and the United States. In alien surroundings, they quickly saw that the problems of each island were not peculiar to that island but were really regional problems; and soon they began to think of themselves as West Indians rather than as particular islanders. Returning home, these persons spread the idea of West

immediately following the end of the war; the rise of trade unions during the war also considerably increased agitation for change.

Barbados Museum and Historical Society Director Neville Connell demonstrated a new awareness in addressing its deficiencies through that institution's acquisitions policy. He wrote to his colleagues at Hull indicating that

> The Council of this Society is anxious to obtain relics of slavery in the form of slave chains, yokes etc. for its Museum which are at present sadly lacking. No relics are obtainable locally and except for a few documents relating to the sale and transfer of slaves there is nothing to remind visitors of this period of the island's history...[98]

The 1956 *Guide to the Barbados Museum* reflects the success of Connell's campaign in this regard with its description of the Hall Gallery. This indicated that

> This Gallery contains specimens of local historical interest. Case No.59 ... displays relics of slavery. Negro slaves were first imported from Africa in quantity to work on the sugar plantations here as a result of white apprentices and bondservants from England having proved unsatisfactory in this climate. In 1629, only two years after the settlement of the island the presence of negroes is first recorded numbering 50. By 1643, the number had risen to approximately 6,000, and in 1838, the year when slavery was finally abolished, the number exceeded 82,000.[99]

Elsewhere the Gallery guide made brief references to the fate of the majority population. The exhibit of a Zouave uniform of a sergeant of the West India Regiment, for example, provided an opportunity to explain the origins of that unique arrangement of... black and white loyalists ... formed into a corps of which the South Carolina was one ... which took active part in the fighting in the islands' and subsequently 'in Africa and in the Ashanti Wars of 1864 and 1873-4.'[100] These references to the black population, brief though they were - for example, the Destruction of St. Pierre, Martinique, the Arawaks and the Jews of Barbados all merited much greater attention in terms of their prominence within the national historical narrative displayed in the Museum's galleries - represented a critical first step in authorizing their existence on the national historical landscape. Nevertheless the earnest tone of this note is contradicted in other correspondence from the former Governor of Barbados' widow, Lady Gilbert Carter, with reference to her arrangements for the disposition of her collections after her death, with which Connell's stance thus seems quite inconsistent. Lady Gilbert Carter asserted that

---

Indian unity. The awareness of a West Indian identity was also fostered by improved communications and air travel between the islands.

[98] Neville Connell, unpublished Letter to the Director of Hull Municipal Museum, Hull, 16 January 1950. BMHS Archives.

[99] Neville Connell, *A Guide to the Barbados Museum,* 2nd Edition, published by The Barbados Museum & Historical Society, 1956, p. 3.

[100] *Barbados Museum Guide,* pp. 4-5.

> Sir Alfred Savage wrote that Nigeria was starting a new museum & they would like to have Sir Gilbert's [African] Collection (in the front hall of Ilaro). Now in my will I left it to the Barbados Museum, but I feel sure the Historical Society will waive this & let it go to Nigeria as it came from there, ... - I sort of thought that Mr. Shilstone [President of the Society] was not anxious to have it - he rightly stressed the idea that the Arawaks were the only *heathens* [my emphasis] which should interest the coloured people in Barbados & that they should be encouraged to forget that they were brought over from there against their will.[101]

In fact the first edition of the Barbados Museum's guide, while explaining in detail the entire process of the sugar industry, made only a single reference to slavery. The 36-page publication contains a single reference to the enslaved, fortuitously in the History section, recounting 'There are examples of the 'pine-apple' penny, issued in the island, on the one side of which is a pine-apple, and on the other the head of a negro, crowned. There are different varieties of this 'slave-money', as it is called, and half-pennies were also in circulation.'[102] These are clear indicators of the ways in which some communities and individuals took definite steps to erase history and, in some sense, any reconnection with past identities.

Similarly processes of conscious repositioning again emerged in the Jamaican context. William Patterson's article publicly protesting the nature of the Institute of Jamaica's exhibits indicates that the Barbados Museum was not alone in the distinctly monochromatic hue of its displays. Regarding the Jamaican historical experience, the writer and human rights activist asserted that

> If you ask the average passer-by where to find authentic stories of those historical events which blazed the path to the ending of slavery in Jamaica he or she will invariably answer "Go the Institute. It is our cultural centre and fills the cultural needs of Jamaicans". [But] "the cultural needs of such a variegated community must be regarded with great objectivity". The question arises: whose culture and for whom? Distortions of the cultural background of a people can have grave psychological effects upon its youth, a degrading and dehumanising effect.[103]

The writer then critically analyzes the Institute's exhibits against this criterion:

> Spend some hours in the Institute of Jamaica. After a careful and impartial survey and you will probably say that: The Institute may be for the white Jamaican, for the Englishman and the American, all that it

---

[101] Lady Gertrude Gilbert Carter, Unpublished letter to Neville Connell, Director of the Barbados Museum & Historical Society, 15 January 1953, BMHS Archives - Gifts.

[102] *"What to See in the Barbados Museum: A Popular Guide to the Exhibits"* compiled by Thomas Sheppard, 1937, p. 10.

[103] William L. Patterson, 'The Role of the Institute as ...Jamaica's Cultural Centre', *The Sunday Gleaner,* 21 April 1957, n/n.

> is said to be - a cultural centre satisfying to their needs. But the value of the contents of this "Centre of Culture" to the divided coloured youth, especially to an ambitious negro lad or lass is very questionable indeed.[104]

Patterson's excoriating interrogation of the exhibition exposes the inherently triumphalist nature of the displays. He adverts that

> The black man has a place in the Institute of Jamaica as a slave, as a freed man who is a faithful servant for the economic rulers, as a subordinate to his technical advisers, as a backward and subservient figure. His culture is presented to him in terms of what those who rule think best for themselves.[105]

In contrast, Patterson points out the glaring deficiencies and deliberate elisions of history in terms of what was *not* present in the assumed national story on display:

> I looked in vain for a portrait of Cudjoe, the mighty warrior for human freedom ... I was referred to a history written by a sympathiser of those whom he had conquered. Cudjoe was caricatured in it, perhaps out of revenge ... I looked in vain for a picture of English gentlemen humbly signing the treaty forced upon them by the Maroons in 1739. I wanted to see pictures of the Tacky Slave Rebellion of 1769, of the Maroon War of 1796, of the revolt of the slaves in 1831. These are the historic events which give character and substance to the culture of the Jamaican.[106]

While acknowledging the presence of the branding irons and the iron cage gibbet on display, Patterson was not mollified by these evidences of slavery which in his view, largely point to an effective criminalization of the black population. He retorts that "on the walls are pictures of contented slaves and their benevolent masters ... This gives no evidence ... of those who bore the brands of slavery and made of these a badge of honour ...".[107] The writer surmises that the abolition of the Historical Gallery was perhaps a deliberate attempt to conceal the "peerless courage of the Negro slaves".[108] He considers that

> An Institute that is a cultural centre for Jamaica should blazen the walls with the struggles of men who valued freedom more than life. Freedom and Culture are inseparable. Here lies the roots of Jamaican culture. In this respect the Institute is a complete failure.[109]

---

[104] Ibid.
[105] Ibid.
[106] Ibid.
[107] Ibid.
[108] Ibid.
[109] Ibid.

Patterson's evaluation provided an in-depth view of where one West Indian country stood in terms of its national museum's capacity to address a growing sense of self-expressed confidence. The ability of Jamaica's central museum institution to reflect that burgeoning identity had been found to be both morally and intellectually deficient on this point.

In curating the *Federation Day Exhibition on Aspects of the History of the West Indies,* Dr. Elsa Goveia, the young advocate historian based at the department of history on the University College of the West Indies' Mona campus, sought to address these deficiencies in public knowledge by promoting the importance of Federation as the foundation for a new nation and a new national identity, and found innovative opportunities to expand public knowledge.

Goveia, in her extensive Introduction to the 1959 exhibit provided, for the first time within the context of history-making in a West Indian educational institution, a seminal statement of the core of West Indian history. She states that 'Some will say that, among such people, history has stood still. But perhaps it would be better to say that, in them, history lives and will speak to us if we listen.'[110] In a masterly recitation, recapitulation and restatement of Caribbean history, Goveia contextualized the importance of the region to the advancement of empire. She then proceeded, through a deliberate reconstruction of West Indian history in several sections, to articulate the technical basis for the specificity of the black man's unfreedom within that history. Goveia elucidates:

> Freedom confers mobility. The slave's position is characterized by fixity. His status is a matter of law, which places him under the control of a master. The master decides his occupation and his place of residence. The law restricts his physical movement. He is coerced by law and by the master's will.[111]

The structure of this exhibit, though only temporary in nature, was a radical departure from the existing permanent history displays at the Institute of Jamaica, and indeed elsewhere in the region. Goveia structured the whole exhibit around the growth and development of knowledge of the New World; the process by which the development of the West Indies fuelled material prosperity elsewhere, leading to the desire to harness its resources and the creation of a slave-based society and economy; effective resistance and challenge to the established order; and finally to the political awakening of the region. She was convinced that 'shame about the past too often fills the place that should be held by knowledge. Knowledge of the past must play its part in our liberation from the bonds of the past'.[112] Her approach was innovative and indeed revolutionary, graphically depicting the bonds of enslavement which tied the contemporary Caribbean to its

---

[110] Elsa V. Goveia, 'An Introduction to the Federation Day Exhibition on Aspects of the History of the West Indies', University College of the West Indies, 1959, p. 2.

[111] Ibid., p. 30.

[112] Ibid., p. 42.

complex historical past in a way never previously articulated.[113] Through her 'creolisation' of the region's history, the experience of the peoples within the historical narrative were contextualized through the process by which the region's landscape, economy, and pysche were shaped.

The exhibition therefore was a reminder of how West Indians came to be who they were today. For many of those who regarded themselves as West Indians, Elsa Goveia laid out the issue:

> It is important to ask what this nation is. If it includes all the people of the Federation, the national Government is the government of the Federation. That Government must be given powers commensurate with its responsibilities. Otherwise it will prove to be as impotent in the face of needs and desires of its citizens as was Crown Colony government in relation to its subjects. Changes of government will be meaningless until we have settled the fundamental question of our national identity. In the earlier struggle for our political rights, it was perhaps enough to be anti-British. Now that we face Independence, and the immense problems which it will bring, it has become absolutely essential that we should know whether we are West Indians.[114]

Conclusions

Early Caribbean museums were predominantly museums of natural history and science. They were not history museums, and few had significant collections designed to relate to the human history of their respective countries. Of course, within some of the museums, there did exist items that would now be considered as historical material, such as documents, portraits, personalia, domestic items, tools and farming implements. Yet these were in no sense collected with the aim of representing the human development of the country. As Tony Bennett indicates, when compared to European national pasts, the colony 'could not lay claim to a past which might be represented on the same footing as the pasts of other nations within the militarised modes of national commemoration which were dominant at the time'.[115]

In this sense, the colony did not have a 'nation' on which to base historical collections. The indigenous population was generally regarded as outside civilized time and history, while pirate, plebeian or planter ancestors were not

---

[113] The sections were: I - Environment, Aborigines and Discovery; II - Discovery and Early Colonisation; III - Curiosity and Scientific Interest aroused by the Discovery; IV - Economic Development of the European Colonies in the West Indies; V - The Established Order in the West Indies during the Eighteenth Century; VI - Challenge and Overthrow; VII -Reconstruction; VIII -Modern Political Developments, including Federation; IX - History and Evidence: How the Past Survives; X - Conservation of the Records.

[114] Ibid., p. 40.

[115] T. Bennett, *Out of Which Past? Critical Reflections on Australian Museum and Heritage Policy,* Cultural Policy Studies, Occasional Paper No. 3, Institute for Cultural Policy Studies, Griffith University, Brisbane, 1988, p. 6.

regarded as worthy of preservation or commemoration, and certainly not the appropriate foundation upon which to build a national identity.[116] The white population still largely saw itself as being British or European, and was content to have its history rooted in that context. The Black majority was not merely marginalized from the scope of museum interpretation, but quite simply did not exist in any formal consideration of colonial history. West Indian museums thus developed in the colonial manner whereby they celebrated the dominance of European culture and society, organized primarily around the exploits of monarchs, great statesmen and military heroes, over 'primitive' indigenous populations. This served to confirm the West Indies' place as part of the Empire, reinforcing the sense of imperial identity, and also re-affirmed the colonies as part of the continuum of Europe's white history. As Graeme Davison has described, state institutions were not ascribed the word 'national' to portray a national distinctiveness: 'Museums and art galleries were national by virtue of their civic and educative role, not because of their exclusively or distinctively national content.' Martin Prösler goes even further in observing that

> ... the world-wide diffusion of museums was tied in with European colonialism and imperialism. Their expansion, then, occurred in close connection with those political factors in globalization which have provided the contemporary *world order* with its basic structure.[117]

The organizing principles which had been adopted as the model for West Indian institutions, inspired by the Great Exhibition of 1851, would remain unchanged - and largely unchallenged - for the next one hundred years.

References

Ade, S., 4 January, 2004. 'The Passions of Suzie Wong Revisited' *Aboriginal Intelligence.*

Anderson, Benedict, 1991. *Imagined Communities: Reflections on the Origin and Spread of Nationalism,* London, Verso.

Barbados Globe, 4 October 1850.

Bather, Francis, May, 1934. "Special Report on the Institute of Jamaica for the Encouragement of Literature, Sciences, and Arts", NLJ MS73.

Bennett, T., 1988. 'Out of Which Past? Critical Reflections on Australian Museum and Heritage Policy', *Cultural Policy Studies, Occasional Paper No. 3,* Institute for Cultural Policy Studies, Griffith University, Brisbane.

---

[116] The colonies did however strive to show the progress they had made, particularly through the Exhibitions, which in some ways can be seen as being typical of nationalism.

[117] Martin Prösler, 'Museums and Globalisation', in Sharon MacDonald and Gordon Fyfe, eds, *Theorizing Museums: Representing Identity and Diversity in a Changing World,* (Oxford: Blackwell & The Sociological Review, 1996), p. 22.

Blouet, O, 1986. 'Sir William Reid, F.R.S., 1791-1858: Governor of Bermuda, Barbados and Malta,' *Notes and Records of the Royal Society,* Vol. 40, #2, pp. 169-193.

Booth, K., 1985. 'When Jamaica Welcomed the World: The Great Exhibition of 1891'. *Jamaica Journal,* August-October.

Carter, Lady Gertrude Gilbert, Unpublished letter to Neville Connell, Director of the Barbados Museum & Historical Society, 15 January 1953, BMHS Archives.

Connell, Neville, 1956. *A Guide to the Barbados Museum,* 2^{n} Edition, The Barbados Museum & Historical Society.

______, unpublished Letter to the Director of Hull Municipal Museum, Hull, 16 January 1950. BMHS Archives.

Cummins, Alissandra, {1994} 1996. 'The "Caribbeanization" of the West Indies: the Museum's Role in the Development of National Identity', in Kaplan, Flora (ed.), *Museums and the Making of "Ourselves": the Role of Objects in National Identity,* London and New York.

______, 1998. 'Confronting Colonialism: the First 60 Years at the BMHS', *Journal of the Barbados Museum & Historical Society,* Vol. XLII, 1994-1995.

Daily Gleaner, The, Jamaica Exhibition 1891: History of the Undertaking', 28 January 1891; 'Holding of the Convention of Negro Peoples: Mr. Garvey Speaks of Art and Urges Hearers to live Artistic Lives', 17 August 1934; 'A Lively Meeting of Jamaica Institute: For Two Hours Coterie of Young Members Criticize the Board of Management', letter to the Editor by Agnes M. Butterfield, Congreve Park, Spanish Town, 30 January 1936; Annual Meeting of the Institute of Jamaica, Lively Indeed', 31 January 1936; 'Art Exhibition Described as Epoch-Making Event', 17 May 1938; Arts Society Honours Mr. Philip Sherlock', 12 December 1938.

Drayton, Richard, 2000. *Nature's Government: Science, Imperial Britain, and the 'Improvement' of the World,* New Haven and London.

Fewkes, Jesse W, 1907. 'The Aborigines of Puerto Rico and Neighbouring Islands' 25th *Annual Report of the Bureau of American Ethnology,* Washington D.C, Bureau of American Ethnology.

Fleming, D, 1988. 'Science in Australia, Canada, and the United States: Some Comparative Remarks', *Actes du Dixième Congrès International d'Histoire des Sciences,* Paris, 1962, (quoted in Sheets-Pyenson, Susan, *Cathedrals of Science: The Development of Colonial Natural History Museums During the Late Nineteenth Century,* McGill-Queen's University Press, Montreal, Canada).

Froude, James Anthony, 1888. *The English in the West Indies, or, The Bow of Ulysses;* London.

Goveia, Elsa V, 1959. 'An Introduction to the Federation Day Exhibition on Aspects of the History of the West Indies', University College of the West Indies.

Healy, C, 1997. *From the Ruins of Colonialism: History as Social Memory,* Melbourne.

Impey, O. and A. McGregor (eds), 1985. *The Origins of Museums: The Cabinet of Curiosities in Sixteenth and Seventeenth Century Europe,* Oxford.

Kidd, Benjamin, 1898. *The Control of the Tropics,* MacMillan, New York.

LeMercier du Quesnay, Frederick, 1965. 'Museums of Jamaica'.

MacDonald, Sharon, 1998. *The Politics of Display: Museums, Science, Culture,* London, Routledge.

Patterson, William L. 21 April 1957. 'The Role of the Institute as ... Jamaica's Cultural Centre', *The Sunday Gleaner.*

Proceedings of the Natural History Society of British Guiana, Georgetown, British Guiana, 1863.

Prösler, Martin, 1996. 'Museums and Globalisation', Sharon MacDonald and Gordon Fyfe (eds), *Theorizing Museums: Representing Identity and Diversity in a Changing World,* Oxford: Blackwell & The Sociological Review.

Report of the Committee of Correspondence of the Royal Agricultural and Commercial Society, 1857-1861, Georgetown, British Guiana, 1861.

Sheppard, Thomas, 1937. *"What to See in the Barbados Museum: A Popular Guide to the Exhibits"* Barbados Museum & Historical Society, Bridgetown.

Stabroek News, 2004. "The Colonist", 13 February 1868, cited in Arlene Munro, *A Short History of the National Museum.*

The Imperial Institute of the United Kingdom, the Colonies, and India, Imperial Institute, London, 1892.

Tortello, Rebecca 'The Great Exhibition of 1891: Jamaica on Show', http://jamaica-gleaner.com/pages/history/storyoo18.html, accessed 30 June 2012.

Tothill, Vincent D, {1939} 2009. *Trinidad's Doctor's Office: The Amusing Diary of a Scottish Physician in Trinidad in the 1920s,* Trinidad, Paria Publishing Company Ltd.

Willis, Deborah and Carla Williams, 2000. 'The Black Female Body in Photographs from World's Fairs and Expositions' in "Race, Photography, and American Culture," *Exposure,* volume 33,1/2, Daytona Beach, Florida.

Chapter 2

Haiti, Museums and Public Collections:

Their History and Development after 1804

Marie-Lucie Vendryes

Introduction

The country's cultural heritage has been a major preoccupation for the successive governments in Haiti since the country adopted the Civil Code in 1825. Even the Constitution promulgated in 1987 includes three articles addressing the necessity to preserve the cultural heritage and entrusting current generations with the duty to develop, promote and transmit this legacy to the following generations. Conscious of this public responsibility, the country's political leaders created places of memory accessible to all, but difficult to sustain.

The first museums in Haiti emerged at the end of the nineteenth century as the primary instances of conservation for movable cultural goods. It is unclear whether these had been inspired by the colonial "chambers of wonders" set up by the Circle of Philadelphists (which became the Royal Society of Science and Art of Cap-Francais in 1785). Doubts remain, because the museum is first mentioned in a posthumous government plan developed by the thinker and ideologist Edmond Paul (1837-1895). In 1927 there were timid attempts to raise public awareness concerning the need to set up a dedicated place for the conservation of cultural goods which are part of the public domain. From 1804, the year of Haitian independence, to the present day, the number of public institutions safeguarding the country's memory and heritage is a marker for what must be termed a failure in terms of preservation and transmission of movable cultural goods. In 1997 the French legal expert Vincent Negri noted in his mission report *Legal Analyses and Proposals for Norms in Museums and for Heritage Conservation in Haiti* that "museums are not embedded in the institutional landscape governing the administration of heritage in Haiti".

He was right. When reassessing the history of public museum institutions after the conquest of the territory and the country's liberation from the oppression of slavery, five major models can be observed. This categorization allows us to distinguish a paradigmatic line that runs through the history of these institutions, all of which were inaugurated with pomp and circumstance and then left to die slowly but surely from neglect. It also allows us to reconsider these institutions in their original context and thus get a better understanding of the reasons that led to their conspicuous absence today. The five models in question are:

1. the palace
2. the museum of the nation
3. the museum of commemoration
4. the temple of remembrance
5. the museum of the fatherland

The Palace

The era of the palace is epitomised by two institutions: the Exhibition Palace (Palais de l'Exposition, 1881) and the Palace of Independence (Palais de l'Independance, 1904).

The Exhibition Palace was housed in a dedicated building on Champ-de-Mars in the capital, Port-au-Prince. In the nineteenth century Europe's industrial and commercial developments had prompted the emergence of universal exhibitions. Aiming to establish itself in Europe's markets, Haiti, the little country in the Caribbean, was keen to be invited to these fairs (Amsterdam in 1883, Antwerp in 1885, Brussels in 1910, etc.) and promote its agricultural and artisanal products. On the national scale, the key factor for the establishment of a palace was the sudden awareness of the country's wealth. The government of Lysius Félicité Salomon (Cayes 1885-Paris 1888) did not beat about the bush. There was no doubt that Haiti's economic potential lay in its natural and cultural resources. Natural specimens, exhibited for the most part with the support of persons in charge of the pedagogical collections in church schools, aroused the visitor's curiosity and instilled a sense of pride in Haitians. On the other hand, the section within the Palace dedicated to decorative arts seemed to prove to many Haitians that they were blessed with creativity. But the adventure of the fair, by its very nature and purpose, is an ephemeral one, since the exhibited collections exist as such only for the time of the exhibition.

In 1904 the Palace of Independence was built as a monument to Gonaives, the historic city where the January 1804 celebrations had taken place. For the centenary of the victory of the revolutionaries who had chased the Napoleonic troops from Saint-Domingue and called out a new country (Haiti) freed from slavery, the government did not cut corners. Some inhabitants from Gonaives who had seen the Palace with their own eyes in the first half of the twentieth century remember it as a prestigious building that accommodated objects and works of art related to the revolutionary adventure. Among others it presented the - imagined rather than real - portraits of the protagonists who had played a decisive role in the history of this revolution. By 1930, however, the Palace had prematurely aged and the collections were left to themselves. In 1952 the building, which had once been the pride of Haiti, was torn down. The remains of its collections (mostly artworks, since according to the evocative approach adopted in the conception of the museum, art has to testify for history) were transported to the National Museum (Le Musée National).

A place of commercial or commemorative exhibitions, the "museal" palace was for a while transformed into a place of general interest catering to large audiences who discovered the country's rich natural and cultural heritage. Haiti's self-sufficiency was obvious, if the country regulated itself and adopted rational procedures. The visitor's pride and sense of belonging were bolstered by the construction of the palace, a prestigious and flourishing place.

The Museum of the Nation

After 1904 the palaces became obsolete as "guardians" of the country's heritage. They slowly vanished, leaving only a few traces behind them. The time had come to stage a certain idea of the *nation*. This nation had led a successful revolution; once it was free and independent, it was both its wish and duty to prove to the rest of the world that it could properly manage itself and its resources. After all, who could forget that it was from its soil that the French colonial power drew its wealth? Or that in 1915 the country suffered humiliation when it was occupied by the USA? By 1938, the year the Americans left the island, Haitian national pride had been titillated. It was therefore necessary to anchor the people's identity and reconquer the territory. In 1940 and 1941, respectively, two new museums were inaugurated: the National Museum and the Museum of the Bureau of Ethnology.

In 1940, the National Museum was founded as a result of the movement in favour of a strong Haitian nation. The museum's mission was to "preserve the memory of the past and [to] glorify it, [to] reconstruct the national pride after the humiliation of American occupation, [to] give the people reasons for hope in the future, [to] understand the present [...]".[118] On Champ-de-Mars, which had become the historic and cultural centre of Port-au-Prince, construction started in April 1940 on a small building designed to accommodate this first *modern* public museum and its collections. These came from the Vincent Foundation, named after then-president Sténio Vincent (1874-1959) and his sister Rézia. The National Museum gathered all disciplines under one roof: history, arts, archaeology, numismatics, mineralogy, botany, textiles, etc. - a heterogeneous collection offered to the nation, private objects entering the public sphere to bear witness to the existence of wealth, authenticity and sound management as legitimate causes for pride and hope.

In 1960, the collections of the National Museum were retrieved from the building on Champ-de-Mars to be housed in the private home of Paul E. Magloire (1907-2001) while the former president was in exile in the USA. This museum, which was located in the Turgeau area in Port-au-Prince, functioned relatively well despite being managed by changing and therefore destabilising administrations.[119] This hesitation in firmly establishing the museum's public mission as a guardian of national cultural goods betrays an indecisiveness concerning the direction that Haitian museum institutions were to take. In 1983 the National Museum was divested of most of its collections for the benefit of a new museum, the Museum of the Haitian National Pantheon (Musée du Panthéon National Haïtien, MUPANAH).

In 1941, one year after the creation of the National Museum, the Museum of the Bureau of Ethnology, opened its doors to the public with the aim to secure objects used in the Vodou cult thus *en déshérence.*[120] It was a department of the Bureau of Ethnology and one of the first *native* ethnographical museums worldwide. Its self-declared mission was to collect the scattered artefacts of a culture that was disappearing because, as it was believed, the campaigns against superstition led by the Catholic Church were targeting the practice of Vodou religion and aimed to destroy the artefacts used in its ritual ceremonies. The mission of the Museum of the Bureau of Ethnology was to "conduct research, collect, preserve and present the material and spiritual culture of Haitians".

Exhibitions were staged with the artefacts from the museum's ethnographical and archaeological collections, which were the subject of relatively serious study and research in the early years of the institution. Unfortunately, the museum's functioning was seriously hampered by a string of incidents, among which were relocations, fires (in 1960, 1984 and 2005), theft and vandalism. This explains why its exhibitions became few and far between.

---

[118] State Law from 1940 creating the National Museum, [*Loi organique creant le Musée National*].

[119] Between 1940 and 1970 the National Museum was placed under the supervision of the State Secretariats of Public Education and Public Works and of the Communal Magistrate of Port-au-Prince. From 1970 onwards, it was under the responsibility of the Office for Tourism and Public Relations.

[120] *En desherence* a term which means without any heirs. Objects that have been discarded which no-one would be willing to own.

Today only fragments and parts of objects remain, encased in plastic boxes standing on shelves in a room that ignores all standards of preventive conservation. (In January 2010 the building collapsed and buried the collection under its rubble).

The National Museum and the Museum of the Bureau of Ethnology promoted a certain concept of the nation. They aimed to raise awareness among the sons and daughters of the nation that they were forming a large family who had inherited a territory, a history, a culture, a language and a legacy. This collective awareness had to be transformed into a public duty of remembrance. Together, Haitians were to nurture and manage this common heritage and promote its uniqueness in the rest of the world.

The Museum of Commemoration

The year 1949 was the occasion for the government to organise an international exhibition to mark the bicentenary of the foundation of Haiti's capital, Port-au-Prince. This anniversary called for lavish celebrations, to which all friendly nations were invited. The city's coastline was redeveloped and revamped thanks to a large illuminated avenue. Pavilions and booths were constructed, which represented "the visible contribution [...] of the workers, the artists and the people". Among the places to visit was the Museum of the Haitian People.

Conceived by Georges Henri Rivière (1897-1985), who was then the director of the International Council of Museums (ICOM), the Museum of the Haitian People formed an integral part of the bicentenary commemorative complex in Port-au-Prince. It participated in the celebration by exhibiting the 'witnesses' of Haitian history and identity. "The Father of French Museology", as Rivière was nicknamed, had designed ten galleries dealing with 'the history of Haiti, from geological times to the present day'. During a second trip to Haiti in 1976, the museologist remarked in hindsight that "unfortunately, without a sound administrative foundation, the Museum survived only a few months after the great manifestation from which it had emerged". In 1949 Rivière had dreamed of a Museum of the Haitian People that would have been able to fulfill the various functions of modern museums, i.e. acquiring, managing, promoting and expanding collections.

The heterogeneity of collections - which were similar to those of the National Museum - made the management of the artefacts a difficult undertaking, as financial, technical and material means were rather precarious. Moreover, the administration's disinterest was blatantly obvious. The Museum of the Haitian People was closed for good in 1958, and most of the remaining artefacts were entrusted to the Bureau of Ethnology for the purposes of its own museum.

The notion of the "formation of the Haitian territory" and the "history of its evolution", inscribed in the approach that underpinned the establishment of a Haitian museum, was new. Nature and culture, in a dialectical relationship, were associated with history to illustrate the defining events in the emergence and construction of Haiti. And then there were also those who, anonymously, had allowed history to unfold, as they had also taken part in these events - the people.

The Temple of Remembrance

"It is on the walls of tombstones that we read the most judicious reasons to live. It is the dead who give best counsel." On 2 July 1955, Secretary of State for National Education, Leon Laleau, pronounced these words during the inauguration of the Musée Paul-Eugene Magloire at Cap-Haïtien. This museum defined itself as a place of memory conducive to "meditation and resolve [sic], where it is possible to learn lessons [...] from the past". It was lodged in a small monument, the house of Anténor Firmin. Eyewitnesses have described the place as "a temple of remembrance". It was indeed imbued with a sense of sacredness, especially with regard to the Christophian cult to which it pandered. Magloire, who hailed from the country's northern capital Cap-Haïtien, was a staunch admirer of Henri Christophe, who had ruled over this region from 1807 to 1820. The museum paid tribute to this revolutionary figure and invited visitors to reflect on his deeds, while encouraging them to learn the lessons from this momentous past. The museum thus cultivated *the memory of history.*

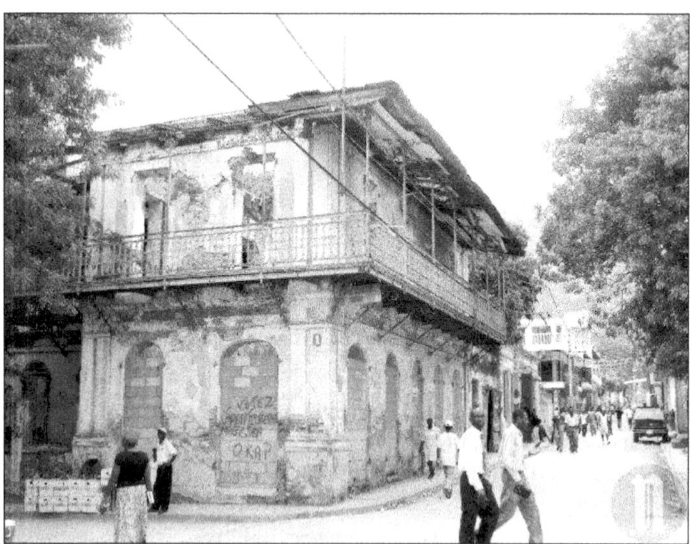

Maison Anténor Firmin, Cap-Haïtien (Photo Credit: Le Nouvelliste)

In 1957, it changed its name to Musée Anténor Firmin. Alas, in 1990 a fire destroyed the building as well as most of the collection of historic documents, plans, maps, military objects (uniforms, arms, honours, etc.) and coins. The building has remained empty ever since and is now in a state of unspeakable dereliction.

The Museum of the Fatherland

While it followed the paradigmatic line of public museums, the construction of the Museum of the Haitian National Pantheon (MUPANAH) in the latter part of the twentieth century was a rather particular endeavour. It evidenced a shift from the notion of nation to that of fatherland, epitomised by its founding fathers. In the museum, the anonymous makers of history therefore had to make way for heroes, as nationalism became *heroic.*[121]

In 1971, after the death of François Duvalier (1909-1971), his widowed wife, Simone Ovide Duvalier, and their son Jean-Claude (born in 1951) commissioned the construction of a mausoleum dedicated to the "Founding Father of the Fatherland". The architectural project was entrusted to the French architect Alexandre Guichard, who proposed a dome capped by eight hyperboloids: a large one over the tomb and seven smaller ones arranged in a semi-circle around it, symbolising the seven decisive moments in the life of "a nation tending towards its becoming".[122]

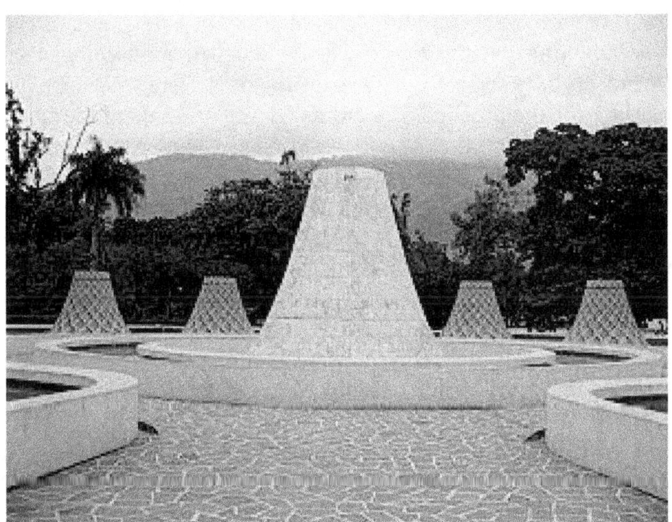

Museum of the Haitian National Pantheon, MUPANAH, (Photo Credit: Jean Frantz Philippe, Juillet 2009)

When, in May 1975, the mausoleum on Independence Square on Champ-de-Mars was inaugurated, it received the mortal remains of three founding fathers

[121] Carlo A. Célius, 'Le Musée, le passe et l'histoire', *ICOFOM Study Series* 35, 2006.
[122] Conversation between Alexandre Guichard and Carlo A. Célius, suburbs of Paris, 2007, unpublished.

of the fatherland: those of Alexandre Pétion (1770-1818), and those, scattered and fragmented, of Jean-Jacques Dessalines (1758-1806) and Henri Christophe (1757-1820). A fourth figure was to join them in April 1983, when the symbolic remains of Toussaint Louverture (1743-1803), which had been retrieved from a mass grave at Fort-de-Joux, entered the mausoleum in 1983. (It cannot be established with certainty whether the mortal remains of François Duvalier, for whom this monument had originally been built, are actually buried in the cenotaph.) Before the end of 1975, a presidential decree outlined the project of a Museum of the Haitian Nation, whose aim was to "analyse and present the history of Haiti in a didactic manner to Haitians and foreigners alike".[123] In October 1982, however, a decree-law abrogated this decree from 1975. This mission was then entrusted to the Museum of the Haitian National Pantheon (MUPANAH), along with the need to "perpetuate and promote the memory of the Founding Fathers of the Fatherland".

For the museography of the MUPANAH, the Haitian engineer A. Mangonès once again turned to Georges Henri Rivière, arguing that there was neither a museologist nor "a genuine museum" in Haiti. Rivière replied that he was "only too happy to serve this island with its prestigious past". Arriving in Haiti in September 1976, he met with the young president-for-life and presented his project. His conceptual choices focused on the constitutive events of the Haitian people, i.e. the abolition of slavery after the victorious battle against the oppressor and the foundation of a new nation. However, all this would be illustrated *virtually.* Claude Pecquet, a museologist sent to Haiti at the end of 1979 by UNESCO to evaluate Rivière's concept, proposed to compensate for the absence of exhibits by thinking along the lines of Andre Malraux's concept of the *Musée imaginaire.* This would have entailed a presentation based on sounds and images. Pecquet's report highlighted the MUPANAH's two contradictory functions: the more static and introspective mission as a space of commemoration (cenotaph), and the more cognitive and experiential, play-based approach as an exhibition space that needs to be animated and activated (museum). He also recommended that its scope should extend beyond its initial intention (paying tribute to the founding fathers of the fatherland) - and emphasise the historic evolution of the Haitian nation.

This double mission marked the heyday of the MUPANAH from 1983 to 1986, when it was placed under the responsibility of the Haitian National Institute of Culture and Arts (Institut National Haïtien de la Culture et des Arts), whose board of administrators was headed by Michèle Bennett Duvalier. After February 1986, when the Duvaliers were forced to leave the country, the MUPANAH was fortunately spared from public wrath. To this day people visit the museum, where they are offered a "reading" of the country's history that "evokes past events and interprets the present and the future". School classes continue to visit it as well, as do the members of the Haitian diaspora who are trying to reconnect with their origins. Furthermore,

[123] Presidential Decree from 1975 establishing the Museum of the Haitian Nation and defining its mission.

ambassadors of foreign countries traditionally place a wreath of flowers in front of the grave after presenting their credentials to the president of the Republic.

In 2006, the collections of the MUPANAH, Haiti's only functional public museum, comprised more than 1750 objects. The museum is unfortunately unable to fulfill its mission of "recording, collecting, gathering, classifying, restoring, acquiring and preserving pieces, documents, objects and furnishings of artistic, historic, archaeological or other value to form part of the national heritage".[124] And since it must also "coordinate the governing bodies' actions aiming to establish museums throughout the country", it cannot possibly play the role it has been assigned. Its responsibilities, which can be compared to those of a national directorate of museums, will not translate into tangible results unless it is given adequate means to do so and a clear vision is defined.

The MUPANAH, an autonomous agency of the Haitian Ministry of Culture, is a lonely crusader on the museum field in Haiti. This is not surprising to the extent that it encapsulates the four previous models (palace, museum of the nation, museum of commemoration, temple of remembrance). The choice of events worthy of remembrance concentrates on illustrious feats of arms, while those responsible for them are presented as heroes.[125] The spatial translation of these choices has dictated the architectural approach, resulting in a stately building in the shape of a small palace that seems to emerge from the ground. These choices are also visible in the museography, as witness the light streaming from the central hyperboloid into the cenotaph, the off-centred, peripheral cells with display cases and walls clad in images, or the great crescent space for temporary exhibitions. All other museums were deprived of their (historical, artistic, archaeological, ethnographic, numismatic, mineralogical, botanical, textile ...) collections and were literally left to die, as only the MUPANAH was to epitomise the concept of fatherland and sharpen people's civic and political awareness. This concept, transposed into the museum, has encouraged the intrusion of politics into the realm of culture.

Conclusion

Normative documents on Haiti's heritage state that the decision to protect the country's cultural goods is based on their artistic as well as their historic value. Protecting the country's heritage requires the establishment of sustainable spaces of conservation. But the decision to establish such spaces is dependent on the choices of the governing parties, whose influence on the life of cultural institutions in Haiti is pervasive.

The ubiquitous presence of governmental representatives in public heritage institutions leads to a strong political bias. Due to the way in which they

[124] Decree-Law from October 1982 creating the Musée du Panthéon National Haïtien (MUPANAH).

[125] Carlo A. Célius, op. cit.

have been conceived, these institutions are bound to transform into public platforms for politically vested events. This political activity marks the cultural infrastructure, while concealing the institutions' actual missions. The prevailing approach, which is based on short-term events, undermines the perennial mission of heritage conservation. On the other hand, the country's endemic political instability continually brings to the fore new leaders who, once they are in office, simply adopt their predecessor's approach. Politicians, it seems, still fail to understand the real meaning of heritage conservation. And in everyday practice confusion prevails, as national heritage sites, public collections and private goods are effectively indistinguishable.

In this context of political instability and influence on cultural heritage institutions, it is difficult to implement a stable and coherent museum policy that would accommodate a cultural and museological approach based on the social and economic development of the country. The museum, as the place *par excellence* of heritage conservation, has not yet found its own voice within Haitian society.

Chapter 3

The History and Evolution of Cuban Museums

José Linares

The island of Cuba has been a real crossroads where for geographical, historical and cultural reasons, European, American and Caribbean factors have coincided. Any analysis should therefore take into account this multiple perspective in order to find a nation with its own identity.

The museum phenomenon in this part of the world still needs a special study and a preliminary analysis of its historical, political and social nature. For obvious chronological reasons it cannot be analysed synchronically with either the European evolution of museums nor with North America, even though the museum establishment and development process might demonstrate certain common features. These include the conditions produced by different roots deriving from autochthonous populations, from territorial domination and occupation processes and from the origin of its occupants. Above all, its specific political and cultural evolution makes it a phenomenon with an underlying differentiated process of identity affirmation, consolidation and formation as a nation.

One approach to understanding the history and evolution of Cuban museums must start with their genesis: Collecting.

The earliest collecting in Cuba was predominantly scientific. In a "New World", the territory and inhabitants had first to be identified and known. The main way to achieve this was through natural history, biology - a wider discipline - and progressively archaeology and anthropology, which were then newly-formed sciences.

The origins of our collecting and the foundations of the first private scientific collections, then natural science museums and later on new and more diversified museums are to be found in this process. After achieving Independence from Spain in 1899 collecting interests were aimed then at historical and patriotic values. Museums kept very diverse sets of collections and objects; as time went by they gradually became more specialised, and integrated wider aspects of human creation: culture and art.

The first sources refer to a "natural history museum" established by Juan Cristóbal Gundlach (a German naturalist settled in Cuba) at his country estate, one mile away from Cardenas, in the western Matanzas province. Subsequently, through the actions of another scientist and collector (Francisco Blanes) and the patriot Oscar M. de Rojas, the entire collection was given to the museum founded in the same city in 1900.

The first Cuban museum of Anatomy was also created in the early years of the nineteenth century, in the old Augustinian monastery in Havana. It later became the Natural History and Pathologic Anatomy Museum in 1874, an institution that after several transformations was turned into the current and much richer Historical Museum of Medical Sciences bearing the name of Carlos J. Finlay, the Cuban doctor who discovered the source of transmission of yellow fever.

Other important museums appeared in provincial towns and in the capital city - Havana - as a result of commendable efforts by those citizens who had treasured valuable collections from their inception.

Firstly, the Museum and Municipal Library in the eastern city of Santiago de Cuba was created as an initiative of patriot Emilio Bacardí Moreau. It was later housed in a 1927 building which now bears the name of its inspirer and founder. This museum holds important collections of aboriginal archaeology, national history, local art and a very unusual, though small, South American pre-Columbian art collection, as well as some Egyptian pieces.

In the first half of the twentieth century, the third among three institutions in charge of "taking care of the memory of a nation that showed periodical symptoms of chronic amnesia"(1) was created by official decree in 1910. It was founded in 1913 and would become, after a very eventful existence, the present-day National Museum of Fine Arts.

The University of Havana's Museum of Anthropology was created as a teaching institution in 1903, bearing the name of the Cuban scholar Dr. Luis Montané. It treasures an exceptional collection of Indo-Cuban and Caribbean anthropology and archaeology, sciences with many common interests.

The birthplace of the most universal of all Cubans - José Martí (1853-1895) was turned into a museum in 1925.

Lastly, in the 1940s, due in large part to the sterling efforts of the community, a museum was created in city of Camagüey (towards the east of the island), which eventually became the Ignacio Agramonte Museum, named for an outstanding regional patriot (1841-1873).

This was the status of Cuban museums in 1959. Seven museums in the whole country without appropriate buildings, organised without either scientific bases or museological or museographical criteria, lacking both specialized staff and collection cataloguing systems for their collections, without defined research lines and with a very poor relationship with the public. Statistics show that the number of visitors to these seven museums was 2500 in 1958; that is, one out of 2000 inhabitants and an average of 357 visitors per institution.(2) That situation existed despite the efforts of many people who were personally committed to the survival of these institutions, but were faced with an official lack of interest.

From 1959 onwards, and supported by a strong political will, the sociocultural scene of the country began a long and deep transformation process. Museums became a focus of attention; an emergency action plan was proposed in order to overcome the existing situation and subsequently, to implement actions based on scientific and technical concepts, as well as to assimilate the most advanced museological knowledge. In practice, the restructuring of the abovementioned seven museums was begun. The cataloguing and conservation (and restoration if possible) of their collections could no longer wait and other scattered cultural assets had to be saved. Training of staff in different specialities in the field of museums was urgently needed; this included architects and designers able to update the image and presentation of museums. Given the lack of museologists, university graduates in history, art history and related disciplines were also brought into museums.

As in most Caribbean countries, Cuba lacked any foundation in the fields of either museum management or museology, the latter only later established as a specialized discipline. The first references were obtained through technical assistance from European countries, including the Eastern Bloc, and from the United Nations Educational Scientific and Cultural Organization (UNESCO), a UN specialized organization that also contributed support with the preparation of seminars and other training events.

In parallel with the abovementioned actions, new museums appeared with rich collections of objects from around the country, which developed into important cultural institutions including:

- Napoleonic Museum, Havana, 1961, from a rich collection of art objects, books and documents treasured by a wealthy Cuban sugar baron;
- National Museum of Decorative Arts, Havana, 1964;
- Pharmaceutical Museum, Matanzas, 1964 (the nineteenth-century Triolet Pharmacy);
- Guanabacoa Ethnographic Museum, Havana, 1964 (currently Guanabacoa Municipal Museum, first museum devoted to Afro-Cuban syncretic rites);
- Indo-Cuban Archaeology Museum, Banes, Oriente province, 1965.

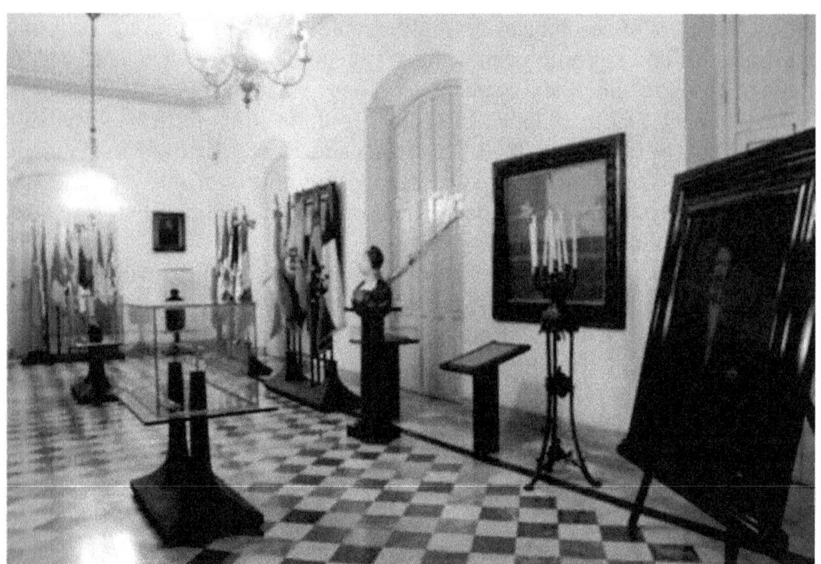

Museum of the City, Havana (Photo Credit: Rodolfo Martínez, 2009)

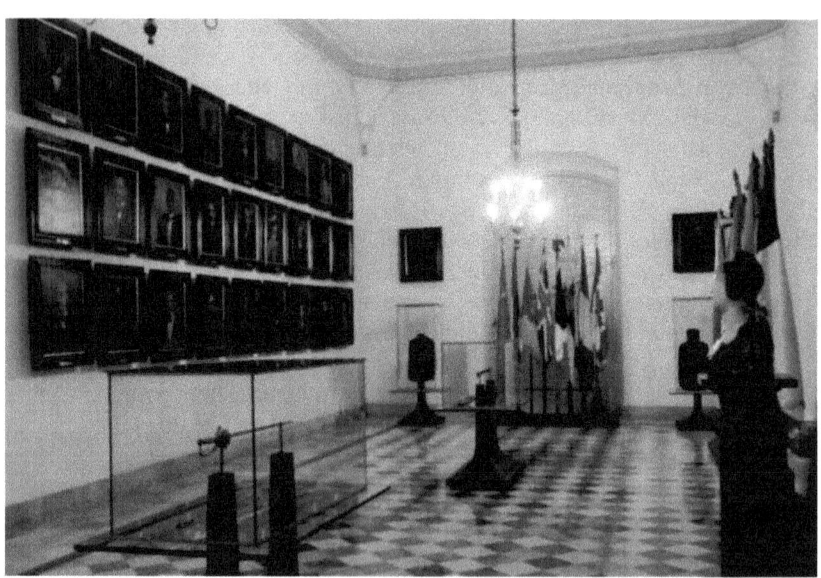

Museum of the City, Havana (Photo Credit: Rodolfo Martínez, 2009)

The turning point of Cuban museology, when a certain maturity was achieved, occurred in the second half of the 1960s with the creation of the Havana City Museum (1968), and the Colonial Art Museum of Havana (1969). Given their importance, the value of their collections, their buildings, and the museological and museographic approaches assumed, these museums permanently opened the way to new concepts. Similar contributions were made to the remodeling of the Ignacio Agramonte Provincial Museum of Camaguey and the Emilio Bacardí Municipal Museum of Santiago de Cuba. Both had existed before 1959 and were remodelled between 1968 and 1972. In addition to the internal museological aspects and the effective interaction with the population, diversified functional programmes and a museographic design enabling a more participative visitor experience, were introduced. This was unprecedented in Cuba and, I dare say, throughout the Caribbean region, the only important exception being the National Museum of Anthropology and History, Mexico, Federal District (1964).

The great importance of these museums and those which followed later lies in the fact that a modern museum is presented positively to the public. It is able to approach its vision of the subject in an attractive way that favours an object-spectator dialogue, moving away from the traditional museum approach and the concepts dominating these institutions until that moment.

Subsequently, and within the framework of the basic statements of the Constitution of the Republic, a legislative body was created in order to legally protect both the moveable and immoveable heritage and to create the so-called municipal museums. (3)

The enactment of the Law of Municipal Museums (1979) enabled the application of the new museology in Cuba. This law established that (Article 1):

> A museum will be created in every municipality of the Republic, where documents, photographs or other objects related to the national and local history reflecting the people's traditions, outstanding episodes of its struggle, the facts and life of its important personalities in the different times, and referring to its economical development, culture and institutions, will be preserved and displayed for their knowledge and study.

Today, more than 30 years after the enactment of the above-mentioned law, these museums are a reality. Although they do not all fully correspond to the strictest museological aspirations - often due to the lack of local resources - the most important achievement is the systematic work that they have developed, and continue to develop. The preservation and protection of both moveable and immoveable assets is continuously and actively pursued, as is the safeguarding of the intangible heritage, at permanent risk of disappearance. It is far more feasible to identify and protect this heritage at the regional level. This has been possible because municipal museums have been integrated - in most cases - into the community, of which they form a vital part. The identification and implementation of local particularities has allowed them to improve and enrich their contents.

The significance of the UNESCO Round Table of Santiago de Chile ("The importance and development of museums in the contemporary world") held in May 1972 should not be overlooked. To a large extent, Cuba assumed the challenges to museology mentioned in the Resolutions, and faced "the social, economical and cultural changes taking place in the world and above all in many of the underdeveloped areas" and headed in this direction without neglecting the current museums or abandoning the category of specialized museums.

A series of specific features which determined the quality of the solutions can be identified in new museums created from the 1980s onwards. Most of these are located in pre-existing buildings that were not conceived as museums, and many of them are housed in buildings of high historical or artistic value. This always means challenges regarding the feasibility, co-existence and dialogue between architectural and museographic values, and the adequate relationship of collections to the space. The Cuban experience is very important in this respect because, beyond the design criteria applied, it has made the current, somewhat old-fashioned conceptions, more flexible in terms of the theory of "architectural intervention".[126] In addition, it has opened a productive debate probably based on the action of the post-World War II generation of Italian architects with regard to buildings' restoration and museums' arrangement. (5)

New Cuban museums have given a high value to light, considering lighting as an important element of design which enhances the museum space, allowing a better appreciation of the displayed works, and contributing to a more effective object-subject communication: new technologies favour new and safer lighting equipment. This communication - object-subject - so debated today, becomes more important when the preponderance of the objects in the museum has been displaced by the subject, communicated by new technologies, information and search media rather than by direct didactic information. This can be achieved in different ways, by means of learning and new options and sensations, leading to individual interpretation.

New museological approaches to the ordering and organisation of the exhibitions of collections, options for signage and programming, readings and tours, museography based on a new way of "presenting" using focal points and spatially differentiated areas, all contribute definitely to this aim. It has also been important to exhibit fewer objects, to reduce and use written information properly, which if not done might well distract the visitor's attention in many cases.

Management of collections, presented in different ways, and temporary exhibitions ensuring their own permanent movement as well as the variety of offerings to the public, are important in achieving these goals.

Finally, as far as economic resources permit, the use of new technologies allows first of all, for the better preservation of objects (an inalienable responsibility of every museum) and helps to enrich exhibitions by creating real interactivity, not necessarily depending on the amount of computers and buttons that the subject can press at will.

A singular experience is the museum network of Havana's Historical Centre within the "integral management" model of Old Havana, which was included on the World Heritage List in 1982, together with its fortifications. In

[126] Architectural Intervention is a cross between installation art and architecture. It is an artistic practice where the architect's most important skill is spatial conceptualization.

the middle of a crisis in the country, the functions of the City Historian's Office were defined in 1993 by the Decree Law 143 of the State Council of the Republic of Cuba. The Office is granted the highest authority to promote the preservation and restoration of the monumental heritage in Old Havana.

Within this frame, a wide network of museums and house museums has been created which recovers, preserves and exhibits Havana's very rich heritage. It has been allowed to use important buildings as museums, and to carry out important cultural work which has had a significant impact on the population and its active participation.

From accumulated, duly processed and critically analysed experiences - while what is done is not always successful - it has been possible to improve the museum facilities in recent years throughout the country (many are still pending), and to set up or re-establish important museums, especially art museums, which have become paradigms for Cuba, and which could also be models for the Caribbean if they were better known.

In order to emphasise this aspect, it is worthwhile to analyse, at least briefly, a case study. This is the National Museum of Fine Arts, founded in 1913 as a National Museum, but which had a very eventful history with no fixed location until 1954 when the "Palace of Fine Arts" was inaugurated. Despite its name, this museum exhibited the most diverse collections of history, arts, ethnography and other disciplines. After 1959 its mission was redefined as a museum of arts and the other collections were transferred to other new, important museums.

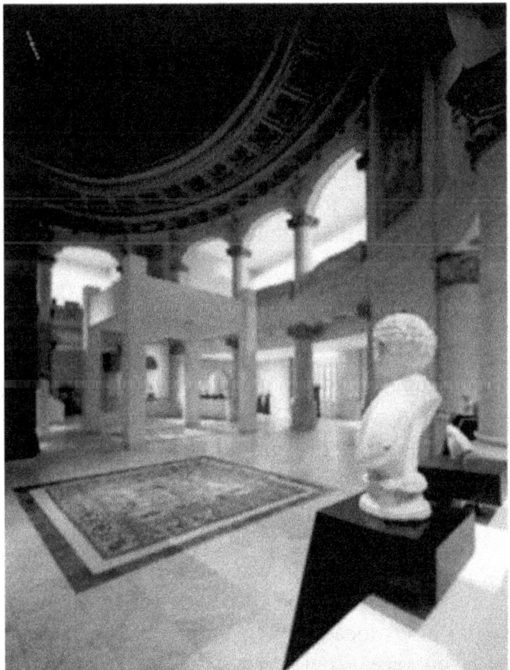

National Museum of Fine Arts, Havana (Photo Credit: Rodolfo Martínez, 2009)

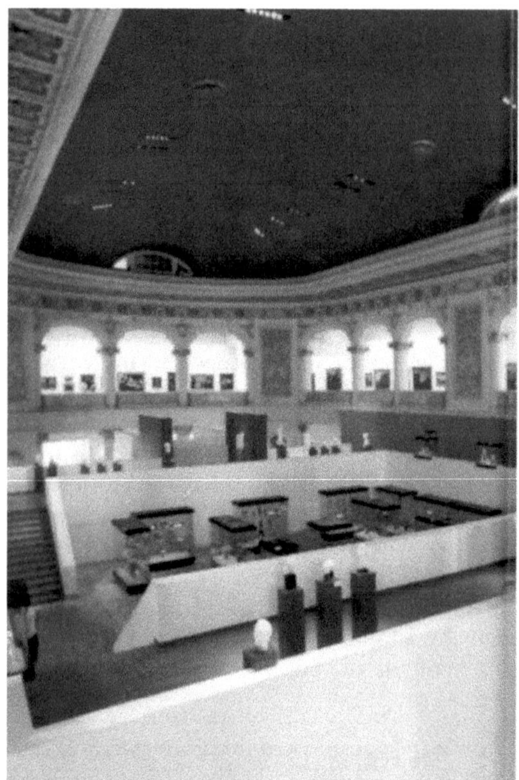

National Museum of Fine Arts, Havana (Photo Credit: Rodolfo Martínez, 2009)

Thus the museum enriched its collections of Cuban and universal painting and sculpture very quickly. These were presented tightly packed in the spaces of a 1950s building that was far from what a modern art museum should be, even though the original project had aimed to satisfy important spatial requirements at that time. This was not however, the case with either the storage areas or the technical systems needed for the correct preservation of its heritage.

The problems, mainly related to insufficient space - a chronic evil in almost every big museum in the world - circulation, technical systems and others, became critical. Despite some attempts to rectify the situation, only the decision of the State to address all these problems affecting this highly valued heritage led to studies to find a definitive solution. These studies, begun in 1996, became executive projects in 1999, with the work finally culminating in 2001.

The first issue to be addressed in facing the complex situation was the need for more space. The decision was made to divide the collections into two large groups of "Cuban Art" and "Universal Art", and to house them in a group of three buildings located in an important area, near the existing Palace of Fine Arts. This area had developed as a result of expansion and urbanisation immediately after the demolition of the City Walls (1863); and the redesign of a wide strip in which the urban and building criteria assumed codes of scale, traffic and architectural types totally different from those in the historical core.

The whole complex would then include the existing Palace of Fine Arts, the former headquarters of Asturian Societies in Cuba, (a magnificent and monumental eclectic building dating from 1927) that would house the "universal art" collections, as well as the modified Militia House (1764) which would become the administrative headquarters.

It is a project that considers, first of all, intervention in three existing buildings, different in date and architectural features, and their adaptation to the new uses proposed, primarily in the two museum buildings.

The Palace of Fine Arts (National Museum), which houses the Cuban Art collections from the seventeenth to the twentieth century, and had been purpose-built as a museum, involved an intervention of general restructuring, and a new architectural expression different from its original configuration. The general works were aimed at reorganising and redesigning inner spaces, organising circulation to allow freer movements inside, and giving visitors the option of not having to walk through the entire building (as was originally the case with the ramp located at the back of the central courtyard). Lifts for the public in the main hall and two stairways (with two glass-covered semi-cylinders on the longer sides of the building) were introduced, allowing visitors to access in a differentiated way, the eight large exhibition areas corresponding to the time periods established for Cuban art. Each exhibition area is air-conditioned with stable temperature and relative humidity, and protected with an integral communication and security system.

Perhaps the most important aspect is the treatment of light in the museum; a combination of natural and artificial light with proven advantages offered by this choice, although not exempt from difficulties and design complexity. Natural light penetrates through the rows of high windows in the entire perimeter of the building and the central courtyard and on the last floor through holes made originally to obtain a source of zenithal light.[127]

Natural light is filtered through special glass to the interior and reflected inwardly on the exhibition walls by curved surfaces that at the same time, due to their reflecting condition and treatment, eliminate ultraviolet radiation on the museum pieces. Lighting levels are controlled by sensors determining the required amount at different times of the day and according to the amount of natural light, and from the artificial light sources located around the borders of the ceilings, in front of the windows, according to the illumination parameters established for better visibility and protection of artworks (up to 250 - 300 lux).

[127] Zenithal lighting is a technique in which you attempt to apply a global lighting scheme, generally as if the light were directly overhead, like sunlight filtering downward from high windows, domes, skylights, towers etc.

The building dedicated to the "Universal Art" collections posed very different intervention problems. As it was a building with important heritage values and richly decorated architecture, the preservation of its own values and the adaptation of its inner spaces for exhibition of paintings and sculptures required, first and foremost, the optimal co-existence between the building and the exhibition. This was most particularly the case in respect to the splendid ancient art collection of Egyptian, Greek and Roman antiquities donated by the Count of Lagunillas to the National Museum.

The "restoring" intervention was therefore aimed at rescuing the original values of the building and the accentuation and hierarchical organisation of public circulation areas, beginning with the entrance, and the big, sumptuous staircase crowned by a huge skylight with decorative stained glass. In other spaces (originally administrative offices), differentiated museographic architecture was used to facilitate proper lighting design (reflected and punctuated or accentuated), and for the installation of the central air-conditioning ducts.

The decorative and chromatic treatment of the oval space (double height, 4 and 5 levels of the building) was respected and a museographic structure with light-material architectural elements was used on the two levels. This allows three different points of view of the collection, with differentiated and characterised spaces where the valuable pieces are exhibited and protected in showcases lit with a "fibre-optic" system.

Furthermore, the building has two original underground levels that allowed the creation of storage areas for the artworks in optimal environmental conditions (humidity and temperature) and optimal security and protection. (7)

Conclusions

A brief overview of the origin, development and current situation of museology in Cuban museums has been provided, describing the main aspects and factors involved in this process. This has not been exempt from difficulties and is still very far from satisfying the expectations of the authorities, the museum staff and the public.

Today, the "Cuban museum network" has 328 institutions in the whole country (15.7 per cent are located in the capital city, Havana). Some of the national museums, of an exceptional nature because of their highly valuable collections and significance, are of international renown. Other monographic museums and 'memorial' houses are very interesting for the general public, and for the museum field worldwide, as many of them are related to facts, phenomena and collections from different parts of the world, in particular from the Caribbean. Finally, municipal museums are characterised mainly by their influence on the community and their integration into the life of the population and its general culture. In addition, their participation provides a good demonstration of the use and interpretation of the principles of the *integral museum* and the so-called *new museology.*

The most important goal now is to work systematically based on the experiences and results obtained and to assess and process the universal experiences, especially in our geographical area, which suffers common problems in many respects.

References

Nüñez Vega, Jorge, *The Cuban intellectual field, 1920-1925,* American Debates, No. 5-6, January-December 1998, Havana.

Arjona, Marta, 1984, *Museums in Cuba* (exhibition catalogue), ICOM Cuban Committee, Division of Cultural Heritage, Havana, Cuba.

Law No. 1. Law of Protection of Cultural Heritage, in the Official Gazette of the Republic of Cuba, Year LXXV, No. 29, Havana, 6 August 1977.

Law No. 23. Law of Municipal Museums, in the Official Gazette of the Republic of Cuba, Year LXXVII, No. 15, Havana, 19th May 1979.

For further information see:

Linares, José, 1994. *Museum, Architecture and Museography,* Cultural Development Fund, Havana, Cuba (printed in Spain).

Notes from the book:

Linares, José, 2001. *"THE NATIONAL MUSEUM OF FINE ARTS", history of a project,* Office of Publications of the State Council, Havana, Cuba, first edition.

The project of the National Museum of Fine Arts and the book abovementioned have received the most important national architecture awards and several international awards, among them some granted in Latin America and the Caribbean. Honourable Mention for the book: "Conjunto Museo Nacional de Bellas Artes; historia de un proyecto" Ed. Del Consejo de Estado, La Habana, 2001; Award of the City of Havana to Architecture and Engineering, 2001. Publication; 3rd Ibero-American Biennial of Architecture, Santiago de Chile, 2002; Biennial of Architecture, Quito, Ecuador, 2002. Awards for the project: National Museum of Fine Arts, Award of the City of Havana to Architecture and Engineering, 2001. Recuperation; National Award for Conservation and Restoration of Monuments, 2003. Special Award of the jury. 3rd Biennial of Caribbean Architecture, Santiago de Cuba, 2002 (rehabilitation category: construction work). 22e Congrès Panaméricain d'Architectes; 6e Biennale d'Architecture Caribéenne, Guadeloupe, 2004 (heritage category).

Chapter 4

The Natural History Collections of the University of the West Indies (UWI)

Mike G. Rutherford

Despite the relatively small size of the country, Trinidad and Tobago is home to a wide range of natural history collections. Over the course of the last two centuries many naturalists have come to Trinidad and collected huge numbers of specimens. Significant collections have been deposited in museums in Canada, Germany, The Netherlands, the United Kingdom and the U.S.A. but equally important collections have also been kept in the country.

These include the Barcant butterfly collection at Angostura Ltd.; the Centre for Agricultural Bioscience International (CABI) insect collection; the Caribbean Epidemiology Centre (CAREC) collection of birds, mammals, reptiles and insects; the Institute of Marine Affairs (IMA) marine collections; the Percharde mollusk collection at the Pointe-a-Pierre Wildfowl Trust and the remaining collections of the National Museum and Art Gallery, formerly known as the Royal Victoria Institute. This last collection is unfortunately a fraction of its former size as most of the original specimens were lost in a fire in 1920 (Tikasingh, 2003).

These collections contain thousands of important specimens, however, the most varied and important natural history collections are those held at The University of the West Indies (UWI) St. Augustine campus. The National Herbarium and the UWI Zoology Museum between them hold around 100,000 objects and it is the history of the these collections, along with the natural history specimens held by the other UWI campuses in Jamaica and Barbados, that will be the focus of this chapter.

University natural history museums around the world fall into two broad categories: - those that have large accessible displays for the general public as well as their research collections - what have been referred to as 'full-service' museums (Humphrey 1991) - and those that function largely as stores of specimens for research and/or teaching. The ability to function as a full-service museum often depends, not surprisingly, on the money available to build, maintain and staff such an institution.

University natural history museums occupy a special place in the world of museums, as they are often more important for their research collections than they are for the specimens on display. Many university collections aren't generally open to public viewing and objects are often kept only for scientific study. This hearkens back to the early days of natural history collections in Europe when most of the collections were private. Public access was the least of the curators' concerns, and scientific research, mainly with a taxonomic focus, was the primary purpose (Farber 2000).

The University Museums and Collections (UMAC) committee, part of the International Council of Museums (ICOM), has around 200 members in 40 different countries and lists over 840 university-related natural history and natural science collections from around the world. This includes zoology, geology, paleontology and botany collections.(1) This list is by no means comprehensive, but does indicate that universities around the world hold a significant amount of natural history specimens.

The focus for this chapter is The University of the West Indies (UWI). UWI is a multi-campus regional institution of higher learning. It was established in 1948 as an external College of The University of London and became fully independent in 1962. The 16 English-speaking countries and overseas territories that support and are served by UWI are Anguilla, Antigua and Barbuda, The Bahamas, Barbados, Belize, Bermuda, British Virgin Islands, Cayman, Dominica, Grenada, Jamaica, Montserrat, St. Kitts and Nevis, Saint Lucia, St. Vincent & the Grenadines and Trinidad & Tobago. There are four campuses - Mona in Jamaica, St. Augustine in Trinidad, Cave Hill in Barbados and The Open Campus. The last one is not a physical campus as much as a focus for long distance learning and only has small resource centres scattered throughout the member countries; as such there are no collections associated with it. The first three campuses, however, all have well-established natural history collections of varying size and content. Who made them, how they were built up, what they are used for, and what the future holds for them will be examined in this chapter.

UWI Cave Hill

The UWI Cave Hill campus in Barbados is home to a herbarium and a small entomology collection. Currently the entomology collection is not curated to any significant degree, but the herbarium has been well looked after in recent years.

Botany Collections

The Department of Biological and Chemical Sciences houses the Barbados National Herbarium. It was established in 1977 by combining botanical collections from three sources - the Department of Agriculture, the Barbados Museum & Historical Society, and the Lodge School.

The first of these collections is the oldest, dating back to 1900. The majority of the specimens were collected by three agricultural scientists: John R. Bovell, the Superintendent of Agriculture; William George Freeman, who went on to serve in the Trinidad & Tobago Department of Agriculture; and J. Sydney Dash the Agricultural Assistant. These men were involved in all aspects of agriculture in Barbados and the surrounding region and conducted a wide range of research. Although their work would have provided them with many specimens for the herbarium, they were also keen on collecting in their spare time. In all they contributed several hundred flowering plants to the collections.

The second collection was started in 1935 by the geneticist, sugarcane breeder and Assistant Director of Agriculture, Andrew Elphinstone Sinclair (A.E.S) McIntosh, along with several amateur botanists; over the years they collected around 1300 plants.[128] The final collection of around 700 specimens came from The Lodge School, and was built up by the secondary school students and their headmaster, the Rev. Harry Beaujon Gooding and his cousin Evelyn Graham Beaujon Gooding again around the 1930s.[129] E.G.B. Gooding was responsible for many books and papers about the plant communities on the island, and was one of the authors of the 1965 book *Flora of Barbados.*

Over the last decade much work was done to bring the herbarium up to a higher standard with the collection of more specimens, but the most important work began in 2005 when a project between the Barbados Museum & Historical Society and UWI was launched. Funding from the Barbados Government, the Peter Moores Barbados Trust and UWI was used to create a virtual herbarium. The aim was to allow access by the general public, researchers and students to this regional collection. This was achieved in January 2009 with the launch of the searchable database containing scanned copies of every specimen. (2)

The collection holds around 4000 pressed and dried flowering plant specimens, along with smaller numbers of bryophytes and algal specimens, and is currently curated part-time by the Senior Lecturer in Biology, Dr. Louis E. Chinnery.

---

[128] This was the Barbados Museum & Historical Society's collection started by McIntosh and a group of enthusiasts.

[129] Several of their specimens appear as duplicates in the BMHS collection.

Zoology Collections

The entomology collection is a remnant from a larger collection assembled by Munir Alam during his work at the Caribbean Agricultural Research and Development Institute (CARDI). After his retirement the collection was split between the Ministry of Agriculture and UWI. The collection held at Cave Hill consists of three cabinets of 15 drawers each containing a variety of insect groups, with specimens from Barbados and the Lesser Antilles (Peck, 2009).

UWI Mona

The UWI Mona campus in Jamaica has two major collections - a herbarium and a geology museum - as well as several minor zoological collections. The collections are used for a variety of teaching and research purposes.

Botany Collections

The UWI Mona herbarium was established in 1949 by Dr. Charles Dennis Adams, who would go on to work in Trinidad and be instrumental in the development of the herbarium there as well. The collection contains some of the oldest herbarium specimens in Jamaica, dating back to the 1880s, and was used extensively by Adams to write the 1972 book *Flowering Plants of Jamaica* (Frodin, 1984).

One of the most important collections in the herbarium is that of William Harris, who started as the superintendent in the Botanical Department of Jamaica and ended up as the Assistant Director of Agriculture and Government Botanist. Harris was born in Northern Ireland, moved to Jamaica in 1881, and spent the next 40 years tirelessly studying the island's plant life. His collection consists of over 900 plants, many of which are Jamaican endemics.

The other collection of note is that of Paul Sintenis, a German botanist and professional plant collector who gathered a huge number of plants from Puerto Rico between 1884 and 1887. This included many duplicates which were sent to herbaria all over the world (Acevedo-Rodriguez & Strong, 2005).

The majority of the specimens, however, were inherited from the Hope Herbarium in Hope Botanic Gardens in Kingston. The gardens, managed by the Department of Agriculture, were established in 1873 and became a major experimental station for crops such as sugarcane, coffee, cocoa and bananas.

Most of the collection of over 35,000 specimens is currently stored in new metal cabinets and is split into three main groups - Regional, Monocotyledons and Dicotyledons. As well as the Angiosperms, there are smaller collections of Gymnosperms and Pteridophytes, but these were acquired in an *ad hoc* fashion and more work is needed to make them a useful resource (Buddo, 2010). Some specimens remain in older wooden cabinets, but once further funding is achieved they will be rehoused. The herbarium is currently under the charge of a curator, Mr. Patrick Lewis, and is open to staff, students and the wider public.

In 2005 UWI Mona and the Institute of Jamaica (IOJ), an umbrella organisation that covers all aspects of Jamaica's heritage, started a joint project to create the Jamaica Virtual Herbarium. This was an effort to make some of the collections held by the two institutions more accessible, and was part of a worldwide trend to facilitate information retrieval. The project was undertaken as part of a PhD by Philip Rose, who was responsible for the electronic cataloguing and development of a purpose-built website. The first collections to be catalogued were those of Harris from UWI and George R. Proctor from IOJ. These consisted of approximately 900 individual specimens from each collection with representatives from 10 plant families. (3) Each herbarium sheet was catalogued and scanned and added to an online database that was launched in 2009. In the future it is hoped that more specimens will be added to the database so that eventually the complete herbaria of UWI Mona and the IOJ will be available online (P. Rose, pers. comm).

Geology Collections

The UWI Geology Museum (UWIGM) contains geological, mineralogical and paleontological materials from Jamaica and the Caribbean, and has been functioning as a publicly accessible museum for 40 years. The Department of Geology, where the museum is based, was formed in 1961, and by 1965 the gathering of specimens for teaching purposes had resulted in the founding of the UWIGM as a private collection. Over time, as the collection increased in size and importance, proper storage space was needed. Eventually the UWIGM was brought into public existence in 1969 when the specimens and cabinets of the Geological Survey of Jamaica were donated to the museum (Brown & Langner, 2002). The first curator was Dr. Peter Jung, an expert on fossil mollusks who was at the time on sabbatical from the Naturhistorisches Museum in Basel, Switzerland (Donovan *et.al.* 2004). In 1970 the museum was opened for public viewing.

Several important collections form the backbone of the museum. The earliest collection dates back to the 1850s and was the work of Lucas Barrett. In 1859 he had been appointed Director of the Geological Survey of Jamaica at the young age of 22, and set about studying the mountains and seas of the island. He worked out the age of the limestone that makes up some of the Blue Mountains by studying the fossilised shells found there. One of these shells was a type of rudist bivalve new to science, and was named *Barrettia* in his honour. Tragically his promising career was cut short when he drowned whilst using a diving suit in the sea off Kingston, aged only 25.(4) His collection consists of 153 samples of rocks, minerals and fossils, many of which were collected in eastern Jamaica. Although collected for research, the specimens were also for a potential geology museum, something he had been keen on since his arrival on the island. After his death the specimens were sent back to England. It was only in 1975 that they were acquired by UWIGM from the Sedgwick Museum in Cambridge.

A century after Barrett, the Geological Survey of Jamaica came under the leadership of Verners A. Zans, a Latvian geologist who arrived in the country in 1949. He undertook many studies on the rocks and minerals of the island and also collected recent mollusks and corals. His work resulted in the publication of a new geological map of Jamaica in 1958. Many of his samples were amongst the first objects acquired by the Department of Geology upon its foundation; there are approximately 400 specimens in his collection.

In 1966 Howard R. Versey became Director of the Geological Survey. His work on limestone formation resulted in a collection of roughly 100 foraminifera that were added to the UWIGM collections after he had completed his M.Sc.

Current staff and students in the Geology Department have also contributed greatly to the collections. Another collection of foraminifera was built up by Professor Edward Robinson from 1969 onwards, and numbers around 2000 objects. Professor Simon Mitchell has so far amassed over 10,000 specimens of rudists, corals, mollusks and rocks, including approximately 500 type and figured specimens. Gavin Gunter's collection of about 400 cretaceous period objects was acquired as part of his PhD thesis.

As well as academic collections, there have been objects donated by geologists working in industry. Anthony Porter, who worked for the Geological Survey and then the West Indies Alumina Company, donated a collection of 135 agates in 2009; and Raymond Wright, former head and co-founder of the Petroleum Company of Jamaica, has donated specimens to the museum dating back to the 1970s.

The last major part of the collection was obtained from the Institute of Jamaica and the Survey Department in 1979 and totals over 9000 objects. This added specimens from around the world as well as objects collected by geologists such as Charles Taylor Trechmann and Lawrence Chubb, both of whom were experts on the rudist bivalves. Chubb actually came to Jamaica to retire, but instead spent the last 21 years of his life helping with survey work and even took over as director from 1961 to 1966. His final work was the 1971 monograph on Jamaican rudists (Brown & Langner, 2002).

The current full-time curator is Dr. Sherene James-Williamson who completed her PhD within the department. In total the museum houses more than 20,000 catalogued specimens. Some of these objects are currently on electronic databases such as MS Excel and Access. It is hoped that soon there will be a publicly accessible database joined with other UWI collections. The museum is visited by around 2000 people per year, mainly from schools and colleges across Jamaica; many are organised primary school tours looking at rocks and minerals in general.

A recent project, supported by funding from the Canadian High Commission, resulted in the creation of an Interactive Learning Centre. This is the first phase in the UWIGM Rejuvenation and Modernization Project, and is intended to provide better teaching and training facilities for the museum.

One of the highlights of the collection is a cast of the fossilised skeleton of an extinct sea cow, *Pezosiren portelli,* discovered during a joint research project between Howard University, Florida Museum of Natural History and UWL Daryl Domning, one of the researchers, named the specimen in 2001. It is well known in paleontological circles because it is the only sea cow fossil to have been found with legs, and it provides a unique look into the transition of a species from land to sea. Although the original fossil is currently in the USA, it is hoped that once suitable storage conditions have been attained in the UWIGM, this important specimen will one day be brought back to Jamaica (S.James-Williamson, pers. comm).

Zoology Collections

The UWI Mona terrestrial invertebrate collection is currently under the charge of Dr. Eric Garraway, co-author of the 2005 book *Butterflies of Jamaica,* and is curated by Dr. Catherine Murphy. Originally the Department of Life Sciences only maintained a teaching collection and reference material was sent to the IOJ, but from around 2000 the department started to assemble its own collection. Specific collections were made for Masters and PhD studies including Arctiid and Noctuid moths, aphids, carabid beetles and land snails. At a very rough estimate there are thought to be 50,000 insects, many collected during student field studies, but the vast majority of these are yet to be curated (C. Murphy, pers. comm.).

Other collections held by the department include marine phytoplankton and marine zooplankton, in particular the crustaceans, collected by Dr. Mona Webber; marine bony fish collected by Dr. Karl Aiken; freshwater fish collected by Dr. Eric Hyslop; mangrove ascidians collected by Prof. Ivan Goodbody, and a small collection of sponges (Buddo, 2010).

UWI St. Augustine

As mentioned at the beginning the UWI campus in St. Augustine, Trinidad is home to two major collections - the UWI Zoology Museum (UWIZM) and the National Herbarium of Trinidad & Tobago.

Zoology Collections

The collections held by UWIZM date back to the 1920s. Before UWI existed, the St. Augustine campus was home to the West Indies Agricultural College which in 1924 became the Imperial College of Tropical Agriculture (ICTA). The early collection was basically a repository for researchers investigating animal species of agricultural importance, and as a resource for teaching (Tikasingh, 2003). Insects formed the bulk of the specimens, and consisted of pest and beneficial species associated with the various crops under study - cocoa, maize, coffee, cotton, tobacco, citrus, pineapple and banana, to name a few. Many of these were collected by the Professor of

Entomology and Commissioner of Agriculture, Henry Arthur Ballou, a prolific author on many aspects of entomology throughout the Caribbean and beyond.

In 1933 Martin Adamson was appointed Senior Lecturer and Head of the Department of Entomology. He started to collect a wider range of animals, including marine invertebrates such as echinoderms and crustaceans, and also terrestrial animals such as beetles and amphibians. He had earned his undergraduate degree at The University of St. Andrew in his home country of Scotland, and during his time at ICTA he gained his PhD from the University of California. He was with ICTA until his death in 1945.(5)

His successor, Professor Thomas Winfred Kirkpatrick, Head of Department from 1946 to 1959, expanded the reference collections further with a wider variety of insects. As well as producing many journal articles he also wrote the well-received book *Insect Life in the Tropics,* which contains photographs and drawings of many of the insects in the collections. Around the same time his colleague Michael Emsley added more non-pest insects, as well as establishing a snake collection, some of the information from which he used to write his 1977 publication, *Snakes, and Trinidad and Tobago.* Unfortunately his original specimens have either disappeared, or over time the labels have become disassociated from them, as during a recent cataloguing of the reptiles none were recorded as being collected by Emsley.

From 1960 to 1964 the reptile collections were increased further due to the work of Professor Garth Underwood. He was a keen herpetologist who started his career at the University College of the West Indies in Jamaica before moving to Trinidad to become the Head of Department. He collected and studied reptiles from all over the Caribbean during his time at UWI, many of which are deposited in the collection. In recognition of his work, the lizard *Gymnophthalmus underwoodi* was named after him. He presided over the department at a time when Zoology began to be taught separately from Agriculture, and so a wider ranging teaching collection was required.

Professor Julian S. Kenny, who served as Head of Department from 1970 to 1990, collected widely, but was particularly keen on amphibians and fish. He was author of *The Amphibia of Trinidad* in 1969, and went on to write many books and articles on all aspects of Trinidad and Tobago's wildlife.

His successor, Peter R. Bacon, also added a variety of specimens ranging from barnacles and mollusks, to turtles and plankton. Bacon had gained the first Zoology PhD from St. Augustine in 1969, and went on to conduct studies of Trinidad's wetlands and threatened leatherback turtle populations. (6)

Over the years many collectors have contributed to the museum: some have bequeathed items in their wills, and some were collected as part of Masters or Doctoral studies. Examples include the shell collection of Sybil Atteck, one of Trinidad's most famous and influential artists; the P. Thompson mollusk collection; freshwater decapods from Wayne Rostant and Dawn Phillip; marine decapods from Jan Stonley; fossils from Robert Kennedy; freshwater insect larvae and fossils from Mary Alkins-Koo; social insects from Christopher K. Starr and Alan W. Hook, freshwater fish from Julian

Kenny and Dawn Phillip; marine fish from Robin W. Bruce; bats from Frank M. Clarke; octocorals from Doon Ramsaroop; marine invertebrates from staff aboard the Research Vessels *Oregon II* and *Discoverer,* and the Texaco collection of marine mollusks, to name but a few.

One of the most colourful collections, both literally and in terms of the life and death of the donor, was the Sir Norman Lamont collection of Lepidoptera. Lamont was a Scottish baronet with an estate in Trinidad who had served as a Governor of ICTA and was a prolific writer on many subjects.(7) At the age of 79 he was gored by a bull and died of his wounds. His collection of local butterflies and moths was split between ICTA and the National Museum of Scotland in Edinburgh.

In January 2010 I became the first full-time curator of UWIZM, and I have spent the last two years cataloguing, cleaning, and opening up the collections. One of the first tasks undertaken was to provide a website with collection-level descriptions of all specimens; this provides information to the family level of all the specimens stored in the UWIZM. (8)

The current holdings of the museum stand at approximately 25,000 specimens split between two storerooms. The Land Arthropod Room contains around 20,000 pinned and identified insects from around 200 different families, made up of six cabinets of butterflies and moths, six cabinets of ants, bees and wasps, five cabinets of beetles, three cabinets of bugs, one cabinet of flies and smaller numbers of other orders. There are also small collections of immature insects, arachnids and myriapods in spirit.

The Zoology Room houses the spirit and dried non-insect collections. The specimens in alcohol are made up of approximately 100 amphibians, 400 reptiles, 700 freshwater fish, 500 marine fish, 100 bats, several thousand marine and freshwater crustaceans, a few hundred marine invertebrates and a small number of birds and mammals. The room also houses the dried collections of sponges, corals, echinoderms and approximately 4000 mollusk shells. Skeletal specimens include various skulls and whole skeletons of domestic animals, African mammals and vertebrates from Trinidad and Tobago.

Currently there are spreadsheets listing the mollusk, fish, reptile, amphibian and mammal collections and there are paper catalogues of some of the smaller groups. The UWIZM staff and student volunteers are in the process of cataloguing and photographing the entire collection. Eventually the records will be made accessible on-line using Past Perfect 5.0 as the database software. In the meantime the UWIZM has been opened up to visits by students, staff and the public, and a variety of organised tours are on offer.

Although not strictly a part of the natural history collections there are a small number of archaeological remains held in the museum. Along with the collections stored at the UWI Archaeology Centre, based on the St. Augustine campus, UWI does have a significant number of archaeological specimens. The most important and well known specimen is the 'Banwari Man', a 5000-year-old human skeleton from the south of Trinidad that has been stored in the Zoology Room since 1978.

Botany Collections

Although the National Herbarium of Trinidad & Tobago is a national collection, because its history is so closely entwined with the University of the West Indies, and as it is housed on the St. Augustine Campus, its inclusion here is appropriate. The herbarium has its origins in the Royal Botanic Gardens in Port of Spain which were established in 1818. For many years the superintendents of the gardens collected specimens, but it was only with the appointment of the fifth superintendent, John Hinchley Hart, in 1887 that a properly organised herbarium began. Hart and his assistant, Paula McLean, spent the next 30 years organising, preserving and cataloguing the specimens, and it is largely due to McLean's devotion that the early collection is in such good condition.

The Department of Agriculture offices in St. Clair provided housing for the collection, and from here it was used by botanists and researchers working in the departments of Forestry and Agriculture, as well as the Royal Botanic Garden and ICTA. One of the most important publications from this time was the *Flora of Trinidad & Tobago* compiled by Ernest Entwistle Cheesman, William George Freeman (recently moved from Barbados), and Robert Orchard Williams. Cheesman was the Professor of Botany at ICTA and also a world expert on bananas - he even had a species of banana named after him, *Musa cheesmani.* The first volume of the flora was published in 1928, with further volumes coming out over the next 80 years.

Over time the collections came to be of the most use to ICTA as more botanical research was undertaken and new publications produced, so the herbarium was transferred to the campus in 1947. At first it was stored in the Plant Pathology Building, before moving to its current home in a purpose-built room in the Sir Frank Stockdale Building.

In 1960 ICTA became the Faculty of Agriculture of the newly formed University College of the West Indies, which by 1962 had become The University of the West Indies. From 1957 to 1967 the Professor of Botany and the person with responsibility for the growth and maintenance of the herbarium was John William Purseglove. Along with the help of talented staff such as Norman W. Simmonds and with the assistance of overseas taxonomists, more volumes of the *Flora* were produced and more specimens were collected. Simmonds had left by 1959 to carry on a career as a world-renowned plant breeding expert in tropical agriculture (Spoor & England 2001).

After a promising start for the herbarium being run by UWI, financial difficulties in the early 1970s forced the Head of Department, Francis William Cope, to approach the Government for assistance. This led to the Ministry of Planning and Development agreeing to finance the herbarium indefinitely, and to it becoming the 'National Herbarium of Trinidad & Tobago'. However it stayed on campus and was still administered by UWI through the Department of Life Sciences.

With the funding secured, the use of the collection picked up again in 1976 when Dr. Charles Dennis Adams started. He revived the herbarium by promoting plant research and taxonomic work, and also pushed for the establishment of a full-time curator. Yasmin S. Baksh-Comeau was appointed to the newly created position in 1980, and has been at the herbarium ever since.

Since then the herbarium has expanded to include a dedicated library staffed by a full-time librarian, a permanent secretary and a variety of postgraduate and intern students all working on the collections. The current herbarium has recently benefited from an extensive refurbishment, with the old wooden cabinets having been replaced by sealed insect-proof and waterproof metal cabinets. It has hosted over 15,000 guests and has provided over 20,000 identifications of plant specimens, as well as increasing the number of specimens held overall to around 70,000 (Acham, 2009).

The catalogued collection consists of approximately 40,000 Angiosperms, 3,500 Pteridophytes, 600 Marine macro-algae, 550 Bryophytes, 500 Fungi and 50 Gymnosperms. The majority of these are in the form of herbarium sheets although there are a few envelopes and seeds as well.

Perhaps the most significant undertaking of the past few years has been the joint project between Oxford University and UWI, funded by the UK Darwin Initiative, to complete a vegetation survey of Trinidad and Tobago and make the herbarium collections accessible through an online database. Over 25,000 new specimens were collected, and so far around 20,000 herbarium sheets have been digitised and added to the database.

In the future it is hoped that the herbarium and UWIZM will both benefit from purpose-built storage and display areas and, with plans currently being developed for a dedicated St. Augustine campus museum, this is looking increasingly likely.

Conclusions

Looking at the natural history holdings of UWI as a whole, a rough count gives a total of close to a quarter of a million specimens. This is broken down into 110,000 botanical, 100,000 zoological and 20,000 geological specimens many of which, however, still need proper identification and cataloguing.

How best to use this treasure trove of biological specimens could be the subject of much debate, but underlying all the possibilities the most important requirement for the future is arguably accessibility. Letting the wider world, both the general public and scientific researcher alike, know what there is and where it is will make these collections more valuable. Utilisation of traditional museum techniques, such as creating displays and providing exhibitions, and the more modern techniques of developing virtual displays, would provide access to the general visitor or enquirer. Provision for the scientific researcher requires more detailed online databases, as well as good storage facilities with well-conserved specimens and access to good working spaces. However, perhaps the most important requirement for all of the collections is to have dedicated, knowledgeable, well-trained staff - collections need curators!

References

Acevedo-Rodriguez, P & Strong, M.T. (eds.) 2005. *Monocotyledons and Gymnosperms of Puerto Rico and the Virgin Islands* Contributions from the United States National Herbarium Volume 52:1-415.

Acham, S. 2009, *122 years of Splendour - National Herbarium is a trove of botanic wonders.* UWI Today, December, 2009, The University of the West Indies.

Baksh-Comeau, Y.S. & Chaboo, C, 1988. *Natural History Museums do exist in Trinidad and Tobago* U.W.I. Bio spec tram Vol. 1.

Brown, I.C. & Langner, D.M, 2002. Type and Figured Specimens in the Geology Museum, University of the West Indies, Mona Campus, Jamaica. *The Geological Curator,* p. 299-304, Vol. 7, No. 8.

Buddo, D, 2010. *Assessment of Capacity-Building Needs for the Convention on Biological Diversity Capacity and Needs for Taxonomic Knowledge* Accessed November 2010 through http://www.nepa.gov.jm/projects/final_reports/Biodiversity_add_on/Taxonomic_Knowledge_FINAL.pdf.

Donovan, S.K, Jackson, T.A., Brown, I.C. & Wood, S.J. 2004. *Small is beautiful? Progress and collections of the Geology Museum, University of the West Indies, Mona.* Winkler Prins, C F . & Donovan, S.K. (eds), VII International Symposium 'Cultural Heritage in Geosciences, Mining and Metallurgy: Libraries - Archives - Museums': "Museums and their collections". *Scripta Geológica Special Issue*, 4:100-107.

Farber, P.L, 2000. *Finding Order in Nature* The John Hopkins University Press, Baltimore.

Frodin, D.G, 1984. *Guide to Standard Floras of the World,* p. 290 Cambridge University Press, United Kingdom.

Humphrey, P.S, 1991. *The Nature of University Natural History Museums* p. 5-11 Natural History Museums: Directions for Growth, Ed. Cato, P.S. & Jones, C. Texas Tech University Press, Lubbock.

Peck, S, 2009. The beetles of Barbados, West Indies (Insecta: Coleoptera): diversity, distribution and faunal structure. *InsectaMundi* 0073: 1-51. Center for Systematic Entomology, Inc., Gainesville, FL.

Spoor, W. & England, F, 2001. Dedication: Norman Willison Simmonds – plant breeder, teacher, administrator. *Plant Breeding Reviews* Volume 20: 1-13, Ed. Jules Janick, John Wiley & Sons, Inc.

Tikasingh, Elisha S, 2003. The History of Zoological Collections in Trinidad and Tobago. *Living World - Journal of the Trinidad and Tobago Field Naturalists' Club.*

(1) http://publicus.culture.hu-berlin.de/umac/database - accessed November 2010
(2) http://ecflora.cavehill.uwi.edu/vhmain.php - accessed November 2010
(3) http://www.jamaicavirtualherbarium.com/ - accessed November 2010
(4) http://www.nahste.ac.uk/isaar/GB_0237JSTAHSTE_P0277.html - accessed November 2010
(5) http://www.mainlib.uwi.tt/divisions/wi/collsp/summaries/martin

adamson.htm - accessed November 2010
(6) http://caribbean-icons.org/science/peter-bacon.htm - accessed November 2010
(7) http://en.wikipedia.org/wiki/Sir_Norman_Lamont,_2nd_Baronet - accessed November 2010
(8) http://sta.uwi.edu/fst/lifesciences/zoology.asp

Chapter 5

The National Gallery of Jamaica:

A Critical History

Veerle Poupeye

Jamaica's main cultural institution, the Institute of Jamaica ("Institute"), is mandated to encourage Literature, Art and Science in, and about, Jamaica. The Institute was founded in 1879, as a members' society, and was one of several such colonial cultural institutions to be established throughout the British Empire around that time.[130] The Institute initially approached Jamaican culture with a strong colonial bias, in which Jamaica was regarded as worthy of documentation because of its economic resources, its ethnographic and natural history curiosities, and its importance to colonial history, but in which European cultural values were firmly upheld. Under pressure from the principals of the nationalist movement in the late 1930s and 1940s, the Institute became more receptive to the emerging cultural expressions of national identity. This "nationalization" was consolidated after Independence, in the 1978 Institute of Jamaica Act which established it as a government agency in the Ministry of Culture. In the process, the Institute produced some of Jamaica's key art institutions: the Edna Manley College of the Visual and Performing Arts, which started in 1950 as the Jamaica School of Art and

---

[130] In the Caribbean, the Royal Victoria Institute in Trinidad was another. It was established in 1892 and is now known as the National Museum and Art Gallery of Trinidad and Tobago.

Crafts and became autonomous in 1995; and the National Gallery of Jamaica ("National Gallery"), which was established in 1974 and currently operates as a semi-autonomous division of the Institute.[131]

The National Gallery is Jamaica's national art museum and gallery and is mandated, as articulated in its mission statement: "To collect, research, document and preserve Jamaican, other Caribbean Art and related material and to promote our artistic heritage for the benefit of present and future generations." The collection currently consists of nearly 2000 works of art in media ranging from painting and sculpture to installation and digital photography and in a wide range of genres and styles, although most conform to conventional notions of "fine art". Its holdings range from Pre-Columbian to contemporary and most of it is Jamaican, in the sense that it was produced by artists who can be defined as Jamaican or have worked in the island of Jamaica, although there is also a small international collection with a Caribbean focus.

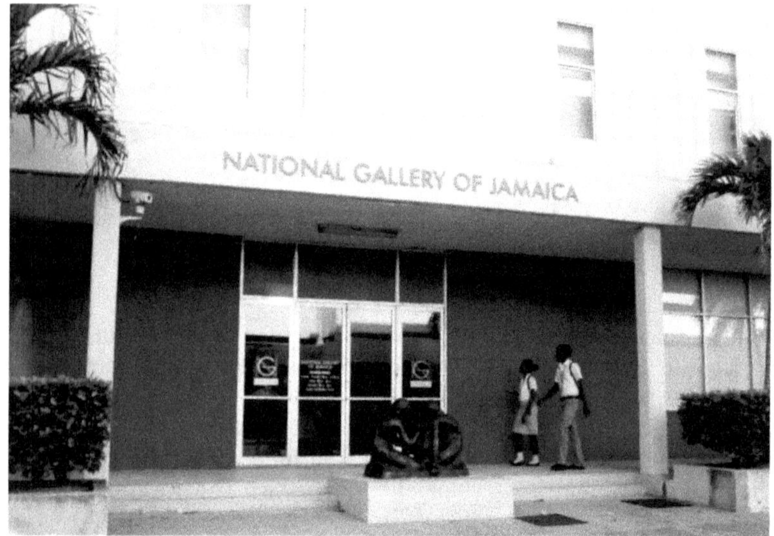

Entrance of the National Gallery of Jamaica in its current building on Orange Street in Downtown Kingston, (Photo Credit: National Gallery of Jamaica)

In its current location in a modern building on the Kingston waterfront that was originally designed to house a department store, the National Gallery has about 30,000 square feet of exhibition space, which makes it the largest art gallery and museum in the Anglophone Caribbean.[132] About half of this space houses permanent exhibitions that provide an overview of the history of art in Jamaica; the rest is used for the National Gallery's exhibition programme,

[131] It is anticipated that the National Gallery of Jamaica will eventually become an autonomous organization, with its own enabling legislation.

[132] The National Gallery was until 1982 located at Devon House, a nineteenth-century mansion just north of the New Kingston business district.

typically four to five exhibitions per year, most of which are internally curated. The National Gallery has active education and outreach programmes and is the main research and publication institution on Jamaican art. Some of the National Gallery's activities, such as its intermittent Caribbean Invitational exhibition series, are Caribbean-focused but the primary concern of all programmes is with what can be broadly defined as "Jamaican art".

Defining "Jamaican art" has in effect been a major preoccupation in the National Gallery's permanent and temporary exhibitions and publications. Definitions of art are a highly politicized concept. According to Eugene Metcalf:

> Art represents and sanctifies what is valued in a society; the ability to create and appreciate art implies heightened human sensibility and confers social status and prestige. A people said to be without art, or with a degraded form of it, reputedly show themselves lacking in the qualities that dignify human experience and social interaction. They are said to be 'uncultured,' 'Primitive,' unable to participate in refined society. Definitions of art are therefore highly political. They are major battlegrounds on which the struggle for human and social recognition is waged. A people can ill afford to let others control the definitions by which their arts are classified and evaluated.[133]

Institutions such as the National Gallery face a difficult and, inevitably, contentious task in addressing these issues and, by virtue of what they are mandated to do, have to articulate art-historical narratives and canons, while being mindful of how conventional art-histories and hierarchies have represented pre-colonial, colonial and post-colonial cultures. As national institutions their mandate is fundamentally tied to official post-colonial cultural nationalism, of which they are key instruments.

This chapter examines how definitions and narratives of Jamaican art have evolved in groundbreaking publications and exhibitions on the subject, particularly as they pertain to the National Gallery, many of which reflect an acute awareness of the political implications of such definitions and narratives.

Early Definitions

The first systematic attempts at documenting a local cultural history began at the Institute. The Englishman Frank Cundall was the Institute's first Secretary and Librarian - effectively its Director - from 1891 to 1937.[134] In addition to

---

[133] Eugene W. Metcalf. *Black Art, Folk Art, and Social Control.* (1983): 271.

[134] Cundall was born in London in 1858. His date of death is uncertain but it seems to have been soon after his retirement from the Institute of Jamaica in 1937. Prior to his arrival in Jamaica in 1891, he had worked on several international exhibitions in England. He had, among others, been Chief Assistant Secretary to the Royal Commission of the Colonial and Indian Exhibition in 1886 and wrote a book, *Reminiscences of the Colonial and Indian Exhibition,* on the subject. Cundall and

developing its natural and cultural history collections and the West India Reference Library, Cundall was a prolific researcher and writer on those subjects and during his tenure authored virtually all Institute publications. He is usually described as an historian, but he had in 1891 published a book on seventeenth-century Dutch landscape and genre painters, so he appears to have had a background in art history. Cundall's mission was clear: while the establishment of the Institute implied an admission that there were things about Jamaican history, culture and the physical environment that were worth documenting and preserving, he was also concerned to demonstrate the civilizing effects of colonialism, especially the view that British colonial governance had been of benefit to Jamaica, now equipped to progress as a modern outpost of the British Empire.

Cundall's many Jamaican publications included catalogues of the collections he was acquiring for the Institute. His Portrait Gallery was accompanied by a biographical guide to the historical figures portrayed, most of them English colonials who had played a role in Jamaica's history, which was first published in 1904 and updated in 1914. His emphasis in compiling and documenting this collection was on historical rather than aesthetic value, and only on what was deemed historically valuable from a colonialist perspective. Many of the portraits in the Gallery were made outside of Jamaica and several were copies or reproductions and only some of the originals later made it into the National Gallery's collection.

Cundall's most ambitious publication was a regularly updated Jamaica settler handbook that was remarkably similar to those that had been produced by planter-historians such as Edward Long (1774) a century and a half earlier.[135] These handbooks, published from 1891 onwards, mainly addressed practical issues facing colonial settlers. In the annual editions an increasingly significant proportion was dedicated to the cultural history of Jamaica, which Cundall was attempting to document. The Jamaica in 1918 edition included an annotated list of "engravings of Jamaican scenery" that had been acquired by the Institute. The notes focused on why, where and for whom those prints were made but, again, not on their aesthetic merit. Jamaica in 1928 had an illustrated chapter on arts and crafts, the earliest published survey of Jamaican art history. This chapter focused on pre-twentieth century colonial architecture

---

the early Institute of Jamaica played a key role in the organization and accompanying publications of the Jamaica International Exhibition of 1891. (National Library of Jamaica, n.d.)

[135] The earliest edition seems to have been *Jamaica in 1891: A Handbook for Intending Settlers and Others* and was produced for the Jamaica Exhibition that year. The 1895, 1896, 1897, 1905, 1918 and 1928 editions have been preserved in the National Library of Jamaica collection, a 1922 edition is held in the Eustace Maxwell Shilstone Library of the BMHS, but additional ones may have been published. This handbook is not to be confused with the *Jamaica Handbooks* which had been published annually by the Colonial Office since 1881 and only contained the "cut and dry" data that were more attractively and readably presented in the Institute's handbooks. Cundall also took over publication of the latter in 1926.

and other colonial art forms, but brief mention was made of Taino and African-Jamaican pottery and of traditional basketry.[136] Cundall, however, glumly concluded that "artistic talent [was] lying almost dormant in the colony"[137] because of the lack of a supporting infrastructure and patronage. Cundall may not have contributed to any clear definition of Jamaican art, but he collected and documented what are now considered as prime examples of colonial art in the island, and contributed to the art-historical data that became the "raw materials" for later accounts of pre-twentieth century Jamaican art. He also helped to create the myth that there was no worthwhile indigenous art in Jamaica prior to the nationalist movement.

While Cundall was placing the colonial perspective on record, the poet and musician Astley Clerk was working on a manuscript titled "Art in Jamaica" (c1929-43), which was not completed or published, perhaps because it was too ambitious a project for its time.[138] Clerk, a coloured Jamaican who died at age 76 in 1944, was fiercely nationalistic, to the point where he designed his own Jamaican flag and wrote his own national anthem, both well before Independence, and researched and self-published several items on Jamaican music and other aspects of the popular culture.[139] In his manuscript and research notes, Clerk attempted to detail everything that could reasonably be part of a Jamaican art history up to the 1930s, starting with the Amerindian legacy. Unencumbered by distinctions between "fine art" and "craft", his documentation includes furniture and curios and he makes a particular effort to uncover evidence of African-Jamaican traditions, especially those related to magic and religion. Much of the photo-documentation accompanying the manuscript is of the early coconut and wood curio carvings of David Miller Sr and Jr, who produced tourist curios from the 1920s, and he obviously regarded these as important evidence of African-Jamaican traditions. The Millers later produced more ambitious sculptures and were recognized as major artists.

Clerk's chapter structure starts with the Taino, followed by the Spanish, African, Maroon, African-Jamaican, English and Jamaican. He had documented and completed sections of each chapter, except for the final part on Jamaican art, and we therefore do not know how he would have defined and related that to the genealogy suggested by the other sections. His limited focus on the English legacy, compared to the planned sections on African, Maroon and African-Jamaican art, suggests that he found the African-Jamaican legacy most significant and, had this research been completed and

---

[136] The Taino, previously known as the Arawak, are the now-extinct Amerindians who inhabited Jamaica at the time of Columbus's first arrival in the island in 1494.

[137] Cundall, p. 79.

[138] This manuscript and Clerk's notes and press clippings on the subject were recently acquired by a private collector, who kindly provided me with access to these documents.

[139] Peta Gay Jensen. *The Last Colonials: The Story of Two European Families in Jamaica* (2005), 68-70 & 84.

published, it would have provided an early challenge to the common notion that there was no historical continuity in African-Jamaican art. Clerk's manuscript was a sign of things to come, and he received a Silver Musgrave Medal from the Institute in 1937 for his contribution to cultural research. Similar sentiments were expressed by other early nationalists, for instance in a 1934 newspaper article by the artist Edna Manley, the English-born wife of barrister and nationalist politician Norman Manley:

> Who are the creative painters, sculptors and engravers and where is the work which should be expressions of its country's existence and growth? A few anaemic imitators of European traditions, a few charming parlour tricks, and then practically silence. Nothing virile, nor original, nor in any sense creative, and nothing, above all, that is an expression of the deep-rooted, hidden pulse of the country - that thing which gives it its unique life. To go into the cause for this barrenness is too big a subject for a newspaper - perhaps it is a still unrealized island consciousness; of one thing I am sure it is not - that there is nothing to be expressed.[140]

Edna Manley's article presents a call for action and an agenda for the future development of Jamaican art and it is significant that this is construed as having to address a critical absence of legitimate and compelling Jamaican art. And, in the words of Krista Thompson, "by emphasizing the problem of black representational absence, artists like Manley could legitimate the significance, indeed the necessity, of their roles in the nationalist movement".[141]

Norman Manley, five years later, presents a more positive picture of an already emerging national movement in his 1939 essay, "National Culture and the Artist", and argues: "Political awakening must and always goes hand in hand with cultural growth"; and: "National culture is a national consciousness reflected in the painting of pictures of our own mountains and our own womenfolk. [...] Becoming one people [...] is the ultimate good; absorbing all the influences from outside and remaining sturdily ourselves". [142] Not surprisingly, "National Culture and the Artist" is widely regarded as the foundational text of that period.

Under public pressure to change its policies, the Institute started to support modern Jamaican art with regular exhibitions and acquisitions, most of them of "fine art", although the publications that accompanied these were rudimentary. Most were simple brochures with just a list of the works in the exhibition. Only rarely did these contain an introduction or, even, biographical notes on the artists. One reason for this may have been a lack of resources at the Institute around World War II, while the focus at the time was on encouraging and promoting the emerging nationalist school rather than, as yet, on documenting and analyzing.

---

[140] Edna Manley. 'Jamaican Art.'*Jamaica Gleaner,* 13 September, 1934,18.
[141] Krista Thompson. 'Black Skin, Blue Eyes' (2004): 28.
[142] *Manley and the New Jamaica: Selected Speeches and Writing 1938-1968* (1971), 72.

One notable exception to the lack of analytical content was the catalogue of the 1945 Exhibition of West Indian Paintings, the first regional exhibition of modern art in the Anglophone Caribbean. The exhibition was a joint project between the Institute, the Trinidad Arts Society, which was founded in 1943, and the British Council, which had become an active player in the promotion of modern art throughout the West Indies. In addition to Jamaica and Trinidad, it also included work from then British Guiana, Barbados and Saint Lucia. This exhibition thus also reflects the regionalization that accompanied the British policy shift towards self-government in the West Indies and later resulted in the short-lived West Indies Federation.[143]

The modest catalogue included an introduction by George Wingfield Digby, an English expatriate who later became Keeper of Textiles at the Victoria and Albert Museum. While Wingfield Digby had been actively involved in the Jamaican art scene, there were local intellectuals who were qualified to write this introduction, but it was clearly deemed desirable to have an endorsement from a "cultured" colonial. The first part of Wingfield Digby's essay was a lesson in art appreciation that focused on how the formal aspects of painting should be analyzed.[144] The assumption was thus that local audiences needed to be educated about "art" before they could appreciate the products of their own nationalist schools, although these supposedly emanated from "the people."

In the second part of his essay, Wingfield Digby ventured a definition of modern Jamaican painting.[145] He first observed, redundantly, that modern Jamaican painting usually represents Jamaican subjects but added that these are "seen uncompromisingly through Jamaican eyes",[146] which he detected particularly in the bold, sometimes even crude treatment of tropical color and light. He also argued that the "Jamaican school" - and he was the first to use that term - was characterized by sobriety and restraint and repeatedly used the word "virility" to summarize its characteristics. This he contrasted with the supposedly compromised and effete "North Coast" paintings that were sold to tourists[147] - one of the first times the "real" Jamaican art was juxtaposed with tourist art.[148] Wingfield Digby however made no mention of the nationalist, anti-colonial political context of modern Jamaican art, although mentioning that might not have been politic in an exhibition sponsored by a colonial organization such as the British Council.

---

[143] The exhibition was slated to travel to Canada afterwards, but it is not clear whether that actually happened.

[144] George Wingfield Digby. "Introduction" (1945).

[145] That he had nothing to say on the work from the other territories may stem from the fact that he was simply not familiar with other West Indian art, perhaps also because the works in the exhibition had not yet arrived in Jamaica at the time the catalogue had to go to press.

[146] Ibid., p. 5.

[147] Ibid., p. 6-7.

[148] Tourism has always been concentrated on the island's north coast, hence the name.

After Independence, a small but growing corps of locally born cultural scholars and art writers emerged, fuelled by increased access to advanced studies abroad or at the new University of the West Indies (UWI), and changing attitudes towards indigenous culture. The theatre and art critic (and later diplomat) Norman Rae was the first locally born writer to start producing serious and incisive criticism in the early 1960s, most of which was published in the *Gleaner*. He also wrote a short essay on Jamaican art for *Ian Fleming Introduces Jamaica* (1965), an upscale guidebook aimed at the "informed reader", with essays by Fleming, who wrote the introduction, and local specialists, all drawn from the elite, on the various subjects covered.[149] While Rae was primarily concerned with sketching the artistic landscape of the 1960s - from the "avant-garde" members of the Contemporary Jamaican Artists Association to emerging Primitives such as Kapo - he ventured an indirect definition. Emphasizing, like his predecessors, that modern Jamaican art was primarily about finding an authentic and legitimate artistic voice, he wrote:

> Jamaican painters generally do not aim at the titillatingly decorative 'native' object or art/craft, the stylish decorations designed for the tourist market that one finds proliferating in many other Caribbean and tropical countries. The ever-present determination not to let the glittering island vistas lead them astray makes them avoid this.[150]

Rae's argument that avoiding seduction by the "Technicolor beauty" of the island was the main challenge facing local artists was not new, as we saw in Wingfield Digby's 1945 essay, but never before had it been made so explicitly in what was, furthermore, a primarily tourist-oriented publication. This well illustrates the uncomfortable manner in which the development of modern Jamaican art and culture correlated to the country's growing economic dependence on tourism.

This concern with juxtaposing the "real" Jamaican art with tourist art however became less acute in the late 1960s and 1970s, which may be a reflection of the increased self-confidence of the Jamaican cultural movement. Definitions however remained essentially reactive, always arguing that modern Jamaican art evolved in reaction to those forces that had attempted to deny the island its own cultural identity. This shift was evident in *The Arts of an Island* (1970) by Ivy Baxter, the first full-length book on the arts of Jamaica, which barely mentions tourism.[151] As a black Jamaican, she came from a more modest social background than any of the previous cited writers,

[149] Fleming died before the book was published. It was edited by the local journalist and satirist Morris Cargill.

[150] P. 169-170

[151] Baxter was a Jamaican cultural researcher who had been attached to the University of Florida in Gainesville, probably as a graduate student. She was also a dancer and choreographer and the founder in 1950 of Jamaica's first modern dance troupe, the Ivy Baxter Creative Dance Group, which sought to combine classical ballet with traditional Jamaican cultural forms.

which reflects the social broadening of the involvement in cultural scholarship and patronage after Independence.

Baxter states in her introduction that she wants to integrate the study of the visual and performing arts of Jamaica into a larger historical, sociological and cultural discussion. Although her first-hand documentation of popular culture and efforts at historicizing and contextualizing Jamaican art represent a pioneering effort, the sketchy narrative she actually presents is descriptive rather than analytical, riddled with minor factual errors and almost exclusively concerned with the performing arts. There is one short chapter on the visual arts, which comprises an anecdotal overview of developments from the Taino until the 1960s. Baxter also discusses the development of the local cultural infrastructure, including the emergence of commercial art galleries in the 1950s and 1960s. Like the rest of the book, this chapter is, regrettably, not illustrated. The promised attempt at an integrated discussion appears in her final chapter, where she argues, albeit only in general terms, that the arts of Jamaica represent a gradual emergence of a viable, modern cultural identity, shaped by the people's responses and survival strategies in the face of a troubled and diverse history - the nation-building process for which the early nationalists had been clamouring.

Although the anti-colonialists had challenged well-established colonial views of Jamaican culture, there is not much evidence on how these early definitions and narratives on Jamaican art were received. There must have been conflict and dissent, if only because pro-colonial sentiments and interest groups did not magically disappear in the late 1930s, but these are drowned out in the written record by the urgent calls for national cultural development. It is only in the 1960s that signs of a polarization of opinion about the actual and desired nature of Jamaican art began to appear. The political radicalization of that era led to accusations of elitism against the nationalist mainstream, in periodicals such as *Abeng* (1969), while the internationalist Contemporary Jamaican Artists' Association (1964-1974) sought to challenge the dogmas of cultural nationalism. But even then there seems to have been a sense of common cause among those involved with art in Jamaica, with none of the acrimony that later came to characterize the Jamaican art world, when the articulation of Jamaican art history began in earnest.

Building Blocks of a Narrative

The opening of the National Gallery of Jamaica in 1974 represents a turning point in the development of the literature on Jamaican art and the Gallery quickly became the main publisher on the subject, most of it in the form of exhibition catalogues. With few exceptions, these catalogues are modestly produced and locally printed with black and white illustrations only. As a body of work, however, they are an invaluable resource on Jamaican art that also documents how the institution, its research, exhibitions and narratives have evolved. There was not enough space at Devon House, the original home of the National Gallery, to have a permanent exhibition and the National

Gallery's narrative was articulated through its temporary exhibitions programme, a process that started systematically when David Boxer, who had a 1974 Ph.D. in art history from Johns Hopkins, joined as Director/ Curator in 1975.[152] These early exhibitions and publications are best understood as building blocks of the National Gallery's emerging narrative.

The National Gallery's articles of association had mandated the institution to exhibit and collect the Jamaican art that came out of the nationalist uprising of 1938, the date designated as the beginning of the Jamaican Independence movement. This definition posed several problems: it failed to provide modern Jamaican art with any deep, indigenous historical groundedness; it did not accommodate any art that was not nationalist; and, in a specific problem for those who wished to place Edna Manley at the centre of modern Jamaican art, it did not account for the fact that her most groundbreaking works were created before 1938. This definition was soon challenged by Boxer in his first major exhibition, *Five Centuries of Art in Jamaica* (1976), which was also the National Gallery's first survey exhibition.

Five Centuries sought to provide "an opportunity to study contemporary Jamaican art against the varied background of past art produced in Jamaica or under Jamaican patronage".[153] Boxer thus added colonial art to the narrative of Jamaican art, starting with the Seville Carvings. He had intended but was, as he explained in the catalogue, unable to also include the pre-Columbian era because of the lack of significant artefacts in Jamaican collections at that time. One year earlier, in the catalogue of *Ten Jamaican Sculptors,* for an exhibition at the Commonwealth Institute, Boxer had argued that Jamaican art history "would hardly begin with the first Jamaicans, the Arawaks [Taino], for they contributed little to the Jamaica we know today". By the time of *Five Centuries,* he was willing to incorporate the Taino into a longer, developmental view of Jamaican art history.

The amount of attention given to pre-twentieth century art, most of it colonial, may at first seem contradictory to Boxer's nationalist project but this is, as Tony Bennett has argued, a characteristic part of nationalist historical narration in new nations:

> In so far as they are 'imagined communities' - ways of conceiving the occupants of a particular territory as essentially unified by an underlying commonality of tradition and purpose - nations exists through, and represent themselves in the form of, long continuous narratives. [...] This process of stretching the national past so as to stitch it into a history rooted in deep time is particularly evident in

---

[152] Prior to Boxer's recruitment, the NGJ had an administrator at the helm and decisions about exhibitions and acquisitions were made by a sub-committee of the Board of Directors. Boxer was the sole curator until 1980, when the Assistant Curator position was established and there has been since the late 1990s also a senior curator position.

[153] Boxer, p.92

> the case of new nations where, however, it also gives rise to peculiar difficulties. In the case of settler societies which have achieved a newly autonomous post-colonial status, this process has to find some way of negotiating - or leaping over - their only too clearly identifiable and often multiple beginnings.[154]

Boxer's negotiating strategy is to present modern Jamaican art as the necessary culmination of Jamaica's deep art history and he writes:

"What is here we believe can admirably demonstrate the richness of our past, and can provide a suitable context within which we can view that segment of the exhibition - The Twentieth Century [...] which will perhaps be most meaningful to the majority of our visitors."[155]

While he thus sought to validate the past, Boxer did not abandon the definition of Jamaican art in the true sense as a product of modern anti-colonialism, but he still had to account for the existence of modern Jamaican work with nationalist overtones that predated 1938. This was done with *The Formative Years: Art in Jamaica 1922-1940* in 1978. It was the first National Gallery exhibition and publication in which 1922 was used as the starting date for modern Jamaican art, although no justification was as yet provided for the choice of this date, except that the two earliest works in the exhibition, two Edna Manley sculptures, were from 1922.

By documenting the nationalist, Modernist work that was produced between 1922 and 1940 by Edna Manley, Alvin Marriott, Albert Huie, Carl Abrahams, Burnett Webster, the photographers Denis Gick and Roger Mais, and the painter Koren der Harootian, an Armenian refugee who was influential as an art teacher in the late 1930s,[156] the exhibition and catalogue effectively diffused the previous focus on 1938 as the starting date of modern Jamaican art. In *The Formative Years,* Boxer also refined his position on pre-twentieth century art, which he more explicitly subordinated to modern Jamaican art. While he acknowledges the contribution of colonial artists "to an interesting and even significant history of art", he adds that:

> "There is no painter, there is no sculptor from this period we can point to and say: 'This is a Jamaican artist; this is someone painting Jamaica and her people through Jamaican eyes'. Indeed, the true Jamaican artist is a product of the 20th century."[157]

The Formative Years also included work by John Dunkley and David Miller Sr. and Jr., which required some chronological gymnastics with the estimated dates for undated works, since they had produced few significant and dated works before 1940 but Boxer was determined, from early on, to include them

---

[154] Tony Bennett. *The Birth of the Museum* (1995), p. 148.

[155] Boxer, op. cit., p. 1.

[156] Koren der Harootian's name is also spelled as Khoren der Harootian or Khoren Harootian.

[157] Boxer, op. cit., p.1.

in the national canon. Although this was not elaborated on, he actually used the term Intuitive for the first time to describe these artists in the catalogue.[158]

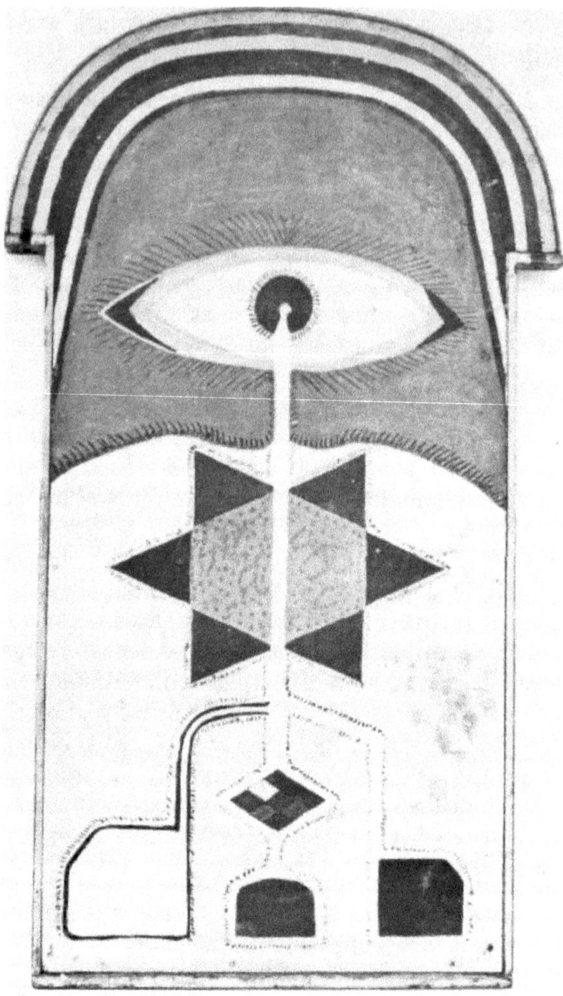

Cover of the *Intuitive Eye* (1979) catalogue, (with reproduction of Everald Brown's *Ritual Sign - Tree of Jesse* (1972)) (Photo Credit: National Gallery of Jamaica)

One last crucial addition to the National Gallery's emerging narrative - the canonization of the Intuitives as a crucial school within the Jamaican school - came in 1979, with the *Intuitive Eye* exhibition. In the catalogue, Boxer defines the Intuitives as follows:

> These artists paint, or sculpt, intuitively. They are not guided by fashion. Their vision is pure and sincere, untarnished by art theories

---

158 Ibid.

> and philosophies, principles and movements. They are for the most part self-taught. Their visions, (and many are true visionaries) as released through paint or wood, are un-mediated expressions of the world around them - and the worlds within. Some of them ... reveal as well a capacity for reaching into the depths of the subconscious to rekindle century old traditions, and to pluck out images as elemental and vital as those of their African fathers.[159]

Boxer implicitly contrasts the Intuitives with the mainstream and argues for their ultimate superiority, by attributing to their work the cultural authenticity and legitimacy for which the entire Jamaican art movement had been searching. Key to this claim is the notion that these artists have evolved independently from Western cultural norms.

Boxer's early exhibitions reflected his political and personal interests and we should not overlook that they challenged then-dominant understandings of Jamaican art and culture. In spite of this, the National Gallery's early exhibitions were generally well received locally, by the public and by reviewers, who all seemed supportive of the new institution's pioneering efforts. The first signs of serious dissent appeared in the critical reception of *The Intuitive Eye* exhibition, which more fundamentally challenged the established hierarchies of Jamaican art. The *Gleaner* art critic, Andrew Hope, had given *The Intuitive Eye* a relatively good review, but had suggested that the younger Intuitives were technically deficient and should be sent to art school.[160] This resulted in his first public disagreement with Boxer - the start of what would become a protracted war of words between the two (Hope 1979, viii; "Anonymous Eye" 1979, n).

"Jamaican Art 1922—1982"

Boxer's articulation of a Jamaican art history culminated in his essay, "Jamaican Art 1922-1982", which was first published in 1983. This essay was commissioned to serve as the main catalogue text for the like-named touring exhibition, which was toured in the USA, Canada and Haiti by the Smithsonian Institution Traveling Exhibition Service (SITES) from 1983 to 1985. While not the first overseas touring exhibition of Jamaican art, it was, and still is, the most ambitious and widely circulated such survey. The catalogue essay has been the principal historical text on Jamaican art since it was first published in 1983, and has also served as the basis for the National Gallery's permanent exhibition, as it was first installed in 1983 when the National Gallery moved to its more spacious current location on the Kingston Waterfront.

After first establishing that Jamaican art is "the art that has developed as an integral part of the nationalist, anti-colonialist consciousness underlying

---

[159] P. 2

[160] Andrew Hope, whose birth name was Ignacy Eker, was a Polish expatriate who served as the *Gleaner's* lead art critic from the 1960s to 1980s.

the cultural and intellectual life of the island since the 1920s",[161] Boxer moves on to sketching its "prehistory". This starts with a brief discussion of the art of the Taino. He praises four woodcarvings of Jamaican Taino zemes, three of which are in the British Museum and one in the Rockefeller Collection in the Metropolitan Museum.[162] He then cursorily mentions the Spanish period (1494-1670) and its main artistic relic, the so-called Seville Carvings (c 1530), a group of decorative architectural stone and stucco carvings made to adorn the Governor's mansion and other buildings in Jamaica's first capital of *Sevilla Nueva.*

The discussion of the English colonial period, which officially started in 1670 when the island was ceded to England, is divided into three short parts. In the first, Boxer discusses work by major European artists commissioned by the plantocracy and imported into the island, especially Neo-Classical commemorative and funerary sculptures such as John Bacon's 1789 Rodney Memorial in Jamaica's former capital Spanish Town. In the second, he surveys the work of itinerant naturalists and topographical artists, most of them Europeans but also a few US-Americans, who produced landscapes, depictions of flora and fauna, and picturesque scenes, often as clients of major planters. In this section he makes special mention of Isaac Mendes Belisario, who, he states, established a painting and printmaking studio in Kingston in 1835 and was therefore one of the first documented artists to practice in Jamaica. Boxer's discussion of colonial art concludes with its most significant and controversial part, in which Boxer claims that no African-Jamaican art of any significance had survived from before the twentieth century, and that very little such art had ever existed. He attributes this to the forced deculturation of African-Jamaicans under colonialism and slavery. This absence, he argues, set the stage for what "real" Jamaican art had to redress in the twentieth century.

---

[161] The *Jamaican Art 1922-1982* catalogue was out of print by the late 1980s. Boxer's essay was reprinted, with some minor modifications, in: David Boxer and Veerle Poupeye, *Modern Jamaican Art* (1998). Citations in the next paragraphs pertain to the 1998 edition of the essay.

[162] The Metropolitan Museum, based on recent scholarship (e.g. Kerchache 1994), now attributes this carving to the Dominican Republic but Boxer has refused to accept this reallocation, a good example of how nationalist agendas sometimes motivate attributions. The 1998 version of Boxer's essay included a footnote in which he described three major Taino carvings recovered in the small town of Aboukir in central Jamaica in 1994 and now housed at the National Gallery (26). Another major carving, a dujo or ceremonial seat, has since been found in the Hellshire hills, not far from Kingston, and is now also displayed at the National Gallery.

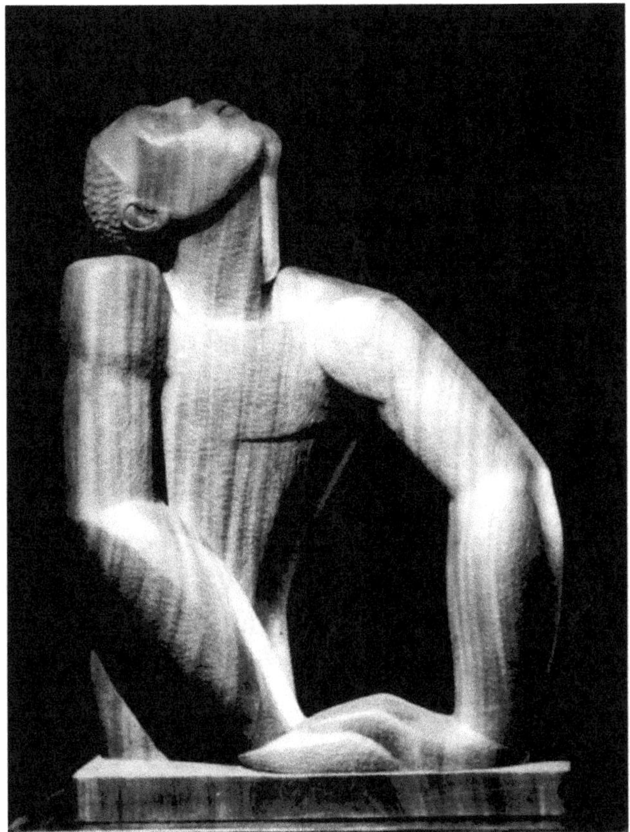

Edna Manley, Negro Aroused (1935), Collection: National Gallery of Jamaica (transferred from the Institute of Jamaica in 1974), period photograph by Denis Gick (Photo Credit: National Gallery of Jamaica)

Boxer's section on modern Jamaican art seeks to establish when, how and by whom this heroic cultural act was accomplished. It begins with a long discussion of Edna Manley's early work which, Boxer contends, was the turning point in the "Jamaicanization" of local art production, and he identifies her arrival in the island in 1922 as the starting date of modern Jamaican art. Boxer, who is the main Edna Manley scholar and the author of a comprehensive 1990 monograph on her work, discusses the early acclaim her work received in England and her influence, in the 1930s, on younger Jamaican artists such as the photographer Denis Gick, the furniture designer Burnett Webster, the sculptor Alvin Marriott and the painter Albert Huie, whose work is described as the earliest stirrings of a national school. The Edna Manley segment concludes with a discussion of the group of carvings she produced between 1935 and 1937 - all Modernist and assertively black - which are signalled as the triumphant breakthrough of nationalist Jamaican art and coincided with her emergence as a prominent member of the nationalist intelligentsia. Most of this discussion focuses on her best known sculpture, *Negro Aroused* (1935), as the iconic art work of that period that has become central to official Jamaican iconography; and it is of note that it was produced by an artist who was, for all intents and purposes, white, foreign-born and a member of the local elite.

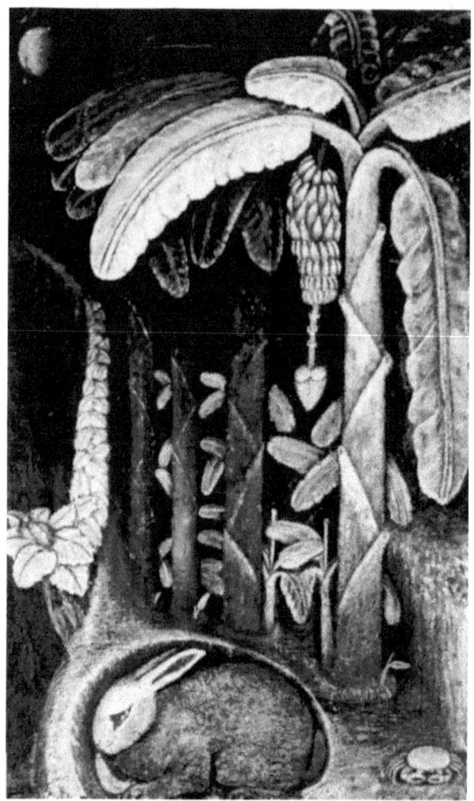

John Dunkley, Banana Plantation (c 1945), Collection: National Gallery of Jamaica (transferred from the Institute of Jamaica in 1974) (Photo Credit: National Gallery of Jamaica)

Boxer's discussion of the early nationalist school continues with what he names "the Early Intuitives", three self-taught artists to whom the term Intuitive was retroactively applied, namely John Dunkley and David Miller Sr and Jr. These artists were presented as personal discoveries of certain members of the nationalist intelligentsia - the "cognoscenti"[163] as Boxer calls them - in search of evidence of "native talent", although he insists on the individuality and visionary quality of their work as the primary reason for their classification as Intuitives. Most of the discussion is devoted to Dunkley, who is labeled as "Jamaica's greatest painter"[164] which thus positions him on a par

[163] P. 17
[164] Ibid.

with Edna Manley. Boxer shores up his claims about Dunkley's significance by citing Edmund Barry Gaither of the Museum of Afro-American Art in Boston, who had written in 1969 that Dunkley was "at best [...] a little short of Henri Rousseau [and] the equal of American Primitives such as Grandma Moses and Horace Pippin".[165]

Boxer then continues with the development of the nationalist school during the 1940s and 1950s, and starts by citing Norman Manley's 1939 "National Culture and the Artist" essay as the foundational text of that period. Two sub-groups are identified. One is labeled "the Institute Group" and consists of the young artists who were tutored by Edna Manley at her pioneering free adult art classes at the Institute's Junior Centre during the 1940s, such as Albert Huie, Ralph Campbell, David Pottinger and Henry Daley, and who consciously pursued the development of an indigenous iconography based on popular life and the physical environment. The second group is presented under the heading "the Independents", and consists of artists whose aesthetic and political pursuits departed from those of the Institute Group, such as Carl Abrahams and Gloria Escoffery, or who worked outside of Jamaica, such as Ronald Moody and Namba Roy, two sculptors who lived in England as adults. Boxer's description of the work of the "Independents", however, implies that there were significant parallels between their work and that of the "Institute Group", so that they could still be regarded as part of a Jamaican school.

The third part of Boxer's essay deals with the decades following Independence, namely the 1960s and 1970s. Under the heading, "Mainstream", Boxer points out that many of the pioneering artists were still active and briefly reviews Edna Manley's later work. He presents the period as one of continuity and change, in which younger artists, who had almost all studied abroad, in Europe, North America or Latin America, built on but also challenged the legacy of the older generation. He then discusses what he describes as the three dominant artists of the 1960s, namely the painters Eugene Hyde, Karl Parboosingh and Barrington Watson, who were more ambitious and adventurous about the formal aspects of their work than their predecessors, and insisted on being recognized as professionals. They were the founding members of the earlier-mentioned Contemporary Jamaican Artists' Association.

The discussion begins with Watson's academic landscapes and history and genre paintings on Jamaican themes which, Boxer rather mischievously states, appealed to "those whose artistic eye had been trained by the museums of Europe [and who] quickly elevated Watson to the role of the Jamaican painter par excellence".[166] The subsequent reference to the local commercial popularity of Watson's formal portraits, nudes and erotica is also subtly disparaging. The discussion then shifts to Hyde and Parboosingh, who are presented as artists who successfully applied the lessons of Modernist

[165] Ibid.

[166] P. 19

expressionism, whether abstract or figurative, to innovative and often provocative Jamaican subject matter, such as Parboosingh's sympathetic portrayals of ganja-smoking Rastafarians of the early 1970s. Boxer writes with great appreciation about Hyde's Casualties series of the late 1970s, which relate to his own artistic sensibilities, although these works openly criticized the social deterioration during the Michael Manley regime and Boxer was a close associate of the Manleys.

The next part, a subsection of the larger section on the 1960s and 1970s, is headed "Surrealism and other Influences" and two artists are highlighted. One is the Australian expatriate painter Colin Garland, who is credited with pioneering the sort of fanciful, meticulously executed Caribbean Surrealism that has been very successful in the upper echelons of the Jamaican and Haitian art markets, which may be the reason why Surrealism is foregrounded over other influences in this part of the essay.[167] The other is the painter and sculptor Osmond Watson (no relation to Barrington), whose Black Nationalist work is labeled as a hybrid of Cubism and Surrealism, to which he was exposed while studying in London. Finally, Boxer discusses "the Younger Generation within the Mainstream", younger artists who had emerged in the 1970s, most of them after studying abroad or as graduates of the Jamaica School of Art, which had started as an informal, part-time institution in 1950 but introduced full-time diploma programmes in 1962. This group includes the sculptors Winston Patrick and Christopher Gonzalez and the painters Milton George and Hope Brooks. Their formally and conceptually innovative work more decisively departed from the nationalist tradition and announced directions that would become more dominant in the 1980s. Boxer would probably have situated his own work here, had it been discussed in the essay.[168]

The section on the 1960s and 1970s ends with a long and enthusiastic discussion of the "Later Intuitives", who are discussed in what seems to be their order of appearance on the national scene from the late 1940s onwards, starting with Mallica "Kapo" Reynolds, Gaston Tabois, Sidney McLaren and Everald Brown, who are all clearly flagged as "masters", and are followed by several younger, less well-known names who are discussed in less detail. As with Dunkley, Boxer makes a point of mentioning the support these artists had received from well-known international Primitive art enthusiasts such as José Gómez-Sicre, a Cuban emigre who was in charge of the art programmes of the OAS and during the 1970s and acquired several Jamaican Intuitive works for the OAS collection; and the Haitian Primitive art promoter Selden Rodman, who, it was reported, had ranked Kapo "as a painter [...] probably equal to the late Hector Hyppolite of Haiti".[169] Boxer also mentions Kapo's

---

[167] Garland taught at the Jamaica School of Art where the Haitian painter Bernard Séjourné was among his students in the late 1960s. Séjourné was an exponent of the so-called School of Beauty in Haitian art, which depicts Haitian women in a meticulous, elegantly mannerist style and has been very popular with the Haitian elite.

[168] Two of his paintings were, however, included in the exhibition.

[169] P. 14

association with Edward Seaga, who had been that artist's most influential patron since the 1950s. The Later Intuitives are informally divided into realist (Tabois and McLaren) or symbolist (Kapo and Brown). Some attention is paid to the religious background of the "symbolists" - Kapo was a Zion Revivalist while Brown was a religious Rastafarian - and Boxer mentions the growing importance of Rastafari in Jamaican culture. Boxer rounds off the section on the "Later Intuitives" with mentioning his *Intuitive Eye* exhibition of 1979 as the landmark event that led to the naming and recognition of the Intuitives, and adds a jab at what he calls the "conservative critics"[170] in Jamaica who had, in his view, failed to appreciate their cultural significance.

Boxer's essay concludes with a section on "Art Schools, Associations and Galleries" in Jamaica, which includes the National Gallery itself. The final paragraph somewhat deflates the confident assertions of cultural nationhood that are made at the start of the essay, by arguing that the process of national self-discovery was still ongoing and full of "contradictions and tensions", but ultimately concerned with forging links with the "wider community of man".[171]

The *Jamaican Art 1922-1982* essay toes an uncomfortable line between Boxer's efforts to simultaneously establish the necessary autonomy of post-colonial Jamaican art and a legitimizing relationship with mainstream Western art history. A traditionally educated art historian, Boxer represents the history of Jamaican art in the terms he had been trained to use. He gives full rein to his classificatory impulses and structures his carefully periodized narrative to present the story of Jamaican art as part of a larger evolutionary framework that reflects the cultural logic of Jamaica's progression from colony to independent nation-state. Its self-conscious mannerism reflects Boxer's desire to create a national master narrative that ultimately, in the telling final sentence, inserts the "Jamaican school" into the artistic achievements of humankind. Boxer thus asserts, by implication, that post-colonial Jamaica has a full-fledged art history of its own, on a par and compatible with the grand narratives of the metropolitan West.

The *Jamaican Art 1922-1982* exhibition was well received in North America, where it attracted approximately 117,000 visitors,[172] and was reviewed in major newspapers such as the *Washington Post* and *New York Times*.[173] The reviews were almost unanimous in their praise of the Intuitives, but several critics expressed reservations about what they saw as the Eurocentricity of the mainstream.[174] John Bentley Mays of the *Globe and Mail* of Toronto wrote: "The most intriguing paintings and sculptures here,

---

[170] P. 25
[171] P. 26
[172] Rosalie Smith-McCrea. *Jamaican Art 1922-1982 Returns* (2006), p. 2.
[173] See: Benjamin Forgery. "Jamaican Artistry." *Washington Post,* July 14, 1983; and: Raynor, Vivien. "Works from Jamaica Show an Island Evolution." *New York Times,* August 12,1984.
[174] Excerpts from the reviews were compiled and published by the NGJ in the brochure *Jamaican Art 1922-1982 Returns* (1986).

however, are not the polished Euro-Jamaican descendents of [Edna Manley's] *The Beadseller,* but the home-spun, punchy pictures of the self-taught Intuitives".[175]

While the project was supported by many locally, it was lambasted by some prominent members of the art community. Their objections were not so much about its focus on Edna Manley - who was still alive and probably too much of a venerable elder in the local art community to be publicly tackled - but about the prominence given to the Intuitives, who were represented with 27 out of 76 works.[176] Chief among the critics was Andrew Hope, who dedicated a significant number of his columns during the 1980s to questioning the National Gallery's promotion of the Intuitives, along with Boxer's professional abilities and intentions.[177] The following comment on the 1986 Jamaican showing of *Jamaican Art 1922-1982* is typical and illustrates how Hope pointedly refused to use the term Intuitive: "[T]he exhibition lacks a guiding intelligence and seems to have been thrown together with the objective of demonstrating that our Primitives are superior to those painters and sculptors who have received formal training and were 'contaminated' by European influences".[178] The protracted public controversy about *Jamaican Art 1922-82* and the Intuitives amounted to a full-fledged culture war, a struggle for control over the production of the dominant canons and narratives. Boxer's essay is nonetheless a crucially important and indeed canonical text and it has been a point of departure, and a problem, for most of what has been written on the subject since then.

Re-negotiating the Canon

Boxer felt that his initial task of establishing a "baseline narrative" had been completed with *Jamaican Art 1922-1982* and he has actually called what followed the "expository years".[179] Since the mid-1980s, the National Gallery has mainly presented exhibitions and publications that deepened or updated its narrative rather than to change it in any substantive manner, such as the 1990 Edna Manley retrospective and the accompanying book *Edna Manley: Sculptor* - Boxer's ultimate tribute to the artist he had placed at the strategic centre of his narrative.[180] Likewise, Boxer's *Jamaican Art 1922-1982* essay was, save for some minor corrections, re-used "as is" in *Modern Jamaican Art* (1998), which was published by Ian Randle, the University of the West Indies

---

[175] Smith-McCrea, op. cit., p. 11.

[176] Ibid., p. 2.

[177] How this controversy panned out in the *Gleaner,* starting in the early 1980s and continuing until as late as 1990, is comprehensively documented in the National Gallery's newspaper scrapbook collection, with reviews, commentaries, published speeches and letters to the editor by most of major participants in this debate.

[178] Andrew Hope. "Gallery Guide." *Gleaner,* March 31,1986,16.

[179] David Boxer & Veerle Poupeye, "The National Gallery as an Educational Institution" (2001).

[180] Edna Manley had died in 1987.

Development and Endowment Fund and the National Gallery. I was asked to contribute an essay on developments in Jamaican art since 1982, which reflects a modular conception of Jamaican art history, to which contemporary art could simply be added. The corrections to Boxer's essay however included a footnote that acknowledges that pre-Emancipation African-Jamaican art had existed - a minor but significant departure from what had ultimately been an untenable position in a culturally confident post-colonial country where the majority of the population is of African descent.[181]

Since then, there have been three noteworthy modifications, each of which involved validating indigenous art from before the twentieth century. Chief among these was the consecration of Isaac Mendes Belisario (1794/95-1849), as the first Jamaica-born artist on record.[182] The other two are: the recognition of nineteenth-century Jamaican photography and a more explicit admission that African-Jamaican art forms in actuality existed before the twentieth century. These changes, which came about in the last ten years, stem from shifts in Boxer's own research interests, who has now done significant work on early Jamaican photography, and an increased focus on the nineteenth century in Caribbean cultural scholarship, especially around the 2007 bicentenary of the abolition of the slave trade in the British territories.

Belisario is best known for his "Sketches of Character: In Illustration of the Habits, Occupation and Costume of the Negro Population, in the Island of Jamaica", a series of hand-coloured lithographs on the customs and mores of the black population which was published in installments between 1837 and 1838.[183] The series is the earliest and main visual source on Jonkonnu, a creolized Christmas-time masquerade which has survived to the present day, although it is increasingly rare. The current interest in Belisario had started in the late 1990s with research initiated by the Jamaican book publisher Valerie Facey. The most potent endorsement however came from the exhibition *Art and Emancipation in Jamaica: Isaac Mendes Belisario and His Worlds* (2007) which was held at the Yale Centre for British Art to mark the above-mentioned bicentenary and accompanied by a substantial publication. The Yale exhibition had emphasized the historical and cultural context of Belisario rather than his own artistic merit but this was pointedly reversed in the Jamaican version, *Isaac Mendes Belisario: Art and Emancipation in Jamaica* (2008), which was curated by Boxer for the National Gallery, and effectively

[181] David Boxer and Veerle Poupeye, *Modern Jamaican Art* (1988), fn 10, p. 27

[182] There is, in actuality, another contender: the naturalist, anti-slavery activist, politician and magistrate Richard Hill, who was also born in the island in 1795 and belonged to the "free coloured" class. Hill, whose English father had been a miniature painter, produced illustrations of the local flora and fauna that have artistic merit, even though art was not his primary activity. See: Frank Cundall. Richard Hill (1920) and Elizabeth Waugh, "Emergent Art and National Identity in Jamaica, 1920s to the Present" (1987), 36.

[183] Only 12 of the originally intended 48 plates were actually published.

repositioned Belisario as the first Jamaican master.[184] This canonization was reinforced by the subsequent reinstallation of the National Gallery's historical galleries, which were expanded and prominently feature Belisario, and the publication of *Belisario: Sketches of Character-A Historical Biography of a Jamaican Jewish Artist* (2008) by Facey's Mill Press, which was launched at the National Gallery.

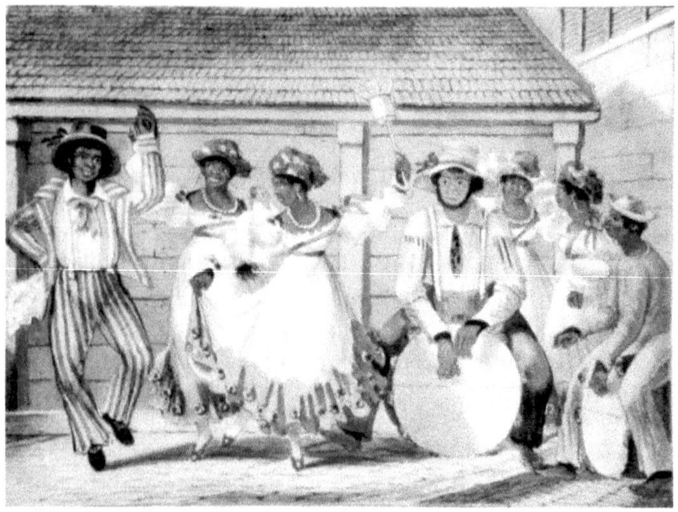

Isaac Mendes Belisario, Sketches of Character - French Set Girls (1837-38), Collection: Hon. Maurice and Mrs Valerie Facey, on loan to the National Gallery of Jamaica. (Photo Credit: National Gallery of Jamaica)

The repositioning of Belisario as the "father" of Jamaican art may seem to challenge Edna Manley's supremacy as its "mother" and earlier claims that true Jamaican art is a product of the twentieth century, but it is significant that his work is situated in the context of Emancipation, since this historical moment has been recognized, recently, as the enabling moment leading up to modern Jamaican nationhood.[185] Belisario's consecration is thus in actuality consistent with the general logic of the National Gallery's core narratives. It is worth noting that he was Sephardic and that the Jewish community did not have full civil rights until 1831; it has been argued that this may have given him common cause with the Emancipation project.[186] Belisario's work also suits the nationalist agenda because it documented and valorized the African-Jamaican popular culture, especially Jonkonnu, which had already in the 1950s been consecrated as a central part of the Jamaican cultural heritage.[187]

---

[184] David Boxer now routinely calls Belisario the "first Jamaican master" (personal communication, 5 July 2008).

[185] See: Petrina Dacres, "Monument and Meaning", *Small Axe.*

[186] Holly Snyder, "Customs of an Unruly Race: The Political Context of Jamaican Jewry, 1670-1831." (2007).

[187] Judith Bettelheim, "Jonkonnu and Other Christmas Masquerades" (1988), 43.

The other two modifications to the National Gallery's core narrative - the recognition of nineteenth-century photography and of Plantation-era African-Jamaican art - are part of the same art-historical reclamation project. The Belisario exhibitions at Yale and the National Gallery each included an African-Jamaican woodcarving that may date from before or around Emancipation, thus seeking to substantiate in material form that such art forms had effectively existed. More recently, in 2011, the National Gallery has also added African-Jamaican pottery to its historical galleries. The inclusion of pre-twentieth century African-Jamaican art has however mainly been a matter of symbolic gestures. This is unlikely to change, since insufficient material has been preserved to provide a more holistic representation.

The recognition of nineteenth-century photography, finally, hinged on the canonization of the French immigrant lithographer and photographer Adolphe Duperly, who had printed Belisario's "Sketches of Character". Duperly's work was the subject of a 2001 exhibition at the National Gallery, which consecrated him as the artist who introduced the modern media of lithography and photography into the island - he started producing daguerreotypes in the mid-1840s and established Jamaica's first photographic firm - and whose documentation of the Jamaican people and environment, like Belisario's, prefigures the iconography of the nationalist movement. While the National Gallery has acquired some early photography, it has not yet included any in its permanent exhibitions although there are plans for a photography gallery.

Despite these adjustments, and the updating and remounting of most galleries, the essential structure of the National Gallery permanent exhibition has not changed since 1983. This is all the more remarkable when one considers that the late 1990s and early 2000s were the most eventful in the National Gallery's history, with far more significant and broader critical challenges than before. Most of these came from artists and other art world stakeholders who vociferously questioned the Gallery's hierarchies and representational practices, and particularly the immense power of its Chief Curator, David Boxer, as the main taste-maker and gatekeeper of the Jamaican art world. These critiques were most cohesively articulated in the work of Indian expatriate art critic Annie Paul, in polemical essays such as "Legislating Taste: The Curator's Palette" (1998). Paul and others, such as the Jamaican-born curator Andrea Douglas and the Bahamian art historian Krista Thompson, also interrogated the underlying politics of the National Gallery's canons and its links to post-colonial social dynamics.[188] Other than providing a greater diversity of curatorial voices, for instance in the guest-curated *Curator's Eye* series which was initiated in 2004, however, these critical challenges have not substantively affected the National Gallery's curatorial

[188] See: Andrea Douglas, "Facing the Nation: Art History and Art Criticism in the Jamaican Context" (2004); and: Krista Thompson, "'Black Skin, Blue Eyes': Visualizing Blackness in Jamaican Art, 1922-1944." (2004).

and narrative strategies; nor has the National Gallery engaged in any critical self-interrogation of its curatorial practices and representational strategies.

Conclusion

While perhaps less urgent and specific than a century ago, the ultimately unanswerable question of how to define, and constantly redefine, Jamaican culture will always be one of the big driving forces in the development of Jamaican art and the narration of a Jamaican art history necessarily remains a core concern for the National Gallery. The lack of substantive change in the National Gallery's canons and narratives may however, undermine its relevance in a rapidly changing and ever contentious cultural context. Contestation is an integral part of post-colonial Caribbean culture and has, furthermore, been part and parcel of the operational context of museums, globally, since the latter part of the twentieth century.[189] The time has come, therefore, for the National Gallery of Jamaica to approach these matters with greater critical self-reflexivity and it is hoped that this chapter will contribute to this process.

References

Barringer, Tim, Forrester, Gillian, and Martinez-Ruiz, Barbaro, eds. 2007. *Art and Emancipation in Jamaica: Isaac Mendes Belisario and His Worlds.* New Haven: Yale Center for British Art & Yale University Press.

Baxter, Ivy, 1970. *The Arts of an Island: The Development of the Culture and of the Folk and Creative Arts in Jamaica.* Metuchen, NJ: Scarecrow Press.

Bennett, Tony, 1995. *The Birth of the Museum.* London: Routledge.

Bettelheim, Judith, 1988. "Jonkonnu and Other Christmas Masquerades." *Caribbean Festival Arts: Each and Every Bit of Difference,* edited by Nunley, John, and Bettelheim, Judith, 38-83. St. Louis: University of Washington Press.

Boxer, David, and Nettleford, Rex, 1979. *The Intuitive Eye.* Kingston, Jamaica: National Gallery of Jamaica.

Boxer, David, and Poupeye, Veerle, 1998. *Modern Jamaican Art.* Kingston, Jamaica: Ian Randle Publishers and the University of the West Indies Development and Endowment Fund.

_______, 2001. "The National Gallery of Jamaica as an Educational Institution." *Caribbean Journal of Education* 23, nos. 1 & 2.

Boxer, David et al. 2008. *Isaac Mendes Belisario: Art & Emancipation in Jamaica.* Kingston: National Gallery of Jamaica.

---

[189] For a discussion of the debates that have recently surrounded museums, see, for instance: Karp & Lavine, *Exhibiting Cultures* (1991), Karp et al., *Museums and Communities* (1992), and Karp et al., (2006).

Boxer, David, 1975. *Ten Jamaican Sculptors (Brochure).* London and Kingston: Commonwealth Institute and National Gallery of Jamaica.

________, 1976. *Five Centuries of Art in Jamaica.* Kingston, Jamaica: National Gallery of Jamaica.

________, 1978. *The Formative Tears: Art in Jamaica 1922-1940.* Kingston: National Gallery of Jamaica.

________, 1983. *Jamaican Art 1922-1982.* Washington, DC and Kingston, Jamaica: Smithsonian Institution Traveling Exhibition Service and National Gallery of Jamaica.

________, 1990. *Edna Manley: Sculptor.* Kingston: National Gallery of Jamaica and Edna Manley Foundation.

________, 1998. "Jamaican Art 1922-1982." *Modern Jamaican Art,* edited by Boxer, David, and Poupeye, Veerle. Kingston, Jamaica: Ian Randle Publishers and the University of the West Indies Development and Endowment Fund.

________, 2001. *Duperly.* Kingston, Jamaica: National Gallery of Jamaica.

Cundall, Frank, 1895. *Jamaica in 1895: A Handbook for Settlers and Others.* Kingston: Institute of Jamaica.

________, 1914. *The Portraits in the Jamaica History Gallery of the Institute of Jamaica.* Kingston: Institute of Jamaica.

________, 1918. *Jamaica in 1918: A Handbook for Settlers and Others.* Kingston: Institute of Jamaica.

________, 1920. "Richard Hill." *The Journal of Negro History* 5, no. 1: 37-44.

________, 1928. *Jamaica in 1928: A Handbook for Settlers and Others.* Kingston: Institute of Jamaica.

Dacres, Petrina, 2004. "Monument and Meaning." *Small Axe,* no.16: 137-54.

Douglas, Andrea, 2004. "Facing the Nation: Art History and Art Criticism in the Jamaican Context." *Small Axe,* no. 16: 49-60.

Fleming, Ian, 1965. *Ian Fleming Introduces Jamaica.* London: Andre Deutsch.

Forgery, Benjamin, 1983. "Jamaican Artistry." *Washington Post,* July 14.

Hope, Andrew, 1986. "Gallery Guide." *Gleaner,* March 31, 16.

Jensen, Peta Gay, 2005. *The Last Colonials: The Story of Two European Families in Jamaica.* London: Radcliffe.

Karp, Ivan, and Lavine, Steven, eds. 1991. *Exhibiting Cultures: The Poetics and Politics of Museum Display.* Washington, DC, and London: Smithsonian Institution Press.

Karp, Ivan, Mullen Kraemer, Christine and Lavine, Steven, eds. 1992. *Museums and Communities: The Politics of Public Culture.* Washington DC: Smithsonian Institution Press.

Karp, Ivan, Kratz, Corinne, Szwaja, Lynn, and Ybarra-Frausto, Tomas, eds. 2006. *Museum Frictions: Public Cultures/Global Transformations.* Durham: Duke University Press.

Manley, Edna, 1934. "Jamaican Art." *Jamaica Gleaner,* September 13, 18.

Manley, Norman, {1939} 1971. "National Culture and the Artist." *Manley and the New Jamaica: Selected Speeches and Writing 1938-1968,* edited by Nettleford, Rex, 108-09. London: Longman Caribbean.

Metcalf, Eugene, 1983. "Black Art, Folk Art, and Social Control." *Winterthur Portfolio* 18, no. 4: 271-89.

Paul, Annie, 1998. "Legislating Taste: The Curator's Palette." *Small Axe,* no. 4: 65-83.

Poupeye, Veerle, 2004. "A Monument in the Public Sphere: The Controversy About Laura Facey's Redemption *Song." Jamaica Journal 28,* no. 2 & 3: 36-48.

Ranston, Jackie, 2008. *Belisario: Sketches of Character - a Historical Biography of a Jamaican Jewish Artist.* Kingston: Mill Press.

Smith McCrea, Rosalie, 1986. *Jamaican Art 1922-1982 Returns.* Kingston: National Gallery of Jamaica.

Snyder, Holly, 2007. "Customs of an Unruly Race: The Political Context of Jamaican Jewry, 1670-1831." *Art and Emancipation in Jamaica: Isaac Mendes Belisario and His Worlds,* edited by Barringer, Tim, Forrester, Gillian, and Martinez-Ruiz, Barbaro, 150-61. New Haven: Yale Center for British Art & Yale University Press.

Thompson, Krista, 2004. "'Black Skin, Blue Eyes': Visualizing Blackness in Jamaican Art, 1922-1944." *Small Axe,* no.16: 1-31.

Waugh, Elizabeth, 1987. "Emergent Art and National Identity in Jamaica, 1920s to the Present." Ph. D. Dissertation, The Queen's University of Belfast.

Chapter 6

The Creation of the National Museum of Bermuda, 1974–2011

Edward Cecil Harris

Introduction

The islands of Bermuda form an isolated archipelago in the centre of the western North Atlantic, some 600 miles from the nearest land in continental North America and roughly equidistant from the Canadian Maritimes to the north and The Bahamas and the beginning of the West Indies to the south. Bermuda made its entry on the world stage in 1505, upon its discovery by the Spanish Pilot, Juan de Bermudez, homeward bound from the West Indies in the late autumn of that year. Unlike the islands of the West Indies, largely within visual distance from one another and connected to the American continents by a short stretch of water to the north and the south, Bermuda rose alone on an oceanic volcano, isolated from indigenous Americans without ocean-going sailing technology, but home for a considerable period to a multiplicity of avian life, including the iconic and endemic cahow. Some nineteen square miles gave life to such endemic plants as a small ecology could bear, including a juniper known as 'Bermuda cedar'. The reef platform of some 250 square miles teemed with fish, the siblings of which could be found off the southern reaches of the Gulf Stream, the largest 'river' in the world, and the reason why the island has a sub-tropical climate and is the northernmost coral atoll on Earth.

Into that natural paradise in the century after Bermudez came both swine and men - the result of shipwreck or exploration - the former creating the first human-generated ecological disaster on the Bermudas; and the latter, aside from the occasional forced sojourn, coming to settle for good in July 1612.

Although a corporate possession of the Bermuda Company (1615-1684) and its largely absent shareholders, the island established in 1620 one of the oldest parliaments in the world, developing from a company town into a seafaring nation after the dissolution of the Company. The Bermuda sloop, constructed in the durable and teredo worm-resistant cedar, was for a period the fastest vessel afloat, and Bermuda-built craft could be found serving under a variety of flags as privateers, merchants, and naval vessels.

The independence of some of the former British American colonies in 1783 changed Bermuda forever. It assumed a military importance formerly held by the islands of the West Indies: this rise to power is indicated in the cessation of major works of defence in those southern islands, and the subsequent creation of immense fortifications in Bermuda and at Halifax in Canada in the nineteenth century. Starting in 1809, a dockyard arose at Bermuda, which became the fulcrum of the North America and West Indies Station of the Royal Navy, and formed an association with Bermudians that only ceased at the end of the Cold War with the closure of British, American and Canadian Forces establishments on what was described as a 'fixed aircraft carrier'.

The natural oceanic heritage of Bermuda is under threat, as is that of many small islands worldwide, while the island itself is now largely an artificial environment, crafted by its residents over the past 400 years. Within that environment, due to the presence of an easily worked limestone, the islanders developed a unique vernacular architecture, particularly for domestic use, and several thousand dwellings and other structures - those that survived the Age of the Bulldozer, ushered in after the Second World War - are considered to be of 'listing' value by the government. Unlike Colonial Williamsburg, largely built anew, the Town of St. George's, established as the first capital in 1612, replete with such buildings yet standing, was inscribed by UNESCO in 2000 along with its associated fortifications as a World Heritage Site. The island is also rich in shipwreck heritage - whatever has survived treasure hunting - and it abounds in fortifications and military heritage that has outlived neglect and lack of interest.

Modern interest in Bermuda's rich history began with Governor Lefroy's abridged transcription of Bermuda's colonial records, published in 1882. Subsequently the Bermuda Historical Society (1895), the St. George's Historical Society (1922), and the Bermuda Historical Monuments Trust (1937) were formed, and at the height of war in 1944 the first local heritage journal, the *Bermuda Historical Quarterly,* appeared, and survived until 1981. All remained relatively quiet in the western reaches of the Atlantic until the establishment of the Bermuda National Trust in 1968, which now owns some 400 of the island's 12,000 acres and a plethora of historic buildings and nature reserves. A group of determined individuals from the Trust set up the

Bermuda Maritime Museum in 1974, appropriately within the ten-acre site of the largest fort in the island - the 'Keep' - on the northern perimeter of the old Royal Naval Dockyard, which had been derelict for some 25 years. To the Keep was added in 2009 all the rest of the fortifications of the Dockyard and the historic buildings within that curtilage, so that now the museum stretches from the large Commissioner's House in the north east, along the long rampart wall enclosing the Dockyard, to the massive Casemate Barracks to the south west.

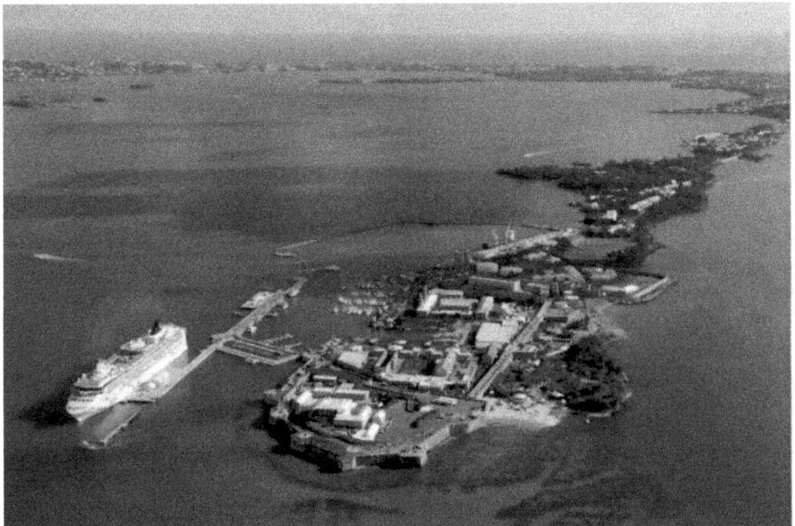

The old Royal Naval Dockyard, Bermuda, from the north, with the ten-acre fort, the 'Keep' in the foreground; the long rampart on the right joins the Keep with the great Casemate Barracks and two adjacent Ordnance buildings, thus, with the Keep, forming the National Museum of Bermuda

The Historic Site and its Restoration

The creation of the National Museum of Bermuda (NMB) from the Bermuda Maritime Museum was prefaced by over three decades of restoration work. The Keep was derelict and overgrown in 1974, and it was only the construction of the buildings in the extremely hard version of the local limestone that saved its marvellous architecture from decay and dissolution throughout several decades of complete neglect. Initial work, in 1974 and 1975, took the form of clearing the site of overgrowth and debris in order to make it accessible, securing the buildings, and making one of them - the 1850 Ordnance Building, now known as the Queen's Exhibition Hall - ready for use by the museum. During the first five years, after the museum was opened by Her Majesty the Queen in early 1975, three buildings in the lower grounds of the Keep were restored and filled with exhibits on various aspects of

Bermuda's maritime history, from small boat racing and fishing to shipwrecks, and from cable-laying to diving. This early renovation and exhibition work was accomplished largely by volunteers and relied on donations from the public, with no financial support from government.

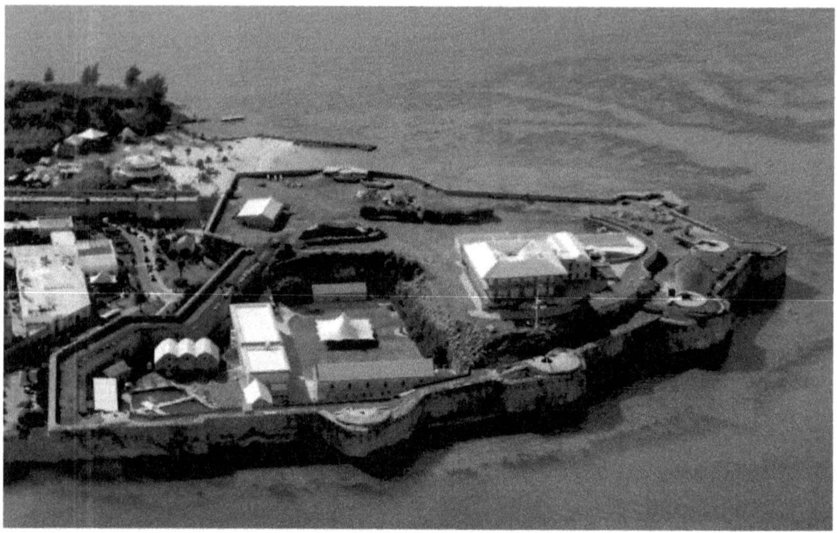

The 'Keep', or great fort, of the old Royal Naval Dockyard, Bermuda, with the large Commissioner's House centre right: the Maritime Museum started in the Keep Yard to the left in 1974, while the Commissioner's House was restored and opened to the public in May 2000

In its first two years the museum attracted upwards of 25,000 paying visitors a year, giving some financial stability to its daily operations, and its success stimulated the government to consider renovating the central area of the Dockyard in 1981. The increase of activity in all areas of the museum led the Board of Trustees to hire a manager in 1980, a post shortly afterwards redesignated as Director. Over the next few years, the other historic buildings of the lower grounds of the Keep were restored, with exhibits on the *Royal Navy at Bermuda*, *Bermuda in the Age of Discovery* and - in the first display not entirely maritime in nature - *Bermuda Coins and Currency*, including examples of the 1616 'Hog Money'. A staff position of Curator was established, as the collection of artefacts, donated and loaned, increased rapidly, and this was supplemented a few years later with the addition of a part-time Registrar.

In the late 1980s the museum began the restoration of the derelict Commissioner's House on the upper grounds of the Keep, representing some 20,000 square feet of future exhibition space. The restoration was completed in 2000. The permanent exhibits in the building, installed over nine years and described in 'Exhibits' below, have been complemented by changing exhibitions of works of art from the Fay and Geoffrey Elliott Collection of the Bermuda Archives, artwork from the Bank of Bermuda Foundation collection, and most recently, a photographic exhibit on the Bermuda longtail bird. The work of filling the House culminated in 2009 with a thousand-square foot mural on the history of Bermuda, which took the artist three years to complete.

From 1980 onwards, subsidiary buildings and parts of the ramparts, bastions and magazines were also renovated or restored for housing for visiting scholars and students, for exhibits, and for boat storage; and a new structure was erected for a conservation laboratory. All in all, the work carried out in the first three decades of the museum represented an investment well in excess of $25 million in cash and kind.

Museum staff and volunteers began work in 2005 on the government-owned Casemate Barracks, a complex of buildings and fortifications erected in the 1840s at the other end of the Dockyard. The Barracks itself served as Bermuda's maximum security prison from 1963 to 1994, with some damage to the historic fabric. Having been derelict for a decade by 2005, it was in need of some rescue work before the buildings were further damaged by vandals and invasive plants. Several years after work began, it was suggested that the area be joined to the Museum, which then would comprise all the fortifications of the Dockyard, making it potentially one of the largest museum complexes in an historic district in the Americas.

The Bermuda government approved that concept in late 2009, and as the museum had by then been in effect carrying out the work of a national institution, the whole area was designated as the 'National Museum of Bermuda'. In seeking to create a national identity based on historical fact, heritage assets must be amassed, recorded and exhibited. In this instance, such asset classes began at the macro level of historic buildings and landscape settings, and continued into the micro groundwork of collecting, preserving and exhibiting artefacts.

Exhibits

When the museum first opened its doors, all exhibits were created, designed and assembled in house with the help of volunteers, and with limited financial resources. Exhibit design and development remained in house for 20 years, with the Curatorial Department responsible for conducting research, creating the interpretive plans, and designing and producing the didactic panels. It was not until the opening of Commissioner's House that exhibit panel design was outsourced to a local graphic design and copy-editing company, and the panels were produced by a professional printing company.

Initially exhibits were of a maritime nature, but with the opening of Commissioner's House as an exhibition space, the museum broadened its focus to become more relevant to the diverse local community, beginning to fill a void in the local cultural landscape which had been apparent to the museum's professional staff and trustees for some time. Four major exhibits in the newly-opened House were the first step along this route: *The Slave Trade*

& Slavery in Bermuda, *Bermuda and the Azores*, *Bermuda and the West Indies*, and *Bermuda's Defense Heritage*. *The Slave Trade and Slavery in Bermuda* explores the New World Slave Trade from Africa to the Americas via the infamous Middle Passage, the hardships of captives in the Americas and the struggle for abolition. *Slavery in Bermuda* follows 200 years of slavery in Bermuda, from the early years of settlement after 1612 through to Emancipation in 1834. The exhibit showcases the artisan and maritime occupations of Bermudian enslaved people and free men, as well as their skill, faith, resistance and solidarity, and traces a Bermudian family's ties to slavery. *Bermuda and the Azores* explores the Portuguese-Bermudian cultural connections, as about one quarter of the island's population can trace its roots to the Azores, and the island's recent history of survival and prosperity owes much to the Portuguese community.

Centuries of sea-borne history link Bermuda to the West Indies. The *Bermuda and the West Indies* exhibit explores the maritime, economic and cultural links between Bermuda and the Caribbean: while geographical isolation sets Bermuda apart, its people share with their Caribbean counterparts the bond of maritime exploits, interwoven families and a mutual legacy of trade, piracy, slavery, hurricanes and shipwrecks. Part of the *Defense Heritage* exhibit featured the Bermudian men and women who served in local forces in the defence of the Island and those who enlisted for overseas service, including 115 who gave their lives in the two World Wars. These exhibits were groundbreaking as no material expression of slavery, of our cultural connections to the West Indies and the Azores, or of the experiences of Bermuda's war veterans had been presented on the island before, or given a permanent home.

Today, however, exhibits are being developed differently. The museum is trying to be more sensitive to competing narratives, and to incorporate multiple voices into an exhibit. Rather than highlighting one narrative, future exhibits aim to interweave the different and competing narratives and multiple voices that reflect the diversity of Bermuda, thus creating a more holistic representation of Bermuda's history, while also incorporating new knowledge generated by research. The museum has also moved to a more constructivist approach to exhibit development, and to developing new exhibits that focus on family learning, group interaction and meaning making.

Administration and Finance

The museum is administered by a volunteer Board of Trustees that is responsible for overall policy, financial oversight and fund-raising involvement and overview. Daily operations are managed by a salaried Executive Director, who answers to the Board of Trustees in monthly meetings. Most of the annual budget for the museum's operations is covered by gate receipts from visitors and by donations from an annual appeal to the membership of the institution, as well as other donations and rental income from the use of the premises in the evening. An Endowment Fund for the museum was established over a decade ago to support the operations of the museum on an annual basis, and to provide full support for the museum for up to a year, should recessionary times dictate. All capital works, including building and other physical projects, exhibits, book publications and any other individual projects are accounted for separately and funds are raised via donations for each such project. In order to garner donations from persons liable for US tax, a 501C3 corporation, the Friends of Bermuda Maritime Museum, Inc., was established in 1982, and a similar organization, the Bermuda Maritime Museum Trust, was set up in the United Kingdom a few years later; both bodies contribute to the work of the museum through requested grants for projects. The Bermuda government has donated funds for particular projects of interest, but does not provide any monies for daily operations: the museum property is leased from the government for a period of 99 years.

The Museum Collections

The museum's initial collection policy was mandated by an Act of Parliament, the *Bermuda Maritime Museum Association Act 1978,* which established the museum with the express aim of collecting and preserving objects associated with Bermuda's maritime history for the "enjoyment and education of the public". It was also given the mandate of promoting and preserving the historical buildings and gun emplacements within the Keep.

When Her Majesty the Queen opened the first exhibition hall at the museum in 1975, all of the objects in the collections were on display. These comprised objects from the collections of the Bermuda National Trust, the Bermuda Aquarium, Museum and Zoo, HM Customs, Watlington & Conyers (shipping agency), and Cable & Wireless, as well as collections of maps and art owned by Trustees and other interested individuals. As the future of the museum was uncertain, situated as it was in the derelict Dockyard at the isolated western tip of the island, most of the items were on 'permanent loan', to be returned should the museum close its doors.

The museum grew, and received more donations from individuals and more outright gifts rather than loans. New collections were acquired, including the Tucker Collection of shipwreck artefacts, loaned by the Bermuda Aquarium, Museum and Zoo; the Forster Cooper Collection of maps and plans of the Dockyard; the Kelly Collection of photographs of Bermuda-related naval vessels; and the Ruberry Collection of glass plate negatives. Other areas of growth included materials related to the Royal Navy Dockyard, commercial and recreational diving, passenger and commercial shipping, and activities such as piloting, fishing and boat racing.

As the museum developed, negotiating its way through its infant years, the collection policy shifted to include collecting significant non-maritime objects, which would otherwise be destroyed, and which could not be taken by another local institution, such as coins and currency, philately, prisoner-of-war mementoes, and collections related to the Bermuda Railway and the Bermuda Electric Light Company. Such objects were to be held in reserve until an appropriate home was found. Now that the museum has changed its name to the National Museum of Bermuda and widened the scope of the collection to include all aspects of Bermuda's history and heritage, the objects held in reserve have found their permanent home.

The museum collections today are diverse and varied in material and subject matter. They encompass the museum site itself (a historic fort dating to the early 1800s and its historic buildings and ramparts); extensive archaeological finds (terrestrial and underwater artefacts); archaeological records; armaments (cannon, guns and ammunition); photographs; documents; works of art and carvings; maps and plans; ship models; textiles (military uniforms, sails, flags, tapestries); rare books; coins and currency; small and large watercraft; tools and equipment (shipping, fishing/whaling, woodworking, farming); furniture; medals, plaques and crests; and digital records (photographs, documents, publications, oral history interviews and film). There are currently over 60,000 items catalogued in the master accession database and the collection is rapidly increasing. Islands tend to trap artefacts, particular larger ones, and that assertion was underscored by the recent discovery of possibly the only known example of a Charles I cannon made of 'special metal', a type of cast iron that is almost as good as bronze for such weapons.

The broadened scope of the collection is now more in line with the spectrum of work the museum has carried out, which has not been limited to maritime history. However, bearing the name 'National' comes with many challenges and preconceived notions that the museum and its collection and exhibits are representative of a collective national identity. The museum is currently developing a new collection policy and thinking critically about its new direction and the role it should play in helping Bermudians construct, negotiate and imagine their own identity. The museum wishes to develop into a space that provides the means to discover and construct a sense of place and identity, rather than create it.

Making the Collections and Research Accessible

Ease of access to research and collections information is imperative to the work of the museum, and has been a focus of the Curatorial Department. Curatorial staff numbers have not changed dramatically since the 1980s, but by capitalising on technology, on partnerships and collaborative projects with local and overseas institutions, and on the work of volunteers and interns, the museum has been able to achieve far more than it has ever done in the past.

Over the last five years the museum has made major changes to the collections information management system via networking, standards-based system design, controlled vocabularies and the development of a single interface to access all collections-related information and research. The Curatorial Department had transitioned from a paper-based system to a non-networked flat-file database around 1990, but the implementation of a museum-wide network around 2005 was the first step in bringing together the 'information silos' that had developed naturally in every department and on every desktop.

The museum's networked system as it stands today has two central servers: one for files - including digital images and digital reference material - and the other a dedicated server for the collections management database. The collections management system itself includes modules supporting essential curatorial activities, as well as access to related digital records and reference materials providing additional contextual information. Data consistency is maintained via the use of strictly controlled terminologies, well-defined field descriptions, and in-house developed authority tables. Even so, close supervision of volunteers and interns helping with cataloguing projects is necessary, as decisions about style and choice in terminology and description are not always cut and dried, and the relationships between objects and other entities can be very complex.

More recently the museum has begun sharing its database structure with other cultural management organisations in Bermuda, with the aim of facilitating cross-institutional research and access at some point in the future.

Research

The museum has established itself as a research institution (the only one in Bermuda), engaged in historical, material culture and underwater and terrestrial archaeology research. It has striven to generate new knowledge, re-interpret Bermuda's past, and publish and exhibit modern scholarship. It has one of the best collections of Bermuda books and Bermudiana, and a reference library focusing on maritime history, which is open, by appointment, to the public. New research, scholarship and interpretation of Bermuda's past is fundamental for generating new knowledge, and underpins all museum education programming, exhibitions, publications and other interpretive material. Archaeological records and research also provide insight into Bermuda's historic role in the Atlantic world, allowing greater understanding of Bermuda's global position.

The museum is strongly anchored in the discipline of archaeology, both land and marine. For over 30 years underwater archaeology has been conducted under the aegis of the museum, partnering with the world's leading marine archaeology programmes, archaeologists and professors to carry out research and conduct surveys on Bermuda's underwater cultural heritage. Terrestrial archaeology has had a similar lifespan, where museum-directed excavations in partnerships with overseas archaeology programmes have extended across the island. Excavations have concentrated on historic forts, and also on residential sites, bringing a new perspective on life in Bermuda between the seventeenth and nineteenth centuries.

The raw archaeological data, archaeological drawings and field notes are all archived at the museum; the finds are accessioned into the museum collection; and the reports are published in the Museum's *Bermuda Journal of Archaeology and Maritime History*. The academic research is then brought to the public through exhibitions, educational programming and other popular museum publications. The *Journal* is not used exclusively for publishing archaeology-related papers, but also includes historical research conducted by the museum in partnership with overseas universities and institutions and independent researchers. The museum has provided support for researchers and carried out projects to reinterpret and generate new perspectives on Bermuda's past, and to give a voice to those people who have been marginalized from Bermuda's history books. In particular, the Curatorial Department conducted original research on slavery in Bermuda and linked archaeological finds from underwater sites to the history of slavery.

Overseas partnerships are invaluable in building the academic reputation of the museum and the scholarly capacity of the island, as there is no local university. Overseas universities, through partnerships, provide a flow of interns, many of whom return year after year to work on a variety of curatorial projects, including assisting with exhibition development, research, and numerous collection management projects. The relationship also attracts local interns and volunteers who are integral to the work of the Curatorial Department. Local students are trained in museum, archaeology and historical praxis to build local capacity and enable the Curatorial Department to achieve far more than it could on its own with only two permanent staff members.

Publications

The museum began to publish the results of research from the early 1980s onwards, and to reprint earlier works long out of print but worthy of presenting again to the public. The museum's newsletter was upgraded in 1987 into a semi-annual magazine, now called *MariTimes* (which has been freely distributed to a number of museums in the Caribbean region); and in 1989 the annual *Bermuda Journal of Archaeology and Maritime History* commenced publication. A number of individual volumes have since been published, including the commencement of a monograph series for the museum in 2007, of which four titles have since been published. Three volumes of a series entitled *Heritage Matters* have been produced for articles from a weekly local newspaper column of the same name; five more are planned. In addition, the museum has a list of a dozen books on Bermuda subjects that will be produced over the next few years. Such works are making cultural and historical information widely available to the public and in particular to schools, where the teaching of Bermuda's history has been lacking in past generations owing to a paucity of published materials on the subject.

Education

There is no full-time educator at the museum, so partnering with educators from local institutions has been vital in carrying out its education mission. To maximize the number of students reached and to carry out more education programmes related to the museum's mandate, the curator has partnered successfully with other local institutions that have established education departments. For example, the museum in 2009 partnered with the Bermuda Sloop Foundation and Bermuda Institute of Ocean Sciences to create an interdisciplinary education initiative based on experiential learning, which targeted local Middle 3 students (13- and 14-year-old students). During the 2009-10 academic year all Middle 3 classes (approximately 500 students) participated in a five-day learning expedition aboard the Bermuda Sloop Foundation's *Spirit of Bermuda.* The year-long project engaged the students in registering, surveying, dredging and restoring artefacts from a previously undocumented local shipwreck found in shallow waters. The students were also trained in navigation and ship handling, explored shipwrecks as ecosystems for new coral reef growth, and learned about the importance of protecting Bermuda's underwater cultural heritage. Without this partnership, the museum alone would not have reached the large number of students, nor produced such a rich learning experience that involved living aboard a 100-foot sailing ship, snorkeling on the coral reef and documenting an unidentified shipwreck. Partnering allowed the institutions to share costs, resources and expertise and reach a wider number of schools and students.

Conservation

Conservation is integral to archaeology and museum work and ensures that the museum fulfills its duty of preserving and caring for Bermuda's cultural heritage for future generations. The museum, since its involvement in underwater archaeology in the late 1970s, has had an operational conservation laboratory. The original lab was however, rudimentary compared with that of today, and had limited equipment and supplies for conserving the broad range of artefacts in the collections. That all changed when the Corange Conservation Laboratory was constructed in 1989 as a purpose-built lab with specialized equipment and chemicals for conserving the museum's growing collections, and in particular marine and terrestrial archaeological finds. In 2010, the museum received a generous donation to update the Corange Conservation Laboratory and purchase new equipment and supplies, supporting its work into the future.

Historical Preservation

When the museum was formed it became responsible for the care and preservation of the then-abandoned Keep fort and its derelict buildings. Much of the museum's work and energy over the past 35 years has been invested in restoring and maintaining the ten-acre property and filling the buildings with exhibits. But the museum's efforts in historical preservation have also extended island wide, in particular outside the museum gates in the Royal Naval Dockyard. In 2007 the museum, by agreement with the Minister responsible for the Dockyard lands and with a group of dedicated volunteers began a programme of pre-restoration work at the Casemate Barracks. The building was constructed in the 1830s at the Land Front end of the Dockyard and initially housed the men who were responsible for manning the Dockyard's fortifications. Eventually it became Bermuda's maximum-security prison, but was left derelict in 1994. Casemates was transferred to the museum in 2009; the intention is to restore the building fully to create more exhibit, education, office and storage space. Further afield, the museum carried out a recent mission to rescue an historic steam-powered winch used at a St. George's marine slip from the mid-1800s until five years ago. This is one of many projects that the museum has spearheaded to rescue and preserve parts of Bermuda's built and moveable heritage.

Advocacy

Since its inception the museum has been an advocate for the protection and preservation of cultural heritage; this role is woven into all aspects of the museum's work, including publication, education and public outreach. One example of its advocacy work was in 2001 when the museum worked closely with the Bermuda government to change the Bermuda law to include the protection of underwater cultural heritage. Ten years ago, the *Bermuda Historic Wrecks Act 2001* was passed with the principal aim of protecting Bermuda's underwater cultural heritage through the archaeological investigation of local shipwrecks. The legislation, according to renowned underwater archaeologist Dr. Jon Adams, is an example of "what can be done by an enlightened administration, supported by a concerned and knowledgeable public. Bermuda sets a powerful example to the rest of the world where in so many states, protection of underwater sites lags woefully behind that afforded to land sites." The *Bermuda Historic Wrecks Act* is based on the 2001 United Nations Educational, Scientific and Cultural Organisation (UNESCO) Convention on the Protection of the Underwater Cultural Heritage. The UNESCO Convention provides legal protection for submerged archaeological sites, wherever they are located (including in international waters); and a framework of rules and standards for the protection and responsible management of underwater heritage.

The Future

Much of the museum's work has involved dealing with large renovation projects, documenting the vast collection, carrying out original research on Bermuda's history and heritage, bringing the museum up to professional standards and making the collections and research accessible. In the future the Curatorial Department aims to focus on more projects to foster active community engagement and participation. Museums have a role in social cohesion, social development and enhancing civic life. The museum intends to develop into a place for visitors to share and connect with each other, provoke new means of understanding and become a place for communities to construct cultural identity, a sense of place and of belonging.

Chapter 7

Recapturing History:

Suriname Museum in Fort Zeelandia

Hilde Neus

> "Monuments of days gone by deserve a place in the Cultural Mosaic of now, because where ever an important body of old buildings is available, it will contribute greatly to the image of and identification with the background from which one now lives and works."
>
> (Albert Helman, 1977: 378).

The Suriname Museum Foundation, host of the largest artefact and antiquarian book collection in Suriname, is housed in the oldest historic building in Paramaribo, Fort Zeelandia. The museum has lived through a tumultuous history of developments over the last 20 years, in different respects. In spite of several setbacks, it survived through the difficult years. The museum in Fort Zeelandia was reopened in 1995 and a number of exhibitions have been organized since, at times made possible with aid from abroad (mainly the Netherlands); at other times with local funding. Since 2000 a productive educational programme has been set up, which has been very successful. The museum aims to disclose its collection to a larger audience by publishing books in the series *'Libri Musei Surinamensis'*. It is argued here that Caribbean museums should pave their own path according to a number of paradigms for finding their way into the future. To make this possible for

Suriname, we are in a constant process of recapturing a fort and recapturing history.

Recapturing a Fort

The Suriname Museum is housed in the old fort at the centre of Paramaribo, the capital. The history of the fort runs parallel to the history of the colony. It is located at the very spot on the Suriname River where the first colonists set foot on shore, and from where further developments took place. The city of Paramaribo saw its growth from the fort and its surroundings onward. This is still reflected in the language today. City in *Sranan*, the vernacular language of Suriname, is 'foto', a word clearly derived from 'fort'.

Because of the presence of an Amerindian settlement at this exact location, from the beginning of colonization the white settlers built their strongholds on this site. Due to malaria and struggle with the indigenous population the early Dutch or French settlers never stayed long. This changed with the arrival of the British. In 1650 Francis, Lord Willoughby, Governor of Barbados, decided to create a colony in Suriname. He travelled up the Suriname River with a number of English planters and, to prevent invaders from attacking, decided to have a fortress built. The outer walls of this pentagonal building were erected entirely out of shell stone; not surprising, since the British used coralstone for their strongholds and some houses on Barbados. In 1667 the fort was captured by the Dutch under the command of Abraham Crijnssen from Zeeland. That same year Suriname officially became Dutch property under the terms of the Peace Treaty of Breda. In return for the loss of Suriname, the British became the owners of New Amsterdam, nowadays better known as New York. The name Fort Willoughby was changed to Fort Zeelandia.

Ever since the Europeans have built forts and drawn maps, a fortress was a prominent feature not to be overlooked. This is not exclusive to Suriname, and not to Fort Zeelandia. Strongholds were strategic buildings; even if the Dutch did not put the fort on their maps, their enemies would. Furthermore, fortresses are striking buildings in size, beauty and often in symmetry. Because of the historical implications of colonization, in which the fort was the centre of usurping power from the days of settlement onwards, it has been the place for punishment. A proverb says: *'tangi fu Spans' bocko mi bin si ini foto'.* (Because of the Spanish bock[190] I have seen the inside of the fort.)

During the period of slavery people were imprisoned in the cells, slaves as well as free, but also dissident military. At several points in history, people supposedly 'fled' from the prisons and were shot in the back. This happened during the Second World War, as well as during the military period of the

[190] A Spanish bock is a form of punishment where the victim is tied by hands and feet and fastened to the ground with a stick at the back of the knees. He is then whipped first on one side, than on the other. This scene was drawn in Brazil by Debret (see http://hitchcock.itc.virginia.edu/Slavery under physical punishment).

1980s. From 1872 until 1967 the building was used exclusively as a jail (Van Putten and Ferrier, 1999).

Anderson gives three reasons why the colonial government in the Dutch East Indies invested heavily in restoring monuments. It coincided with the government's educational policies; it clearly showed colonial hierarchies; and it allowed the state to appear as a guardian of a generalized (and local) tradition (Anderson, 1991: 180). These motives might have played a role when the colonial Suriname government decided to designate the fort as museum quarters. It took from 1967 until 1972 to restore the fort, but in 1972 the premises were transferred to the Suriname Museum Foundation. In 1982 however, because of a military coup, the fort had to be abandoned and the entire collections were stored and exhibitions held in the annex. In 1995 the old fort, and two buildings connected to the museum at the complex surrounding the fortress, were restored with funding by the Dutch government, and the museum reopened. Since then the museum has slowly but surely regained some of its old glory.

History shows that this museum building, i.e. the fortress, has a narrative of refractive violence. A number of people within Suriname society are still reluctant to cross the threshold. This history will never go away, and we have to reinvent the position of the fort within society. We have to recapture its discourse and its value as a historical building, as a memory of violence and as a 'symbol' of grief. The fort cannot be discarded because we want to forget. As a constant reminder of our history, it stands strong and precious.

To Acquire a Collection

The Suriname Museum did collect cultural artefacts of the 'Other', but here the word 'Other' needs to be redefined. The museum does not focus on foreign cultures to be introduced to Suriname's visitors. In this respect it is not, in the strict sense of the word, an ethnological museum. We prefer to call it a 'cultural historical museum', meaning that its collections represent a number of cultures situated within our own national sphere.

During colonial times, the European bourgeois collected many artefacts, also from Suriname, and transported these to the mother country, i.e. the Netherlands. In Europe, collections of rarities, antiques and ethnographic objects grew into museums. This was not just for collecting purposes, but also had educational value: the more people knew about produce, farming and native life in the colonies, the better they could prepare for their travels and endeavours in the tropics.

In 1864 a group of people, the 'Suriname Society for the Preservation of Knowledge', handed over their zoological collection to the State of Suriname, and the Colonial Museum became a reality in 1875. The importance to education was soon acknowledged since the government placed the institution under the supervision of the Inspector of Education. Nevertheless, the institute deteriorated and the remains were turned into the School Museum, which was closed in 1925. By 1930 most of the artefacts had been sold at public auction.

A number of educational institutions sent letters of protest to the Minister of Colonies in The Hague, the Netherlands, but to no avail.

In 1947 the Suriname Museum Foundation was established. The reason for founding it was a growing sense of national awareness that had arisen during the Second World War. By that time, it was customary for foreign visitors to collect valuable cultural items (like Creole head ties, entomological material and Amerindian and maroon artefacts). A law preventing the export of these goods was passed in 1952, but its observance leaves much to be desired.

An exhibition on Suriname in 1953, organized by the Ministry of Education, prompted the Foundation to acquire a building to present its own displays and store the artefacts, and house the colonial library. In 1965 Parliament decided to assign the fortress to the Suriname Museum Foundation. At the beginning, the museum was primarily an institute for exhibition purposes, and just aimed consciously to educate at a later stage. At present, material objects are exhibited in the museum. Cautiously, the incorporation of intangible culture is occurring within the museum walls. The National Archives is in the process of recording (audiovisual) personal oral accounts, but the use of these stories is still limited.

Reading Spaces and Objects

Suriname, on the northern coast of South America, as one of the three Guyanas, consists of an extremely varied population. This diversity came about over time as a result of historical and political developments. In his travelogue *The Middle Passage,* V.S. Naipaul states:

> And one cannot help feeling it unfair that the Dutch should have their own cultural offerings spurned by their former colony. Suriname has come out of Dutch rule as the only truly cosmopolitan territory in the West Indian region. The cosmopolitanism of Trinidad is now fundamentally no more than a matter of race; in Suriname diverse cultures, modified but still distinct, exist side by side (Naipaul, 1975:186).

This cosmopolitan feeling of Suriname society identifies it to foreigners as an example of a multicultural society. Because of its history its demographics consist of a variety of people: indigenous, European, descendants of slaves and maroons, Indians (Hindustani and Muslim), Javanese, Lebanese, Chinese and recently Brazilians. This diversity of people brings a diversity of cultures expressed in all their elements.

In trying to visualize the symbolic shape of Suriname, we could imagine an umbrella, with the various groups of people as its spokes. What it does not have is the shape of a flower, where the heart is formed by one majority and the leaves consist of a number of different ethnic groups. This makes it difficult for the inhabitants of Suriname to answer the question: what is typically Suriname culture? Nation building is thus an intricate process: we all feel as though we are the citizens of this nation, but we also have our own specific cultural expressions within our group. The vision of nation building has changed over time. Just before independence Essed expressed the opinion that integration of various cultures should be encouraged (Essed 1973: 313). Menke, who has analyzed the nation formation efforts of respective governments, sees some tendency to nation creation: the collective efforts of diverse cultural groups within society to (bottom-up) create a nation based on solidarity, common respect and a harmonic attuning to other ethnic groups and their cultures. As he expresses it, some nation creation has been expressed in poetry ('One Tree' by Dobru), and in performance, as in *'Ala Kondre Dron'*, a percussion performance with a harmonic, musicological integration of cultural elements (Menke, 2008: 49-51).

The objects collected by the museum are mostly remnants from the colonial past. The Suriname Museum Foundation has however been able to gather a wonderful collection of Amerindian and maroon artefacts. For budgetary reasons the buying of additional objects lately has been very limited. Creoles (in Suriname the descendants of the slaves) were not in the habit of cherishing things of the past, and most old furniture and other memories were burned. This ethnic group is just beginning to understand the importance of saving one's material heritage. The same goes for Indians and Javanese, who had settled as contract labourers in Suriname, after the abolition of slavery (1863).

Each specific group needs to become aware of its own particular history and heritage. To quote Appiah:

> If we want to preserve a wide range of human conditions because it allows free people the best chance to make their own lives, there is no place for the enforcement of diversity by trapping people within a kind of difference they long to escape. There simply is no decent way to sustain those communities of difference that will not survive without the free allegiance of their members (Appiah 2006,105).

In 2008 the museum built an exhibition on Indian migration, *'Bidesia'*. This event was the reason for gathering old material within the community and adding modern objects to paint a picture of Hindustani life in Suriname. In spite of the temporary nature of the exhibition, these objects were kept together, with the idea of setting up a special museum on Hindustani immigration. The Suriname Museum needs to be an umbrella with different spokes. But if one ethnic group wants to erect a museum that reflects its specific cultural expressions, it is free to do so. It is what the late Jnan Adhin would call 'Unity in diversity'.

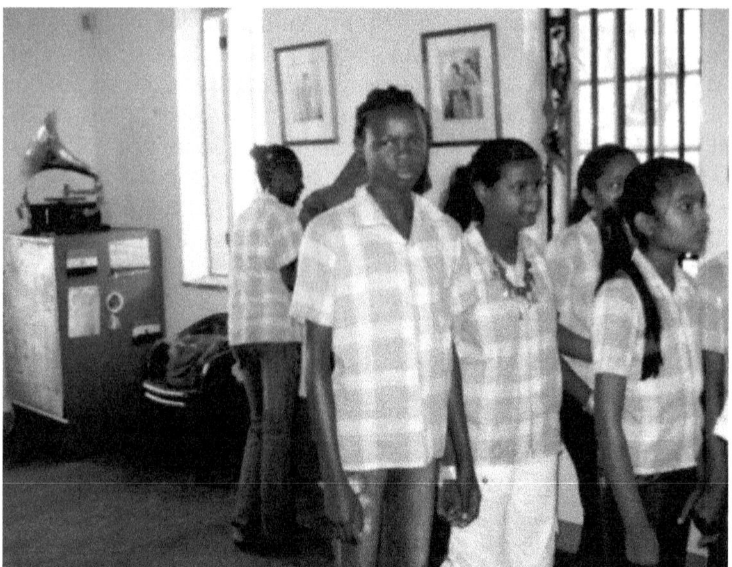

Young Suriname people visiting the exhibition on Indian Migration, *Bidesia*
(Photo Credit: Author)

Richard and Sally Price describe the initiatives taken in the 1990s in Guyane and Belize to create new museums with a modern, national feeling, representing regional identity. In Guyane the project disintegrated because the efforts to 'forge a dignified Guianas identity' meant it became a predominantly French neo-colonial project. Belize incorporated school involvement in the museums' set up, using it as a nation building tool. With elections came another political party, and the programme was stopped. The Prices point out that both initiatives remained 'Musées imaginaires' (Price & Price 1996). In their article they also mention *Suriname,* a museum exhibit in Rotterdam,The Netherlands aimed at representing Suriname identity. In the exhibition catalogue, *Sranan. Cultuur in Suriname,* the variety of its cultures is described and illustrated, alongside a number of articles on cultural expressions (music, dance, literature) which all have their typical forms within the different ethnic groups. When it comes to describing 'Suriname national culture' the author hesitates to identify a definite example of national culture, but focuses on a limited number of expressions the different groups share in, and it is here you can find all ethnic groups intermingled together: visiting the market and other shops and public transport are the main examples (in the capital Paramaribo). The old city centre, Fort Zeelandia, and its neighbouring national square still function as the locations where people gather on national holidays (Van Binnendijk 1992, 85-95). As a country, Suriname gained independence in 1975, and the people designed a number of national symbols. The description of a national Suriname culture remains limited to these symbols; the politics of national objects still needs to be defined.

A Fort as a National Space

Salman Rushdie has remarked:

> If we are to build a plural society on the foundations of what unites us, we must face up to what divides. But the questions of core freedoms and primary loyalties can't be ducked. No society, no matter how tolerant, can expect to thrive if its citizens don't prize what their citizenship means - if, when asked what they stand for as Frenchmen, as Indians, as Britons, they cannot give a clear reply (Rushdie, 2005).

If citizens of Suriname are asked, they will say that primarily they are people from Suriname. Secondly, they will mention their ethnic background: maroon, Javanese, Creole, Hindustani, and Amerindian etc. Or, as Essed has formulated, 'national unity is superseded by the ethno-cultural heterogeneity, that inhibits the rational development of the country and above all, veils the necessary national ideal because of too many group ties' (Essed, 1973). Since then, not much has changed. Menke mentions that many Suriname citizens, because they belong to a certain ethnic group, automatically choose the symbols of this group. But, overall, he sees a positive development: "In Suriname recent unfolding initiatives to understanding nuclear aspects of Suriname society start off with a positive critique o[f] the complex cultural diversity" (Menke, 2009:12).

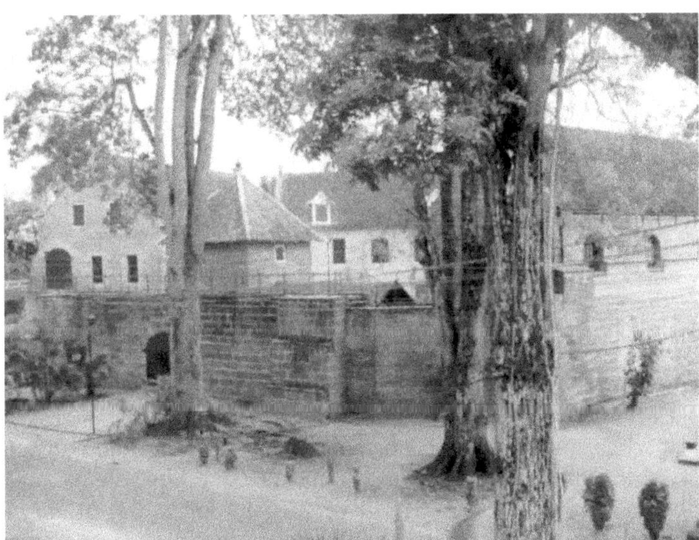

Exterior of Museum at Fort Zeelandia (Photo Credit: Laddy van Putten)

In this context, an important question can be raised: is a military complex with a long-term colonial history suited to housing a collection of folk art? When reading an article on the Open Air Museum in Nieuw Amsterdam, one comes to the conclusion that the author thinks the combination of military construction with folk art is artificial (Kerkhoven, 2008: 344). And again the reader gets the impression that museums in the Caribbean, like many other initiatives, should be facsimiles of European institutions. But we have to acknowledge history. As the proclaimed National Museum in Suriname, it is generated from the formulation of national culture above, so it is impossible for the Foundation to present itself as a 'national museum'. There used to be exhibitions on the different ethnic groups in Suriname, attracting many comments in the 1970s. To portray several groups separately did not fit within the nationalistic views of pre- and post-colonial Suriname people.

But museums in the Caribbean face the fact that history dictates the collection and the premises. The buildings that are fit to house a museum are often colonial military structures.[191] Opting for a new modern building set in ample grounds (as in Guyane and Belize) is often not within the financial or infrastructural possibilities of the state. Of course some institutions are faced with neo-colonial foreign influences, since funding is often derived from the metropole and expertise within the institution is limited (due to lack of training and finances).

As a matter of fact, the Suriname government does not give priority to funding museums. Museums are not even mentioned in the plans formulated by the Department of Culture (Directoraat Cultuur, 2007). Stanley Sidoel, manager of the Directorate of Culture (Ministry of Education) explained in an interview:

> In Suriname, people of many different ethnic and cultural backgrounds live together in a harmonic fashion. Cultural diversity is a normal thing here. Young people take from each other's culture. I believe in cultural absorption, it makes you versatile. Suriname is a multifaceted country (De Graeve, 2009).

It is much easier to conceptualize and realize plans for the visual arts. Artists excel in their separate creative fields; these activities do not necessarily need to be 'national'.

Education: Making History

The Suriname Museum Foundation focuses on two trajectories to bring the museum closer to the public. The first is designing educational programmes so that schoolchildren can visit an exhibition and learn from it. Traditionally, most of the museum visitors in Suriname (and probably in most of the Caribbean countries) are tourists or people who left to live in the metropolis and return for holidays. This raises the problem for museums of how to attract a local public. Since often museums are not especially equipped to accommodate young people, education officers have to find ways to interpret

[191] For example, the Barbados Museum & Historical Society is housed in a former military prison on the Garrison Savannah, Bridgetown.

the collection of objects to the public of Suriname, and particularly to children. This chance must not be missed: it is of crucial importance for museums to play a part in educating young people about their history. The educational centre point has shifted from knowledge to skills. In several European countries the changes in the conception of national history have resulted in the appointment of advisory boards to design a national canon for primary and secondary education: what do we want our children to know about their own history? *(Comissie ontwikkeling Nederlandse Canon,* 2006).

This is also a valid question for Suriname. It is important for schoolchildren to visit museums because experiencing one's cultural heritage is a multifaceted means of looking at history, and subsequently leads to a better understanding of how the past relates to the present.

Before 2000, the yearly average number of schoolchildren visiting the Suriname Museum was 750. In 2001 a new educational programme was created to support the educational services. Through trial and error the department found that school visits take place from February until August. At the beginning of every year a teachers' in-service training programme is organized. The participants are given educational material that supports the exhibition: every school received a museum folder in which to store cardboard sheets with didactical ideas. Ideally, the teachers prepare for their visit to the museum. During the in-service training programme, they have a guided tour of the exhibition so they know what to expect when they visit with their classes. The children receive questionnaires, or little booklets with questions and instructions to interactively go through the exhibition. These materials are adapted to the respective learning levels.

It might seem questionable that the museum does not have a long-term policy, because it could be interpreted as a lack of vision. But again, the lack of finances dictates the policy.

In the Netherlands quite regularly a museum creates an exhibition that contains a subject related to Suriname. And often it is offered to the Suriname Museum Foundation, under certain conditions. When these are favourable, the exhibition is transported to Suriname and erected in the museum. Depending on the subject, the educational services review the exhibition and add a local touch. *Anne Frank* (2002) and *Heritage of Slavery* (2007) just required a few adjustments to the educational programme. At times, the exhibition is not really targeted for students, so extensions have to be made. This happened for instance with *Nursing* (2005), created to commemorate and honour young women from Suriname who travelled to The Netherlands in the 1950s and 1960s to work as nurses. To add to the interest for local schoolchildren, a floor was created to show the history of nursing and medicine in Suriname. Another floor showed nursing in the interior of the country, and the different schooling possibilities for teens to become professionals.

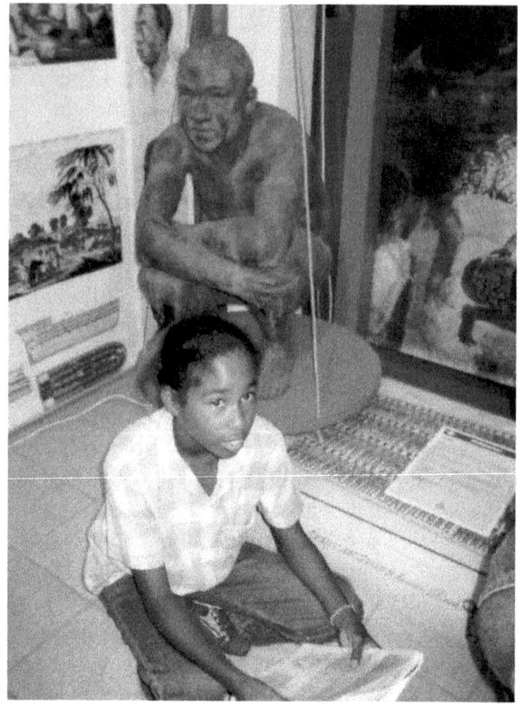

Educational programming on *The Heritage of Slavery* (Photo Credit: Author)

The 2009 exhibition on *Maria Sybilla Merian,* a famous painter who visited Suriname in 1699 to paint the metamorphosis of butterflies, consisted of flat panels with images and Dutch/English text. To make the topic more appealing to students, a section was added with stuffed animals, specimens in formaldehyde and real butterflies and other insects. In some years there is no exhibition available from abroad. Exhibitions with educational programmes on *'Telecommunication'* (2001), *'A cruel slave mistress'* (2004) and *'Bidesia, Indian migration' (2008)* were created in-house by the museum staff.

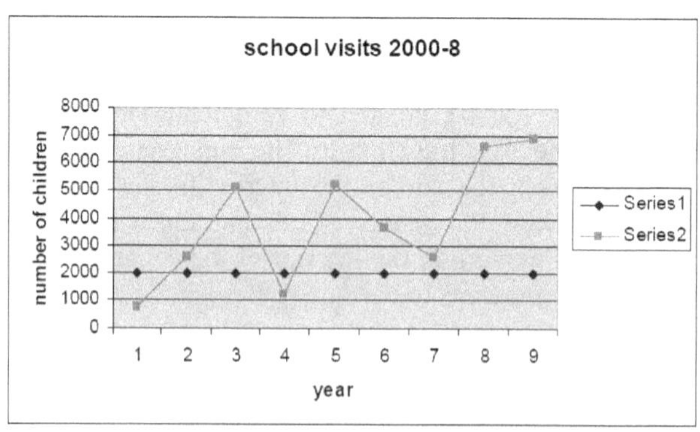

The implementation of an educational programme along set lines (so teachers know what to expect each year) has proven very successful, leading to up to 7000 students visiting yearly. The chart also clearly indicates the necessity of educational experts who are able to draw schools into the museum with attractive topics and programmes.

The department realized that many schools in the interior were excluded from the programme as they were not able to visit the museum because of distance. In recent years, the museum has invited teachers from the interior to an in-service session, and provides their schools with a film and worksheets on the topic. This public outreach has also proven to be very successful.

Publishing: Making History

The Suriname Museum Foundation also focuses on the trajectory of publishing books on material from its own collection. In the past, a little bulletin with articles on Suriname history or the museum was published. This was stopped in 1997 due to lack of funding. To fill the gap, the museum publishes short bi-weekly articles in the largest local newspaper, *'De Ware Tijd'*. These are also put on the website (www.surinaamsmuseum.com). These small pieces (with an image) on museum objects or activities aim to inform the public about the museum.

More ambitious is the *'Libri Musei Surinamensis'* series. By publishing volumes on museum topics, it is possible to write Suriname history and generate some funds. These books also function as a catalogue for the respective exhibitions. *Suriname before Columbus* (Aad Versteeg, 2003) is a bilingual account of research on the Amerindian cultures in Suriname before the European invasion. To aim for a more general public, a limited trilingual version of this book (Aad Versteeg and Stephan Rostain) was published in 2006. Augusta Curiel made glass negative photos of people, city scenes and the interior. A number of these were collected in the volume *Augusta Curiel. Fotografe in Suriname 1904-1937,* (Janneke van Dijk, Hanna van Petten-van Charante, Laddy van Putten, 2007). Number 4 in the 'Libri Musei Surinamensis' series is about a mulatto painter who also made dioramas: *Gerrit Schouten (1799-1839) Met meesterhand vervaardigd* (Hilde Neus and Laddy van Putten, 2008).

Publishing books is a way to make the collections housed in the Suriname Museum accessible. It is not always possible to exhibit certain artefacts permanently. This certainly goes for books and original images. This series brings the collection closer to the general public and thus works as an advertisement for the Suriname Museum Foundation.

Final Remarks

Helman pointed out the importance of historical buildings for national identity and grounding in history so as to face the future. Does this mean people could not do without history? Of course they could. But from that day on they would begin to create their own story, and thus their own history. We are faced with a multifaceted history in Suriname, strongly attached to the fort in the heart of our main city. Because of its gruesome discourse, we do not all share fond memories of the place. But nevertheless it is a concrete marker of events that happened to us as a people, and is rooted in the creation and building of this nation. Therefore it remains the best appointed venue to interpret Suriname's history, be it the (cultural and anthropological) histories of the various ethnic groups that have settled in this country; or the national (political and economic) history that covers all groups.

Attractive to children, inspiring adults with awe, Fort Zeelandia speaks to our imagination as a historical monument and as a museum: a place to safeguard our artefacts and antique books, and a place to display them and interpret them to the visitors old and young alike, so we may know our past to better live in our future.

By creating special education programmes for schools, the Suriname Museum Foundation aims to lure the students to the museum to learn from history and to appreciate their own cultural heritage. Furthermore, the Foundation is able to connect with the public through publications on different themes in history, and striking features within their own artefact or library collections. Through these trajectories it is possible to touch upon different cultures within Suriname society, and at the same time create a sense of the importance of these cultures within the national space.

Acknowledgements

With thanks to Laddy van Putten, director of the museum and Jerry Egger, former director, for adding constructive remarks.

References

Anderson, Benedict, 1991. *Imagined Communities. Reflections on the Origin and Spread of Nationalism.* London: Verso.

Appiah, Kwame Anthony, 2006. *Cosmopolitanism. Ethics in a world of strangers*, New York: W.W. Norton Company.

Binnendijk, Ch. van en P. Faber (ed.) 1992. *Sranan. Cultuur in Suriname* Amsterdam: KIT / Rotterdam: Museum voor Volkenkunde.

Comissie ontwikkeling Nederlandse Canon, 2006. entoen.nu. *De canon van Nederland* Den Haag: Ministerie van OCW.

Directoraat Cultuur, 2007. *Integraal cultuurbeleid* 2007-2012 Paramaribo: STAS Caribe.

Essed, Frank, 1973. *Een volk op weg naar zelfstandigheid* Paramaribo: Stichting Planbureau.

Graeve, Stephanie de, 2009. 'Suriname, land met verschillende gezichten', *De Ware Tijd*, 23 May.

Helman, A. (ed.) 1977. *Cultureel Mozaïek van Suriname. Bijdrage tot onderling begrip* Zutphen: De Walburg Pers.

Kerkhoven, J, 2008. 'Openluchtmuseum Fort Nieuw Amsterdam; Een koloniale omgeving als nationale ruimte', 0S0, jrg. 27, nr. 2.

Menke, J. (ed.) 2008. *Natievorming en natiecreatie in Suriname*. Paramaribo:Stichting Wetenschappelijke Informatie.

Naipaul, V.S, 1975. *The Middle Passage: The Caribbean Revisited*, Penguin, U.K., p.186

Neus, H. and L. van Putten *Museumstof* available at: http://www.surinaamsmuseum.net

Neus, H, 2007. 'Museum Education as a Mode to Equal Opportunities' Unpublished paper presented at the Barbados Conference 'Trajectories of Freedom: Caribbean Societies - Past and Present', UWI Humanities, May 23-25.

Price, R. & S. Price, 2005. 'Museums, Ethnicity and Nation-building: Reflections from the French Caribbean', *Ethnicity in the Caribbean. Essays in Honour of Harry Hoetink*. p. 81-105. Amsterdam: Amsterdam Academic Archive.

Putten, L. van and L. Ferrier, 1999. '50 Years Stichting Surinaams Museum (Suriname Museum Foundation) 1947 - 29 April -1997': *Archiv fiir Volkerkunde* 50. Available at http://www.surinaamsmuseum.net

Rushdie, Salman, 2005. *What this Cultural Debate needs is more dirt, less stupidity*, The Times Online U.K., 10th Dec.2005

Chapter 8

Museography and Places of Remembrance of Slavery in Martinique or the Gaps in a Memory Difficult to Express[192]

Christine Chivallon

Since the 1990s, Martinique, the overseas French *Departement* in the Americas and on the "extreme periphery" of Europe, has undoubtedly entered into the era of patrimonialisation.[193] This phenomenon is hardly original considering that, as J.F. Bayart puts it, our age is marked by the "generalization of mnemonic experience" (2004, 84). Contemporary societies, having lost the serene confidence in a future of progress, relentlessly museumify their past, showing in thc context of globalisation the reassuring landmarks of deeply rooted localism. Martinique is no exception to this trend.

---

[192] This text is a short and different version of a more developed study published in French under the reference: *Chivallon C. 2006.* "Rendre visible l'esclavage. Museographie et hiatus de la memoire aux Antilles francaises", *L'homme, 180: j—42.* A previous English version of this has been published in H. Levy (ed.), *African-Caribbean Worldview and the Making of Caribbean Society,* Kingston, University of the West Indies Press, pp. 114-131. The editors and the author are completely indebted to Horace Levy for the authorization to republish this article.

[193] The term "patrimonialisation" in this case, and throughout the text, means the creation or development of cultural and historical heritage.

The patrimonialisation phenomenon in Martinique could become as generalised as the infamous "cultural consequences of globalization" (Appadurai 2001) if it did not also have to rip away from a completely different process: one of having not been able to constitute with any certainty what could be considered today as heritage.

Martinique's collective past and history are one of buried memories, diffused and diluted by the dominant colonial discourse that has been better able to impose its official chronology.

Patrimony, constructed as a way "to recognize, to defend, and to make fruitful one or more common heritages" (Le Goff 1998, 9), cannot be conceived as a tool endowed with the possibility to attain, as if by magic, transparency and the truth of the past. Through patrimonial action, with museographical language as one of the major components, "the past is what the present needs to legitimize, standardize and create itself" (Preziosi 2004; [1996], 76). This museal self-examination stems from rupture. It intervenes at the moment when the collective needs to locate, name, collect and categorise everything that is supposed to have come from the past as if memory was no longer able to circulate on the habitual paths of intergenerational transmission (Halbwachs 1997; [1950]).

These remarks, within the context of Martinique, indicate how complex the problem of heritage is in societies where memories were maltreated, crushed by colonial powers and produced in the violent conditions of slavery, which can be called a "social death" (Patterson 1982, 38). Societies that display a full mastery of their collective path - the French Nation for example - resort to patrimonial language to create an illusion of identity and use it as a "reservoir to feed historical fictions constructed about the past" (Guillaume 1990, 18). What does this mean for societies that use the same procedures based on a past buried, dominated and trapped by the authority of the colonial system? Does one create a double illusion, one of a reinvented past based on a past that has never been? Or rather, is one right to wait for patrimonial action to participate in the emancipation of memory and its extirpation from the places where it was reduced to silence?

What does today's patrimonialisation bring to the outing of Martinique's slave past and its consequences on social formation? Our study was conducted in 2002 in Martinique involving patrimonial establishments which included genuine museums and old plantations that had added to or substituted their agricultural activities with a focus on museum activities.

Rooting up a Buried Heritage? Official Oblivion and Buried Memories

To talk about heritage in Martinique is to unavoidably bring up the question of collective memory. Rather than enter into the terms of a debate that has widely occupied the social sciences, we will simply recall, especially for non-specialist readers, that this memory is considered to have been so maltreated, crushed by the yoke of slavery and colonialism, that it led to no form of community cohesion.[194] The approach of Édouard Glissant (1981, 130-31), with his still famous expressions such as the "deletion of collective memory", "non-history" and "obscured history", is well known. His approach leads one to believe that no "sedimentation" was possible and thus the collective becomes simultaneously scattered, "compartmentalized" and lost by the "practices of separation and dispersion" (p. 68).

Collective memory goes so far as to be perceived as "an emptiness", in the endeavour that aims to denounce the errors of the slave system. This perception is as easy to develop as the official discourse, endowed with a formidable efficiency, that extols the fusion of Martinique's destiny with that of the French Republic. At the heart of the powerful process of assimilation - that is transmitted through different government apparatuses (the educational system, but also the church and the moral values of French culture) - one finds the extremely official version of history that attempts to weaken the impact of slavery's heritage and to turn it into fiction.

One can thus understand that memories directly formed from within the slave system are buried by the diffusion of the official narrative framework massively occupying Martinique's public space. For this reason, most analyses converge today to interpret the relationship with the heritage of slavery in terms of "oblivion" or "silence" (Chivallon 2005a; Cottias 1997; Price 2001; Schmidt 1999).

Though we can characterize official memory policy and reduce it to a strategy of systematic undervaluing of folk cultural practices, we still know very little about collective memories built within or against the establishment. Research in progress (Chivallon 2002, 2004a, 2005b) or prior research (Chivallon 1998) tends to show the existence of solidly resistant cores formed beyond the policy of oblivion. Further exploration, however, is required in this field to know the terms of the memorial project carried out by the descendants of slaves. Was the intense patrimonialisation deployed over the last few years a way to "discover" these buried memories, as well as the way they lived, transmitted and expressed the reality of the history of slavery?

Entering the Era of Patrimonialisation

To measure the scope of this new era, it would not be superfluous to consult the *"Guides Metis"*[195] series of tourist guidebooks published in 1986. In this edition, there are six museums listed in Martinique, none of which is consecrated even partially to the history of slavery. None of these heritage sites are meant to highlight the physical traces of lifestyles structured by the slave economy. We had not yet to come to the turning point marked by the symbolic decapitation of the statue of Jósephine in 1991 at the Savan Square in the heart of Fort-de-France. The bust of Napoléon Bonaparte's wife was now

[194] For a more in-depth examination of the question of collective memory as it relates to slavery's past, see Chivallon 2002a and b, 2004 and 2005.

[195] *Antilles, Haiti, Guyane,* Paris, Hachette *guides bleus* 1986

headless and its body smeared with blood-red paint – the people knowing that, in 1802, the emperor reinstituted slavery [196] (which had been abolished under the Convention 3) and maintained it in the colonies through the Treaty of Amiens.[197] Its explanatory plaque was crossed out with the terse comment: "*Esklavaj Krim Kont limanité.*"[198]

This type of action constitutes the radical side of the appearance of another memorial discourse in Martinique's public sphere. This new phase was accompanied by many institutionalised and standardised initiatives that mark the transition to a new "regime of historicity" (Hartog 2003) known as "the museum perspective" (p. 201) and for about 15 years has included the slave period in the Martiniquan museums. In 2001, there were 42 museums, seven times more than in 1986,[199] of which five dealt explicitly with the history of slavery. By adding other memorial markers such as the building of monuments (like the "Memorial to Brotherhood"[200] at the Diamant, created in 1998 to honour the memory of enslaved Africans); the naming of streets (as in Rivière-Pilote, where all the streets of the town were renamed according to the history of the local colonised populations); the days of commemoration (like 22 May celebrating abolition won in 1848 by slave revolts); associative activities (like those of the House of Bèlè,[201] in Sainte-Marie, where "masters" of this traditional dance, passed on from the world of African slaves, initiate those who have forgotten its rhythms and gestures) - it is not a stretch to speak of an unprecedented frenzy of heritage projects.[202]

Current heritage policies have also become an affirmation of an identity under the constant threat of prolonged colonialism and the heightened dependence on the context in continental France. During his speech at the permanent inauguration of the Regional Museum of History and Ethnography[203] of Fort-de-France in 1999, the President of the Regional Council,[204] Alfred Marie-Jeanne, an emblematic figure of the independence movement, insisted on how the heritage project must be "a solemn service, for the people, giving them back a part of themselves through works of the past".[205] What has become of this restitution, of this opening up of memory? Do the classic tools

---

[196] Slavery had been abolished for the first time in 1794 under the "Convention", the period where the French revolutionary assembly governed.

[197] Regarding this issue, consult the article by Champion, 1995.

[198] Slavery: crime against humanity.

[199] Source: as cited by the study conducted in 2001 by the l'Agence Regionale de Developpement Touristique de la Martinique, Anse Gouraud-Schoelcher, ARDTM.

[200] *Le Memorial de la fraternite.*

[201] *La Maison du Bèlè.*

[202] For an example of the objects, sites and events that are now considered to be patrimonial, consult Martinique's official tourist website (http://martiniquetourism.com). In regard to the heritage of the Bèlè dance, see the interview with the choreographer Sonia Marc at the site http://afrik.com.

[203] *Musée Régional d'Histoire et d'Ethnographie.*

[204] *Conseil Régional.*

[205] "A Word from the President". Presentational brochure of the Regional Museum of History and Ethnography, Regional Council of Martinique, 1999.

of patrimonialisation reach the desired goal of "making woman/man (historically/culturally) conscious and reconciled with herself/himself'?[206]

Patrimonialisation in Action: A Past that Remains Submissive to the Language Expressed by the Other

The question of "making historically conscious" overlooks the uncovering of a past that has been hidden by official memory policy. This effort must inevitably reference the institutions of slavery that remain the primary matrix of Martinique's social formation. The following analysis is restricted exclusively to establishments that affirm or maintain, even in what goes unsaid, an explicit relationship with slavery. Establishments include either newly founded museums that are often created on historical sites to reconstruct the history of the slave era, or sites where the slave experience actually happened, primarily in *Habitations*,[207] and that could be expected to be converted into "places of remembrance" through the patrimonial activity.

Saying Slavery? Recent Museographical Language

Out of 42 museum establishments, 24 should explicitly take into account the experience of slavery, considering the theme they examine or the location that they represent. It is possible to distinguish two broad categories: museums that make slavery visible and those that make it invisible. Only five museums are included in the first category. In the second are the 19 others, including almost the entirety of all the *Habitations*. In other words, out of all of the recently surveyed museum establishments in Martinique, and despite the frenzy of heritage projects, only a feeble proportion of them - 11 percent - deal with slavery.

At this stage in our progression, we must turn to the extremely relevant typology elaborated by J.L. Eichstedt and S. Small (2002) in their study of museums created on former slave plantations in the Southern United States. Created to interpret what the authors call "white-centric representational strategies", their typology distinguishes five categories:

1. one involving the erasure of slavery and the valuing of plantocracy;
2. one that makes slavery trivial and distorts its meaning;
3. one that uses a "segregated" mode juxtaposing emphasis on the white world against information about the world of slaves;
4. one, qualified as "relative incorporation", that resolutely incorporates slavery into its narrative framework thus destabilizing the glorification of the white world while sometimes, as forgetting this incorporation, moves again into the previous discursive forms;

---

[206] Ibid.

[207] Term used to describe plantations in the French Antilles.

5. one known as "In-between" where the strategy of looking beyond the wondrous descriptions of the plantation's golden age is not yet fully reached thus excluding it from the previous fourth category (p.10-11).

The authors were only able to evaluate the majority of the museum sites from the first two categories. Only three percent of the "plantation museums" in the Southern United States qualify for the fourth category; the one that takes the legacy of slavery into account (p. 65). This approach, focused on "white" plantations, was complemented by a study of 20 additional sites that the authors qualify as being "black-centric" (p. 233). These sites develop "counternarratives" that "contest the dominant narrative and are organized around a different set of valorisations - of struggle and resistance against brutality, of resilience in the face of injustice, and of dignity in the face of inhumanity" (p. 233).

Can such a typology be transposed to Martinique, whose history ends up melting into the destiny of the Republic that maintains the vision of a social world where the category of race is held as being absent? Do the differences between the United States and the French Antilles - on one hand a clear racial bipolarity and on the other, the principle of equal integration "without distinction of origin, race, or religion" according to the French Constitution - show how "the heritage industry" in the Southern United States creates "a racialized regime of representation" (Eichstedt and Small 2002, 6, 9)? Though one cannot ignore the fundamental differences in question (Chivallon 2004b, 71, 75, 130-31), it is not possible to ignore the large contradiction that crosses Martinique's society: the republican system fixed onto a social situation whose structure creates a strong, permanent legacy tainted by racial division. The presence of the *béké* group, who are direct descendants of the masters and colonists in Martinique, is a reminder of racial hierarchy. This group, that continues to base its strategies of social reproduction on the strict observance of conserving racial status, still maintains a place among the dominant elite at the head of Martinique's primary economic engines and thus confirms the surprising longevity of its survival (Chivallon 2004a; Pivois 2000).

This legacy, because it is continually updated, allows the typology elaborated in the context of the United States, though quite different, to be transposed at least partially to Martinique. As we will see, it allows one to recognize unambiguously the first rhetorical strategy - the one of effacement - as it was used within the *Habitations* that were themselves owned by the *béké*.

For the five museums that were identified as visibly displaying slavery's past, one would logically expect that they would create an equivalent to the African-American "counter-narration" and create opposition to the colonial pole. Nothing could be less certain, however, because the message produced is embedded in the texture of classic museographical language, thus creating an obstacle to an approach more faithful to the sensitive realities of slavery. Adding to this characteristic are what could be called "lapses", involuntary gaps in language, or even "missed acts" that make attaining the goal of expression impossible. These five museums were created by the following four public establishments: The Sugar Cane Museum,[208] the *Fonds-Saint-Jacques,* The Eco-museum of Martinique,[209] The Regional Museum of History and Ethnography. The Museum of Folk Art and Tradition[210] in the town of Saint-Esprit, a small association-run museum that is small-scaled compared to the other four, also belongs in this category.

The Sugar Cane Museum is without contest the museum most oriented to the restitution of the slave experience. Installed in the restored buildings of an old distillery, it is the result of work done by an association of history and geography teachers from the prestigious *Lycée Schoelcher* that began their work in 1981. The museum opened its doors in 1987. This project, whose primary vocation was pedagogical, was hailed as a success when the Regional Council officially acquired it in 1992. The presentation of the museum's materials, articulated through the trilogy *"One Land, One Plant, One People",* is organised on a classic chronological axis that goes from the discovery of the island to the end of the reign of centralised factories and also on a thematic axis comprising the two main products resulting from the transformation of sugar cane: sugar and rum. The story of slavery, because it is intrinsically linked with the culture of sugar cane in the New World, cannot be left out of an exhibit meant to recount the agricultural and industrial heritage that created it. For this reason, slavery naturally figures in its own chronology beginning in the middle of the seventeenth century and ending with abolition in 1848. Almost nothing is omitted from the exposition itself nor from the documents made available by the museum including: the treatment, sale, price and marking of slaves, the *Code Noir,*[211] the freeing of slaves, marronage, the hierarchy of slaves on plantations, and attributing names.

The exhibit is accurate, precise, well researched, and includes high quality objects and texts. Though slavery is unambiguously present, it is not, however, central or presented as the substructure of the societies presented. Slavery is associated instead with a category of history - a period and has the same status as the era that succeeds to it ("the period of centralised factories"). None of this allows the spectator to grasp the phenomenal dimension of the human experience of dehumanisation.

The Sugar Cane Museum, like the other four museums, operates by immersion in "something else", in this case technical heritage, which ends up supplanting the message about the institution of slavery. This immersion reveals an identical shift toward a domain other than the foundational domain of the slave system. Both the Eco-Museum in Rivière-Pilote and the Museum of History and Ethnography of Fort-de-France take the same care to express

[208] *La Maison de la Canne.*

[209] *L'Écomusée de Martinique.*

[210] *Musée des Arts et Traditions Populaires.*

[211] *Le Code Noir* ("The Black Code") is a French decree initiated by Colbert and promulgated in 1685 just after Colbert's death. Colbert was Secretary of State of the Navy and Minister of Commerce under Louis XIV. The *Code Noir* was one of the most sophisticated laws addressing the status of the slaves, defining their conditions as "movables" *(Mens meubles)* having virtually no rights.

slavery with much historical accuracy, especially with the exposition catalogues and the signs that explain the course of the exposition.[212] The Museum of Ethnography regularly organises expositions on the theme of slavery. They correspond perfectly with the desire to expose the historical reality of slavery by compiling archives and establishing collections. From this point of view, the "scientific" goal is reached, but what about the understanding of human lives and the depth of the experience of beings confronted with imprisonment in slavery? Emotion is permanently left out of the framework inspired by strict adherence to chronological archives.

It is not for lack of will that the goal of exposure is not reached. Nevertheless, permanent museum exhibits only exacerbate the absence of the lives of slaves and their descendants. This is how the shift works. In Rivière-Pilote, the Eco-Museum, opened in 1993 and installed in an old distillery whose restoration was accompanied by the renovation of an Amerindian archeological site, ends up being swallowed up by the pre-Columbian period. Only one display in the exhibit is dedicated to slavery and the slave trade by a symbolic presentation of shackles. At the Museum of Ethnography in Fort-de-France, which is inside a Second Empire[213] colonial house, the subject is avoided by focusing on the lifestyle of the mulatto bourgeoisie.

The modest Museum of Popular Art and Tradition in the town of Saint-Esprit is quite different. Compared to the other museums of this category, its means are very modest and popular (reprocessing) but successful enough to emphasise folk life styles. Consequently, this place has a rather believable ambiance that displays objects whose logic breaks with that of the strict organisation of the other museums. Though a shift also takes place at this museum - by focusing on the post-abolitionist period - it creates nonetheless the disorganised poetry of the peasant countryside of Martinique: the world of liberated slaves and their descendants *par excellence.*

Le Fonds-Saint-Jacques stands alone. More of a monument than a museum, it is the architectural Mecca of ancient *surcrôtes,*[214] the first units in the production of sugar that are associated with the Reverend Father Labat, a historical figure who resided in Martinique from 1694 to 1705. The site's existence goes back to the origins of colonization. The *Departement* has owned it since 1948. Since 1987, a Cultural Centre, whose vocation is the "management, animation and promotion of the historical domain", has been created. At *le Fonds-Saint-Jacques,* it is the quasi-cult, dedicated to Father Labat, that blocks the message. This priest, who was responsible for a *Habitation* that possessed 389 slaves at his departure (Queinnec 1999, 26) - and

---

[212] See in particular the catalogue "Ecomusée de la Martinique. Histoire vivante d'une culture et d'une communaute".

[213] The "Second Empire" under Napoleon III covers the period from 1852 to 1870.
144

[214] A type of sugar mill.

not "90 workers" as the site's official brochures claim[215] - is the author of a famous travel account (Labat 1993 [1772]) whose "descriptions provoked the indignation of Europe" (Queinnec 1999, 26).

As it is, a new genre of discourse in Martinique, constructed over the last 15 years, resembles the category "of relative incorporation of slavery" and even more often the "In-between" category described by Eichstedt and Small (2002) and explained above. Given the decision makers who undertake these museum projects, it is not the idea of breaking with the golden age of plantations that is difficult to accept (although the "Labat cult" could hint at this), but rather it is the projection into the world of the "pre" or of the "outside" slavery: the pre-Columbian age, industrial technology, the free people of colour,[216] the post-abolitionist period. One wonders, however, if museographical language itself, by inevitably inferring the aforementioned diversions, creates the major handicap to dealing with slavery. Paula Findlen (2004 [1989], 28 and 33-36) shows clearly how museums rely on "encyclopaedic strategies". The Museum, as Donald Preziosi (2004 [1996], 71) reaffirms, "is one of the most central and indispensable framing institutions of our modernity". It is a place of spatial-temporal classification and ordering. It is a powerful instrument of visualisation that renders tangible, through material signposts, the categories of vision and division of the modern world, "of societies, ethnicities, races, classes, genders and individuals, of history, progress, and moralities; of nature itself (p. 80). As "an encyclopedic theater of memory", the museum is "the veritable house of opticality, of vision and consequently, a place for blindness and masquerade, where what is visible is also invisible" (pp. 76 and 80).

What Martinique's museum makes invisible is precisely a culture that cannot be translated by a language so indebted to the rhetoric of modernity. Does Paul Gilroy (1993, 36, 38) not speak of a black cultural ensemble of the New World as a "counterculture of modernity"? For him, it is not about suggesting an anti-modernist discourse but rather a culture that is able to defy the illusory divisions of modernity. Slavery - by placing horror and terror at the heart of the ideology of progress - predisposed the men and women that endured it to hold "the capacity to explode the pretensions of 'the Modern'".[217] This explosion is translated as the emerging of a "polyphonic" culture that cannot be trapped into the ethnic, political and territorial categories of modernity (Gilroy 1993, 19 and 28). This situation permits one to describe the difficult encounter between museums and the collective memory of slavery in Martinique in terms of a hiatus.

---

215 Note the euphemism "workers" to replace "slaves" used in the site's official brochure ("Fonds-Saint-Jacques. Archeologie et Histoire sur les traces du Pere Labat", 4).

216 *Libres de Couleur.*

217 Expression taken from Lazarus (1995, 331) in his commentary on P. Gilroy's work.

Erasing Slavery? Places of Colonial Memory

Two public establishments enter into the category of "erasing slavery": The *Museum of the Pagerie*[218] and the *Chateau Dubuc* site. The first is installed in the birthplace of Empress Jósephine, an old sugar plantation owned by the Tascher de la Pagerie family. In 1944 the veterinarian Rose-Rosette, a local history enthusiast, acquired the estate that had belonged to the *békés*. This amateur museologist, presented as a "descendant of slaves"[219] and at the same time admitting to an "adoration of the *belle Creole",*[220] was able to create as early as 1954 one of the oldest museums in Martinique. It was, until recently, the most visited museum but its attendance has been steadily declining. Intended to present the two sides of the site's history, the world of slaves and the world of masters, according to its founder's testimony,[221] the museum, belonging to the General Council[222] since 1985, is still under the stranglehold of the emphasis on Jósephine's personal trajectory. Several paintings in the entryway depicting cruelty towards slaves and the shackles on display in the single room dominated by Jósephine's personal effects are not enough to make up for the overall tone of the exhibition, because we are on the very premises where the decisions regarding the destiny of slaves were taken. Nothing is used to clearly interpret Jósephine's husband's decision to reinstitute slavery. The contradictory information about Bonaparte, too complex to cover in detail here, tends even to exonerate him.

Le Chateau Dubuc is an even more painful example of the expression of what goes unsaid. The only location that is cut off from the others and ends up creating a symbiosis with its surrounding natural environment; the only site to bear witness to an old past comes back to the present through traces and ruins barely maintained; the only site where the slaves' confinement cells are still visible, could have had the chance to be unencumbered with so-called gestures of heritage had an exhibit not distorted the way one sees it. "Exposition" is much too big a word to describe what is little more than three informational signs - "Morals and Customs of the eighteenth century"; "The Dubuc *Habitation";* "Sugar Production Methods"; - several engravings about the flora and fauna, and three small displays filled with untagged objects - fragments of pipes, rusted tools, pieces of dishes or chipped pottery. Everything becomes clear about what goes unsaid when one notices the absence of the word "slave" from the text about the "Morals and Customs of the eighteenth century".

---

[218] *Musée de la Pagerie.*

[219] *France-Antilles;* "Le berceau de l'lmperatrice", 01-09-99.

[220] *See the article* "Museums" in the "Madras dictionary" (Exbrayat, 1996, 62)

[221] *France-Antilles*, "Le berceau de l'lmperatrice", 01-09-99

[222] "*Conseil Général*'": the institution corresponding to the management of the Departement of Martinique. The Conseil Régional is its counterpart for the Region of Martinique. The fact that the *"Region Martinique"* has only one "departement" gives the expression "Region mono-departementale".

The other 17 establishments that are also in the category of "erasure" all consist of private *Habitations,* domain above all of the *béké* group and more rarely of the bourgeoisie of colour. The majority of them are distilleries (12) that have opened their doors to guided tours followed by tastings in a clear commercial attempt to attract a tourist clientele. From these sites - *la Mauny, Trois-Rivières, Depaz, Dillon* - there is nothing to expect in the way of efforts made to unveil anything other than the method for producing rum, except for the sometimes more elaborate staging of exhibits that take into account the spatial structure of the *Habitation.* This staging, like at the *Depaz* plantation at the base of the *Pelée* Mountain, can hint at the characteristic layout of these old properties where the splendor of the Master's house incarnates Creole elegance.

Two distilleries stand apart from the others, owing to the scope of their heritage project. The *Saint-James* and *Sainte-Marie* Plantations have a distillery that is endowed with a museum that welcomes the largest number of visitors out of all of the other museum sites put together, with 90,000 per year (compared to 35,000 at the Sugar Cane Museum[223]). It must, however, be pointed out that the rum tasting is free! The museum is installed in the old master's house as well as in the distillery belonging to the *Cointreau* group. The commercio-heritage strategy guided by folklorisation will become more intense with the announced, but still unfinished, project of creating a "veritable traditional village of artisans" that will belong to a "zone dedicated to the culture and tradition of rum".[224] In this case, the erasure comes from both the exclusive focus on the *béké* perspective and from the charming and exotic vision, already deplored by Myriam Cottias (1993, 265).

Adding less to this quasi-popular folklore, the *Habitation Clément,* at *François,* displays much more ostentatiously "its" historical truth that caters to the tourist industry. This *distillery-habitation,* belonging to the most powerful *békés* in Martinique, The Hayot Group, whose rum is now produced on a neighboring site, is on the Inventory of classified monuments and historical sites (like most of the museums examined here: *Château Dubuc, la Pagerie, Fonds-Saint-Jacques* etc). This case gets to the heart of the rhetoric, so well described by Eichstedt and Small (2002, 107), of the symbolic annihilation of slavery by focusing exclusively on the materials that deal with plantation lifestyle but omit any relative mention of slaves. The *Habitation Clément* - despite the fact that it takes its name from a mulatto who headed it at the beginning of the twentieth century - is a reminder of the "white gold" period, the centuries of the "grand era of economic growth" and the illustrious proprietors who have succeeded one another at the head of the estate.

This second museum group, which does such a good job of erasing the reality of slavery, makes us confront the patrimonial strategy that brings us back to the idea of the quest for identity, as some authors would describe it.

---

223 *France-Antilles,* 21-22 August 1999 and 28-29 August 1999. *(France-Antilles* is the local newspaper of Martinique)

224 Ibid.

This kind of museum hides fractures and reposes in the warm idea of continuities. It "comes to be an instrument of that (bourgeois) self-fashioning in the sense that artworks, museological objects of desire are constructed as objects whose style or grace is worthy of emulation, whose spirit and vivacity one might admire, whose uniqueness is worthy of remembering" (Preziosi 1996, [2004], 79). Here, the logic of producing identity in the making of heritage is used to the extreme. In the privacy of the island, where blacks and *békés* still confront each other, this logic allows the symbolism of hierarchal values linked to socio-racial groups to endure by almost completely denying the deep rooting of slavery. The gap created by such a use of the heritage-making machine is that this identity strategy makes museums reinforce the social order rather than educate. Paradoxically, it could be said that they do create "places of memory" according to Pierre Nora's definition (1984, xx-xxii). The historian believed, in fact, that there were two phases in the making of these places: a first phase attributed to a living collective memory and the second phase where memory is supplanted by the staging of history. In Martinique, this double "reign" over "places of memory", that makes them both "natural" and "artificial" is only found on the *béké* plantations. This situation comes about because the collective memory of the slave descendants never had the chance to make visible those places that would allow it to circulate. Such places do not run the risk of being (re)fabricated and shown as "places of memory", since even today we hardly know where they are to be found. This situation is the most likely explanation for "new" elements - frescoes, statues, monuments, and newly renamed streets - that quite often have the role of taking into account the memory of slavery. When it comes to the plantations, they maintain complete sovereignty as the places where the particular culture of emphasising racial domination has been handed down. Today, the patrimonial rehabilitation of these plantations bears the mark of the double reign over "places of memory": they are the repetition of colonial memory that continues to affirm its white supremacy in the museographical context.

Patrimonialisation in Martinique: An Unconsummated Divide?

The inability of patrimonial language to allow expression of the living memory of slavery in Martinique must be addressed as we reach the end of our exploration. As was alluded to in my introduction, the characteristics of patrimonial gestures - the fact that these gestures always stem from a strategic appropriation of the past to be used by the present - are not what are being questioned. Rather, it is the language itself, its mechanics and conventions, that makes the job of rehabilitating the history of slavery almost useless. On one hand, this language confines discourse to a framework that is not adapted to the teeming cultural worlds that it undertakes to lay down. These worlds end up shying away from the "chronophage" logic that is enamoured with the categorising order of the history-writing process. On the other hand, the strategic potential of this language allows for the manipulation of identity articulated on the binary separation of "shown-hidden". The rhetoric of places of colonial memory, developed in the world of plantations-as-museums, does nothing more than express the presence of Creole whiteness by erasing the existence of black worlds, whether of slaves or even of "workers".

As far as the statistics on attendance at these sites are concerned, it can be concluded that few people living in Martinique are actually concerned by these heritage projects. In fact, 87 percent of visitors to these museums are tourists.[225] Knowing that only 15 percent are natives of Martinique visiting the country,[226] one can no longer doubt that museums, and other establishments acting as such, address themselves to a foreign audience, thus practically making the island's population a distant spectator to these actions. The reach of this patrimonial projection, however, undoubtedly has other resonances caused simply by its presence alone, without Martiniquans needing to go and visit the museums themselves. Indeed, in Martinique, everyone knows who does what and what belongs to who. The structure of the patrimonial field says more than the message emitted by the museum system. The division between project makers, specifically their membership in clearly typified groups - the *békés,* the bourgeoisie and the black political class, and associative leaders from modest communities - reproduces an order that the republican model's veneer has difficulty wiping out. Here at the beginning of the twenty-first century, the words of Roland Suvelor, one of the most influential of Martinique's intellectuals, words that were reproduced in the newspaper *Liberation* (Pivois 2000) - reiterate an old statement that is still made relevant even in the ultramodern heart of the island: "We are living in a country where the notion of race plays an essential role, permeates our daily lives and influences almost every one of our gestures." If the patrimonial message creates a rupture in the way that it takes possession of the past - with the museal perspective that seeks out archives rather than intergenerational transmission - those who create it are placed in the continuity of the social arena where patrimonial competence is distributed. Museographical creations, therefore, arise more from the reproduction of social race relations than from a divergence from the previous memorial register. Through these creations, a new, but efficient way of leading back to and maintaining old and archaic social positions is passed on. This unconsummated patrimonial rupture thus makes it possible to use Eichstedt and Small's (2002, 9) analysis, despite all expectations, to see, in Martinique as in the United States, that a "racialized regime of representation" enters the museum framework.

Acknowledgements

I would like to extend a warm thanks to my colleague Stephen Small at the University of California at Berkeley, who shared his research with me during

[225] According to the 2001 survey conducted by the ARDTM on museum attendance.

[226] Statistics from 2003 provided by the statistical service at the ARTDM. Regards to Mr Bruno Marques for having sent them.

his two year stay in Bordeaux as the director of the *Centre d'etudes californiennes.* He allowed this work, carried out in Martinique, to have an interpretive and methodological dimension and for that I owe him.

References

L'Agence Régional de Developpement Touristique de la Martinique, Anse Gouraud-Schoelcher, ARDTM.

Appadurai, A, 2001. *Après le colonialisme: Les conséquences culturelles de la globalization.* Paris: Payot.

Bayart, J.F, 2004. *Le gouvernement du monde.* Paris: Fayard.

Champion, J-M, 1995. '30 floréal An X: Le rétablissement de l'esclavage par Bonaparte'. *Les abolitions de l'esclavage,* edited by M. Dorigny, 265-71. Paris: UNESCO et Presses Universitaires de Vincennes.

Chivallon, Christine, 1998. *Espace et identité à la Martinique: Paysannerie des mornes et reconquête collective (1840–1960).* Paris: CNRS Éditions.

________, 2002. 'Mémoires antillaises de l'esclavage'. *Ethnologie Française,* XXXII (4): 601–12.

________, 2004a. 'Espace, mémoire et identité à la Martinique: La belle histoire de "Providence" '. *Annales de Géographie* 113, no. 638–39: 400–423.

________, 2004b. *La diaspora noire des Amériques: Expériences et théories à partir de la Caraïbe.* Paris: CNRS-Éditions.

________, 2005a. 'L'usage politique de la mémoire de l'esclavage dans les anciens ports négriers de Bordeaux et Bristol'. *L'esclavage, la colonisation et après .*

________, 2005b. 'Résurgence des mémoires de l'esclavage: Entre accélération généralisée et historicités singulières'. *Diasporas. Histoire et sociétés* 6: 144–55.

Cottias, Myriam, 1993. 'Société sans mémoire, société sans histoire: Le patrimoine désincarné'. *Encyclopédie Universalis.* 263–65.

________, 1997. "L'oubli du passe contre la citoyennete: troc et ressentiment a la Martinique (1848-1946)". *1946-1996: cinquante ans de departementalisation outre-mer,* edited by F. Constant and J. Daniel, 293-313. Paris: L'Harmattan.

Eichstedt, J., and Small, S, 2002. *Representations of slavery. Race and ideology in Southern Plantation Museums.* Washington: Smithsonian Institution Press.

Exbrayat, A., 1996. *Madras. Dictionnaire encyclopédique et pratique de la Martinique.* Editions Exbrayat: Fort-de-France.

Findlen, P, {1989} 2004. "The Museum. Its Classical Etymology and Renaissance Genealogy". *Museum Studies. An Anthology of Contexts,* by B.M Carbonell, 23-50. Oxford: Blackwell Publishing.

Gilroy, P, 1993. *The Black Atlantic: Modernity and Double Consciousness.* London: Verso.

Glissant, E, 1981. *Le discours Antillais.* Paris: Seuil.

Guides Bleues, 1986. Antilles, Haïti, Guyane. Paris: Hachette.

Guillaume, M, 1990. "Invention et stratégies du patrimoine". *Patrimoines en folie,* edited by H.P. Jeudy, 13-20 . Paris: Mission du Patrimoine ethnologique, Cahier 5, Éditions de la Maison des Sciences de l'Homme de Paris.

Halbwachs, Maurice, 1997. *La mémoire collective*. Paris: Albin Michel.

Hartog, François, 2003. *Régimes d'historicité*. Paris: Seuil.

Labat, J.B, {1722} 1993. *Voyages aux isles. Chronique aventureuse des Caraibes, 1693-1705.* Paris: Phébus.

Lazarus, N, 1995. "Is a counterculture of modernity a theory of modernity?" *Diaspora*, 4 (3): 323-340.

Le Goff, J., ed. 1998. *Patrimoine et passions identitaires.* Paris: Fayard.

Nora, P, 1984. *Les lieux de mémoire*, tome 1, *La République*. Paris: Gallimard.

Patterson, O, 1982. *Slavery and Social Death. A Comparative Study.* Cambridge: Harvard University Press.

Pivois, M, 2000. Couleur békés. *Journal Libération,* n° du 11-08-2000.

Preziosi, Donald, {1996} 2004. "Brain of the earth's body. Museums and the framing of modernity". *Museum studies. An anthology of contexts,* edited by B.M. Carbonell, 71-84. Oxford: Blackwell Publishing.

Price, R, 2001. "Monuments and silent screamings: a view from Martinique". *Facing up to the Past: Perspectives on the commemoration of slavery from Africa, the Americas and Europe,* edited by G. Oostindie, 58-62. Kingston: Ian Randle.

Queinnec, M-L, 1999. Le notariat des îles et l'esclavage. *Esclavage, résistances et abolitions,* edited by M. Dorigny. Paris: CTHS.

Schmidt, N, 1999. Commémoration, histoire et historiographie: A propos du 150c anniversaire de l'abolition de l'esclavage dans les colonies françaises. *Ethnologie française,* XXIX, 3: 453-60.

Chapter 9

New Perspectives in Heritage Presentations in Suriname and Curaçao:

From Dutch Colonial Museums to Diversifying Representations of Enslavement

Valika Smeulders

There is no other fact in social history that has shaped the modern Caribbean as much as transatlantic slavery and the racial ideology that was used to legitimize it. Several 'national' museums in the Dutch Caribbean are located at sites with historical links to slavery. Considering this, one would expect the social history of slavery to be an important theme in these museums. But until 1998 the island of Curaçao, for instance, which began its modern existence as a slave market, did not feature the experience of being enslaved in any of its dozen museums. At the time of writing, this under-representation is changing. Museum exhibitions increasingly include transatlantic slavery history, while alternative and commercially driven heritage trails and sites add new descriptions and depictions of slavery to the heritage market. Using Curaçao and Suriname as case studies, this chapter typifies these representations found in and beyond the classic museum setting. It argues that there are three types of locations where one would and can expect slavery history to be presented. In addition, some heritage producers create new spaces and artefacts to enhance their representations of slavery, adding to the depth of the overall representation of slavery. What effect does this contemporary 'de-silencing' of slavery have? Do these new slavery representations bridge, or rather reconfirm, boundaries like education, income and age between classic museum audiences and non-museum regulars? Consequently, do they bridge, or rather reconfirm, boundaries related to the subject of transatlantic slavery, such as racial identification and national identities between classic museum audiences and non-museum regulars?

Although Curaçao (444 km^2, pop. 152,700) and Suriname (164.000 km^2, pop. 433,000) share the same Dutch colonial background, they served very different purposes during the period of transatlantic slavery and went through very different social developments. Suriname was the classic export plantation economy. Its lush tropical forests enabled Maroons to establish permanent communities. After the abolition of slavery in 1863 different Asian groups were brought in as agricultural contract laborers, replacing the African enslaved. Since the country's independence in 1975, African Surinamese and Indian Surinamese are not only the largest population groups, they are also best represented in political power and cultural policy making.

As mentioned, Curaçao was used as an international slave market in colonial times. There were some small-scale plantations mainly to provide locals with food. Because of the island's geography, Maroons could not build permanent communities. After abolition, there was no large-scale import of labor for agricultural purposes. Over time, the island's economy turned towards the oil industry and tourism. As the largest electoral group, Afro-Curaçaoans have strengthened their political position over the years. At the same time, the light-skinned elite and The Netherlands itself are still very influential in economic decision making. In this context, cultural policy has been slow in reinterpreting colonial heritage representations.

First Representations of National History: Museums[227]

Suriname today sports only a handful of museums. Nevertheless, it boasts a museum tradition dating back to 1875, when the *Koloniaal Museum* was founded. The Suriname Museum (1947) is its contemporary successor. Two other museums deal with colonial history, while a numismatic and a maritime museum were opened recently. Museums in Suriname are small, self-supporting organizations, with a staff of three at the most, helped by volunteers. Thus, operation, organization and external communication are planned and carried out by just a few people. As a result, the director of the

---

[227] New museums and heritage sites have opened after this chapter was written. In the Savonet Museum, opened in 2010 on Curaçao, slavery is incorporated prominently into the main narrative. Slavery is a topic at the Berg & Dal Resorts in Suriname as well. Also, the Dutch traveling exhibition about enslaved children, *Kind aan de Ketting* was displayed in Suriname's Fort Nieuw Amsterdam in 2011. It was the first time this fort hosted a major exhibition on slavery.
Research for the descriptions of exhibitions in this chapter was conducted in 2006/7/8. Exhibitions and presentations may have altered since then.

Suriname Museum, an anthropologist of Dutch origin and education, has a strong defining role.

The Suriname Museum is generally regarded as Suriname's national museum, despite being an independent initiative. It has no government supervision, but does receive subsidies. Since independence, the museum has aimed to reflect the cultural history of the country's various ethnic groups. These are native people, descendants of colonizers, descendants of the enslaved, and descendants of the contract workers who replaced the slaves. Although for some time these groups were permanently represented side by side, the organization has now opted for an integrated national perspective with alternating themes and occasional attention to the histories of specific ethnic groups. Slavery is not a central theme in the museum's permanent display, but the museum does portray plantation history from more than one perspective, and slavery is mentioned in relation to various themes in the permanent exhibits. In general, slavery is a very accepted part of national history, as the commemorative calendar and infrastructure shows.

The Suriname Museum, located in Fort Zeelandia, consists of five buildings. Four of these cover multiple topics, among which are colonial and post-colonial crafts, and pre-Columbian cultures. Maroon history is not a separate theme. The fifth building deals with the history of the plantations, focusing on one in particular. This exhibition consists of three parts: the first floor revolves around coffee production; the second floor is a plantation house period room; and the attic is a kitchen of the time. It is mainly the attic that interprets slavery life. An important motif on this floor is oppression, told by way of the shackles, weapons and descriptions of the sentences that were carried out in the fort. The key story on this floor is that of the mercenary Maroon hunter John Stedman and his romantic involvement with the enslaved Johanna, which gives the history of slavery depth and a human face. The main perspective, though, is still that of the colonizing powers. The antique pieces that serve to illustrate their accomplishments and life of luxury fill two floors, while the reality of slave life is only dealt with in the attic.

The stories of individual slaves have been added to various themes in the rest of the museum. Thus the display of a pharmacy also provides information concerning health care for and by slaves on the plantations, with special attention to Quassie. This slave enjoyed a reputation as a powerful faith healer, and was imprisoned in Fort Zeelandia for raising his voice against the plantation director. In the display of a shoemaker, the story of Jan Ernst Matzeliger is recounted. He was the son of a slave, who migrated to the United States and became famous there as the inventor of a machine that automated shoe manufacturing.

Although Curaçao is smaller than Suriname, the island has more than double the amount of museums. These are small, mostly privately operated organizations, with just a small staff and some volunteers. Several heritage professionals have a Dutch academic education, enhanced by training and experience in Latin America and the USA.

Up until 1998 Curaçaoan museums mostly displayed heritage from a 'white' colonial or post-abolition perspective. Heritage presentations in plantation houses, for example, did not portray the social history of slavery. Just as in Suriname, the oldest museum, the Curaçao Museum (1947), was considered to be the national museum, despite being neither a government initiative, nor state run. The perspective of the enslaved has never been a theme in the museum. For example, a caption for one of the objects on display, a bell used to regulate the lives of the enslaved, reads:

> "Bronze bell used at plantation Sta Cruz to start and stop the working day. Gift by A.G. Statius Muller 31 May 1948."

This puts the family who owned the bell (and the enslaved) at the centre of attention.

The museum has been through a reorganization, and since 2004 has assigned part of its basement floor to Afro-Curaçaoan culture, mainly post-abolition. An employee of the museum explained the choice not to focus on the experience of slavery:

> Yes, because we have decided that you can look at everything from two sides, you see. You can of course foster the emotional, as we call it, negative side - or inheritance, but would we have had our language, our music, our traditional dishes if we hadn't had a slavery heritage? So, let's rather look into our slavery roots and make something beautiful of it.

'National unity' was the central idea behind heritage representations encouraged by the Curaçao government until the 1990s. One of the reasons for this was the economic importance of tourism to the island. It was believed that uncontested, multi-ethnic colonial heritage - such as music and folklore - would appeal to this audience.[228] Official heritage circles finally warmed to including the social history of slavery, due to 30 years of lobbying by local cultural activists, and global trends in slavery presentations including the Kura Hulanda Museum (1998). This latter museum, a private initiative by a non-resident, demonstrated that exhibiting the slavery past did not necessarily have a subversive influence, and could even be of commercial benefit to the island.

So a new heritage institute was founded in 1998: NAAM, the National Archaeological Anthropological Museum Foundation. This organization does recognize the central position of Afro-Curaçaoan heritage within national heritage. In 2006 it organized the temporary travelling exhibition, *The Heritage of Slavery,* the first big exhibition on local slavery. NAAM has very little exhibition space, in which it approaches Antillean history from a multi-ethnic perspective. But since 2007 it does mention interesting, less widely

---

[228] See Rose Mary Allen's account on the use of traditional slave dances for tourism in E. N. Ayubi (ed.), (1996). *Papers of the third seminar on Latin-American and Caribbean Folklore.* Reports of the Archaeological-Anthropological Institute of the Netherlands Antilles, no 12.

known details about Dutch Antillean slavery history, like Olaudah Equiano's link to St Eustatius. NAAM furthermore manages the most important Afro-Curaçaoan collection that has been on display in the Curaçao Museum since 2004. And finally, in 2007, a government-funded new museum was opened that focuses exclusively on Afro-Curaçaoan culture. At the *Museo Tula*, named after the best-known enslaved rebel leader, rebellion and resistance during slavery times are central themes.

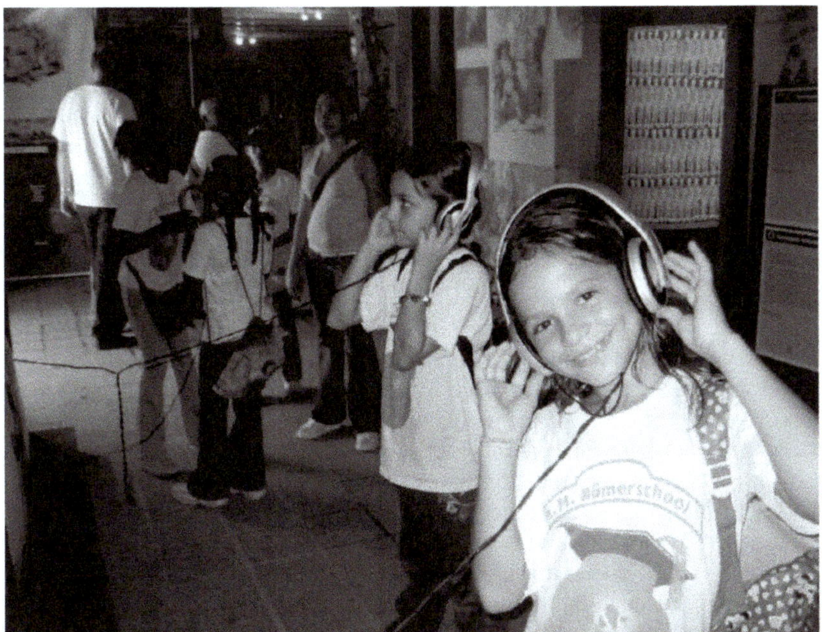

New techniques and young visitors at *The Heritage of Slavery* on Curaçao. (Photo Credit: Author)

Adding Perspective: Cultural Activism

Museums are usually the first institutions to represent national heritage. Nevertheless, some cultural non-governmental organizations feel that these representations can be improved or completed with extra input from their specific perspective, that is, the social history of enslavement. This is done through special tours of existing heritage sites or places not yet marked as sites of remembrance.

Sweet Merodia is such a foundation. It takes thousands of schoolchildren and some 6000 tourists each year to experience Suriname's plantation history from a pluralist perspective. Cynthia McLeod was the first in Suriname to write historical novels based on colonial archive material. Her books have a large audience that crosses all class boundaries. In these novels diverse population groups and cultures come alive, as McLeod describes them and how they related to each other. She includes nuances that in essentialist circles are unpopular, such as that of coloured slave owners (McLeod 1996).[229] The apparent demand for this Surinamese historical perspective inspired McLeod to start the Sweet Merodia Foundation in 1999, named after a plantation in one of her novels. The foundation organizes boat trips past historic plantations, principally for local schools and youth organizations. The trips for youths are funded by offering the same trips for a fee to mostly Dutch and Dutch-Surinamese tourists. Costs are kept low because the six guides, all schoolteachers, work for free. The foundation received financial contributions for the establishment of the organization and maintenance of the materials from the Dutch municipality of Amsterdam and the multinational mining and construction company IAMGOLD NV. Sweet Merodia fills a void in historical presentations and education left by the Surinamese government. Its founder finds this private initiative fair, given the many responsibilities that the administration of a small country like Suriname juggles:

> "[...] I think that you need to relieve the government of this sort of thing. Actually, they should not interfere with this sort of thing. [The government] makes guidelines, [for education] [...] Let the people do the rest."

Rivers were the main means of transport in colonial Suriname. Plantations lined the river banks. Little more than overgrown lands and an occasional house remain of many of them. Using old maps as a reference, the guide reports on what happened at some of these plantations. The participants disembark in two places: the first time to visit the graves of some notable colonial administrators; the second time to see the renovated plantation, Frederiksdorp. This is a tourist resort where visitors can pass time and relax. The tour by Sweet Merodia, however, sheds a different light on this location with an expressive account of the social history of slavery.

Although the guides give prominence to the little-known perspective of the enslaved people, they are wary of polarization in doing so. They emphasize that the living descendants of slaveholders bear no responsibility for the past. The gruesome stories about work-related accidents with the sugar presses are moderated, lest the Dutch/white tourists feel uneasy. A guide says: "Let's keep it pleasant [...] it serves no purpose to go on about that *ad nauseam.*"

Moreover, just as in the books by the founder, McLeod, aspects of history are presented that contradict the essentialist version of the past. The social context that was the norm then, as well as the personal choices and considerations of both slaveholders and enslaved, is mentioned. Moreover, guides are open about their own current quest for understanding slavery history. For instance, one guide relates how she struggles with the question as to why slaves were mutilated when they were financially valuable.

---

229 Research shows that 21.7 per cent of Surinamese slave owners were colored, see: Hoogbergen, W. en Ten Hove, O. (2001). De vrije gekleurde en zwarte bevolking van Paramaribo, 1762-1863. *OSO* 20(2): 306-320.

Curaçao has its own alternative slavery heritage tour: the *Ruta Tula.* This historical tour is organized with the local non-museum visitor in mind, but it's also attended by tourists who do visit museums. The organizers are heritage professionals who work at the National Archive, *Kas di Kultura* and the Public Library, but the *Ruta Tula* is an all-volunteer project.

Tula worked on the Knip plantation in Curaçao, and in 1795 he led his fellow enslaved in a bid for freedom. Slaves from several plantations thronged behind him in an expedition over the island. They eventually had to surrender to the colonial soldiers at the end of fighting that lasted several days. Since 1998, the Tula Route has been an annually organized event, with a bus trip along the key locations of Tula's battles. Young people perform plays on the sites, giving life to this historical event, particularly for non-museum visitors, and familiarizing the participants with the historic relevance of the sites, part of which are currently anonymous wastelands. About 300 people follow the route, for a small fee, and the attendance increases every year.

Commercial Sites: Slavery and Business

Apart from traditional museums and institutions that present national heritage, and the cultural NGOs who add their perspectives to these representations, new, more commercial producers emerge, who present colonial and slavery heritage mostly for tourists. The cultural NGOs' starting point is their goal of educating audiences on slavery history and heritage. Since these organizations generally do not own historical locations, they visit locations of relevance with their audiences. For commercial producers, the opposite applies. They start out by owning a location, which is a possible tourist venue. When those locations have a link to slavery history, these commercial heritage producers have the choice to either emphasize, neutralize, or ignore that fact. Which choice is made is usually a matter of which consumer the producer is aiming for.

Suriname's young tourism industry receives about 138,000 visitors a year.[230] The industry focuses on 'friends and family' and ecotourism rather than international mass tourism. *Danpaati,* a small resort in the Amazon jungle, is such a project, offering the idyll of life close to nature. Traveling into the vast, inaccessible Suriname jungle by air and traditional longboat, the tourist slowly withdraws from the inhabited world. Accommodation consists of small huts and shared sleeping quarters built on the island of Dan. The twelve surrounding Maroon villages provide the foodstuffs, service and entertainment for the tourists' stay. There are excursions through the villages and the natural surroundings, workshops and dance performances. Thus the visitor gets an impression of the Maroons' culture and current living conditions. The presentation does not deal with the theme of slavery in any

[230] WTO Tourism market trends 2005 edition: http://unwto.org/facts/eng/pdf/indicators/ITA_Americas. pdf

depth, yet it is not avoided completely; during the dance performance, a dance is shown that refers to secret communication among slaves.

The enterprise is based on a social project: after the initial phase, the business will be passed on to be run independently by the twelve surrounding Maroon villages. In this way the Bonama Foundation, a Dutch-Surinamese collaboration of care organizations, wants to offer new ways of livelihood to changing (urbanizing) Maroon communities. *Danpaati* is marketed as a small paradise where stressed westerners can find peace of mind, and therefore discussing slavery history is not an easy fit. As a result, tourists only realize the connection between the existence of Maroon communities and the history of western expansion if they are willing to analyze their colonial history of their own accord.

Frederiksdorp is an example of a Surinamese plantation under private ownership that eventually became a tourist destination because of dwindling profits in the agricultural sector. The historical Dutch buildings on the property were restored using Dutch subsidies granted because of the shared heritage aspect. Just as in *Danpaati*, a tourist can visit Frederiksdorp without being confronted with the history of slavery. They can stay overnight in a guestroom built in the overseer's quarters, sip coconut water from fruits grown on plantations that used to be farmed by enslaved Africans, stroll in the gardens past the large pots used in the production of sugar and to feed slaves, and not reflect for a second upon these links to slavery history. Tourists that visit Frederiksdorp aboard the *Sweet Merodia* however, are faced with a different narrative. Walking across the grounds, they learn about the production of sugar and coffee from a social perspective, paying attention to the lives of those doing the manual labor (enslaved, then after abolition, contract laborers). Ultimately, at these sites, tourists get to choose their own level of involvement in the social realities of the past.

Curaçao started out as a tourist destination in the 1950s, aiming for the beach and cruise tourist. Cruise tourists admired the Dutch colonial storehouses built along Willemstad's harbor entrance, which became the island's distinguishing mark. International recognition of this location came in 1997 when Willemstad was placed on UNESCO's World Heritage List. The small island now receives 225,000 visitors a year.[231]

Around the time of UNESCO's inscription of Willemstad, construction of the Kura Hulanda Resort began. A private Dutch initiative, it consisted of the renovation of part of Willemstad, surrounding a hotel. When information surfaced that the location had probably been the docking place for slave ships, the idea of adding a slavery museum and institute to the grounds was proposed. It was the very first time for Curaçao that slavery and the African origins of the island's inhabitants were displayed on this scale, and on a permanent basis. The Kura Hulanda Museum attracts mostly a Dutch, but also an international African Diaspora audience. Local visitors are scarce.

---

[231] WTO Tourism market trends 2005 edition: http://unwto.org/facts/eng/pdf/indicators/ITA_Americas.pdf.

Both resort and museum have commercial as well as social goals. The company expresses a willingness to contribute to the development of the local population, financially as well as culturally. The director talks about a concert by local choirs organized in the museum:

> "[...] by organizing these sorts of things [...] [we] try to raise the cultural social level as well. And [...] we offer a large piece of employment, of course, through the projects we do here. [In this way] we try [...] to make our contribution, economically as well as socially, by showing people [...] that you can and must function at a certain level if you [...] want to achieve quality."

The museum focuses on the history of the transatlantic slave trade and cultures of West Africa. Furthermore there are smaller exhibitions on evolution, world religions and contemporary African art. The main exhibition depicts a very global story of transatlantic slavery and its legacy referring to many of the countries and actors involved, and attention is given to the long process of emancipation and contemporary slavery. The part of the museum that is focused on the social history of slavery uses authentic artefacts, replicas, modern art and the staging of scenes from the past to convey to the visitors the experience of being enslaved. Material colonial heritage, that in other museums is admired, is displayed right next to large, impressive instruments of submission and torture, horrifying visitors. The second largest part of the museum is intended to showcase West Africa's cultural splendour, using large works of art and replicas of houses and a fishing boat.

The Kura Hulanda Museum offers its visitors an experience, by allowing visitors to touch objects, enter a reconstruction of a boat hull and play the musical instruments on display. Furthermore, it organizes 'living history' performances in the evenings, attracting non-regular museum visitors to the premises too. Its approach to transatlantic slavery - global, and at the same time outspoken yet welcoming and interesting to any audience - is trend-setting, and finds a following in other countries.

Presentation Types: 'De-Silencing' Slavery

The foregoing is a sketch of the institutional heritage producers, non-governmental initiatives and commercial producers that present colonial and slavery heritage stemming from different roles and situations during slavery times, within differing national narratives and discourses. These producers cater to audiences that *want* to learn more about colonial slavery, and audiences who don't. Within these frames, different types of slavery presentation can be distinguished: sites of colonial heritage, like plantations and forts; and Maroon sites. At these sites one would expect that presentations of the history and inhabitants would include the experience of being enslaved, or at least the politics and economics of enslavement. In addition to existing material heritage at sites, some heritage producers create new *lieux de memoire,* staging scenes of the past to enhance their representations of slavery, adding to the depth of the overall representation of slavery.

Plantations

Combining luxury accommodations with myths of the uncomplicated, unstressed rural life, plantations have for some time attracted heritage tourists who want to escape from their own hectic everyday lives and relate to the comfortable lives of plantation owners instead (Buzinde 2008; Corkern 2004; Eichstedt & Small 2002; Gable 1996; St. George 1999). Since the 1990s, however, a consciousness has been growing among different audiences and heritage producers that the pleasant aspects of life on the plantation would not have been possible without the repressive practices of chattel slavery. Representing the first aspect without dealing with the second has become an increasingly uncomfortable stance for heritage producers to take. Yet producers at the same time are still interested in attracting audiences interested in leisurely relaxation. As a result, both heritage organizations founded in colonial times and new entrepreneurs try to accommodate two different narratives and their respective audiences. The main narrative continues to be the uncomplicated one of European-colonial accomplishments and the lifestyles of the rich and powerful. To that main narrative, a second narrative is appended that does relate to the African Diaspora and sometimes to slavery. This add-on is offered discreetly so as not to disturb the main narrative: it is located on a different floor or in a different building; or it is offered during special tours. Wherever the main and secondary narratives do meet, there's a hierarchy of narratives: the contributions of the enslaved to national history and heritage are trivialized or ignored.[232]

Forts

The representation of history in forts and other seats of colonial rule is not very different. Colonial forts are often the largest stone historical buildings in the Dutch Caribbean, and therefore have gained a central position in national heritage. As such, they are expected to represent national unity, accommodating different groups. Both in Ghana and in South Africa heritage circles have redefined the use of (some) forts. Although they were used for purposes other than heritage representation or to represent other aspects of history, such as European architecture, several have now been reorganized

---

[232] Examples are Frederiksdorp, Curaçao Museum and Groot Santa Martha. This last plantation exhibition temporarily hosted a traveling exhibition on slavery called *The Heritage of Slavery* in its warehouse. The permanent exhibition on the life of the plantation owners remained unchanged and visitors to the plantation were not informed of the slavery exhibition. Therefore, visitors to the permanent and visitors to the temporary exhibition (which was advertised in the media by the organizer, NAAM, not Groot Santa Martha) were two separate groups.

and have centralized the representation of slavery history.[233] Such a redefinition has not occurred in the Caribbean. In Curaçao, fortresses still mainly serve as government housing. In Suriname, forts that serve as historical representations either showcase colonial heritage or, in the case of the Suriname Museum, interpret plural themes. This last museum does, as mentioned before, refer to slavery in several of its storylines, most importantly plantation life, but also in representations of the pharmacy and shoe industry.

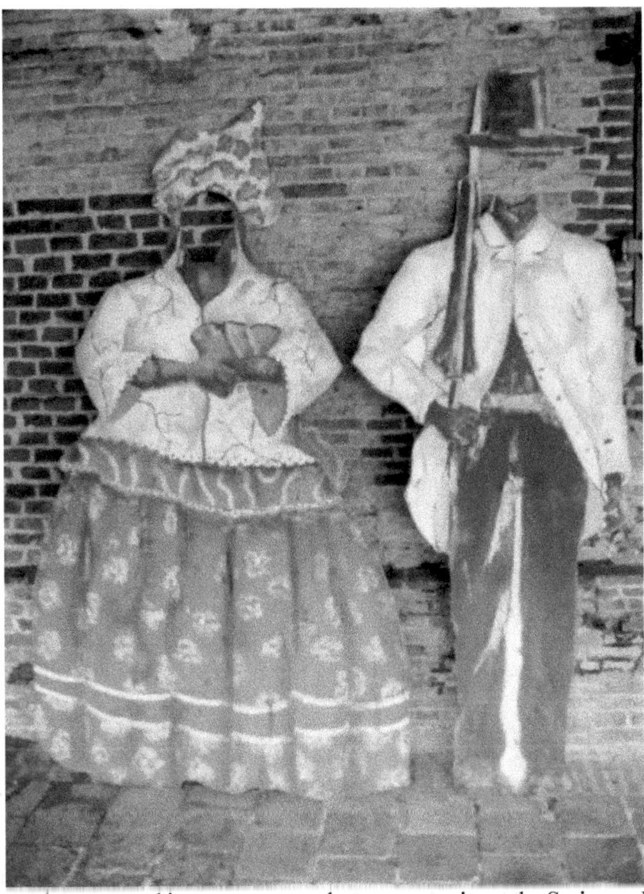

Slavery can be presented in many ways - photo opportunity at the Suriname Museum (Photo Credit: Author)

---

[233] Reasons for these changes are different in Ghana and South Africa. In Ghana, the changes were prompted by the importance of the tourist industry and specifically the wish to please the African Diaspora tourist/pilgrim. In South Africa, the post-Apartheid redefinition of national history in multicultural terms was translated in the allocation of different (ethnic) historical perspectives to different museums. See my forthcoming dissertation: *Slavernij in perspectief. Mondialisering en erfgoed in Suriname, Ghana, Zuid-Afrika en Curaçao.*

Living Heritage of Resistance: Maroon Sites

Whether it is correct to apply the term 'slavery heritage' to the heritage of those who escaped slavery is subject to debate. The fact is that without colonial slavery there would not have been any Maroon heritage. The liberties that the Maroons managed to wrench from the colonial powers, laid down in two peace treaties in Suriname, are a source of pride to many. On the other hand, the debate about the consequences of *marronage* for the slaves who stayed behind has caused tensions in Suriname society. By western standards, moreover, Maroons are perceived as 'primitive', which forms a counterweight to feelings of pride.

In different settings, Maroon communities and heritage are mostly presented as anthropologically interesting. In contemporary museum presentations like the one in the Suriname Museum, one finds little about the social history of the Maroons. Rather, attention is paid to anthropological interpretations of Maroon culture and the Maroons' natural lifestyle. This same approach is seen in tourist destinations; in Suriname, the tourist industry plays up the image of untainted natural life in the Suriname hinterland. Because of the hinterland's inaccessibility, Maroon villages are hard to travel to and are a relatively expensive destination. Consequently, within the overall makeup of Suriname's tourist audience (friends and family and a small group seeking natural beauty off the beaten track) only a select group travels to places like *Danpaati.* They are predominantly Dutch with a personal/work related connection to the country; an audience not looking for confrontation with the Dutch colonial past for which they, as descendants of the perpetrators, might be held responsible. There is considerable ignorance about the Maroons on the part of the Dutch consumer; likewise about the connection between African history and their own Dutch history. The breaking of that ignorance seems to be diametrically opposed to a quiet, relaxing vacation. So for producers aiming for that audience, presenting Maroon culture without highlighting slavery seems to be the most logical choice.

Furthermore, for the Maroon community itself, slavery is a touchy subject as well. Some of the community see themselves, not as descendants of slaves, but of free people. Simultaneously, the fight against slavery and their enforced fugitive life have left negative emotions connected with colonial history, however proud the Maroons may be of their hard-won freedom. Finally, community and individuals distinguish between private matters and matters discussed publicly. The slavery past, and the emotions connected with it, are part of the former.

Curaçao does not have a local Maroon community, as Maroons there either lived in isolation or fled from the island to the South American mainland. Local Maroons do not form part of representations of national history. Just as in Suriname, slavery history is not explicitly represented at Maroon sites. This is different in other parts of the world such as Ghana, where some sites representing the history of resistance to enslavement (as in slave raiders) have been made part of the routes that 'roots' tourists attend as part of their 'pilgrimage'.

New Constructions

Plantations, forts and sites of resistance are locations with an historical, and more or less tangible link to slavery. As explained above, heritage producers of all backgrounds offer representations of slavery at these locations that vary from downplaying that history within main narratives of colonial accomplishments or anthropological perspectives on 'the other', to centralizing the social history of slavery. Heritage producers who are serious about presenting slavery history sometimes commission recreations and new objects to strengthen their representations, stepping away from the focus on authentic material heritage in traditional heritage presentations (Landsberg 2004).

Monuments and other commemorative setups transform sites into *lieux de memoire* for those looking to connect with slavery history in general, or with their personal history and their enslaved ancestors. Although transatlantic slavery was abolished in the nineteenth century, the silence around that history and the ongoing legacy of racism that succeeded it provides fertile soil for emotional connections to that past. At these *lieux de memoire,* spaces are created that allow room for an emotional pan-African perspective on slavery history, including the pain of being enslaved, and admiration for the heroes who emerged from subjection.

Some heritage producers concentrating on slavery want to depict parts of that history for which they can't obtain authentic objects. A trend has emerged to reconstruct objects that transmit to visitors the experience of being enslaved. These reconstructions can be based on a particular object (replica), or on a generalization of such an object (simulacrum). The best example of this is the increase worldwide of reconstructions of ships' holds, intended to simulate the experience of the enslaved people's journey in chains from their homeland to the land of servitude. The Kura Hulanda Museum in Curaçao was one of the trendsetters here. Although in other parts of the world similar items such as recreations of slave dwellings are seen, this is not a big trend (yet) on Curaçao, and certainly not in Suriname.[234]

So Who Cares? Audience Profiles

Museums have traditionally attracted audiences who want to relate to the museum's focus on the history of political power and economic accom-

[234] Recreated ship's holds can be seen in, among other locations, Ghana, South Africa, the UK and the USA. Much discussed are the standardized exits of forts in Ghana aimed at Diaspora visitors, labeled 'Doors of (no) return'. See for example G. Oostindie (2005). The slippery paths of commemoration and heritage tourism: The Netherlands, Ghana, and the rediscovery of Atlantic slavery. *New West Indian Guide,* 75K1&2), 55-77.

plishment. Post-colonial museum personnel, and alternative and commercial heritage producers have since contributed to the exposure of the social history of slavery with new representations of slavery. Does this change heritage audiences as well?

Classic museum audiences and a large percentage of tourists are white (Smith 2009). Research in the USA has shown an increase in percentages of African-Americans among tourists and among museum visitors. This is attributed to a rise in economic living standards for some African-Americans on the one hand, and to specific efforts from grassroots organizations and museums to stimulate African-American museum attendance on the other (Falk 2009; 1995). Research on Curaçao and in Suriname has shown that one and the same slavery exhibition *(The Heritage of Slavery)* can attract just classic museum audiences, or expand that to non-museum regulars, depending on the marketing strategy used. Utilizing marketing channels used by the working-class group, and emphasizing the personal relevance of that particular exhibition for descendants of the enslaved, a new group of museum visitors was attracted to the exhibition on Curaçao, in contrast to Suriname (Smeulders 2009).

Congruent with my findings in Ghana and South Africa, visitor books in the Dutch Caribbean confirm the idea that museums that do not invest in outreach programmes primarily attract visitors of higher education and income groups. This class difference is somewhat less pronounced at a younger age because children do attend in school settings, but at later stages of life working-class descendants of the enslaved generally do not return to museums on their own (Falk 2009; 1995). So class differences cross over into ethnic differences. This is a result of the traditional museum focus on the elite, to which both the working class and descendants of the enslaved - in Wolf's terms 'the people without history' - could not relate.

But it is also a result of the political use of the concept of 'race' to legitimize transatlantic slavery, and, in its aftermath, inequality between groups in society. Some traditional museum visitors relate to the perpetrators and the colonial perspective, and can feel offended by new exhibitions that expose slavery history. Meanwhile others relate to the victims of slavery and the heroes of the African Diaspora and feel that slavery exhibitions are long overdue because slavery history was silenced for so long. For museums it is therefore very difficult to produce exhibitions that accommodate the perspectives of different visitor groups. This sometimes leads to some segregation in audiences.

So while the main audience is still white, despite the de-silencing, at the same time, when audiences do become more coloured, this seems to go hand in hand with some segregation. 'De-silencing' representations by themselves, therefore, seem unable to bridge boundaries between classic museum audiences and non-museum regulars, and between different ethnic identifications related to the roles of enslaved and enslavers. At the same time, the fact that large percentages of these audiences are white, confirms what is apparent at representations of other histories of exclusion: histories of exclusion are universal and therefore are of interest to any audience, not just the descendants of the victims involved (Landsberg 2004).

Conclusion

Representations of colonial history in the Dutch Caribbean are transforming into representations that include the social history of slavery. This transformation occurred locally, gradually and relatively smoothly in Suriname, where the former colonizer ceased to be a local economic and political power after the country's 1975 independence. In the absence of that former colonizer, the different local ethnic groups, who theoretically can all relate to being oppressed during colonial times, could reformulate their national historical representations to include oppression and slavery as important topics. However on Curaçao, descendants of enslavers are still an economically (and thus politically) powerful group locally. Consequently, national historical representations, seeking to avoid contested heritage and unify different groups, avoided the subject of slavery as long as possible. The global de-silencing of slavery helped change this attitude, and since 1998 the number of Curaçao representations focusing on slavery is expanding at a remarkable pace.

The producers of these new representations are not only colonial museums that are gradually incorporating post-colonial perspectives, but also commercial heritage producers aiming for diverse audiences, and cultural activist organizations that complement these representations from the perspective of the concerned. While in Suriname perspectives defended by cultural activists have been influencing historical representations for decades, the first big change in colonial perspectives in Curaçao only came in 1998, when a non-resident entrepreneur proved that slavery could be commercially interesting for the tourism industry. Representing slavery is therefore done or not done out of concerns of national unity, out of group frustration with existing national representations, and out of commercial interests. The new representations are found at historic locations like plantations, forts and Maroon sites and at newly defined *lieux de memoire.*

Those that visit these museums and other heritage sites, including some new slavery exhibitions, are mostly the traditional heritage audiences. The attendance at sites still reflects differences in economic and educational means between groups and, therefore, it reconfirms rather than transcends boundaries between the descendants of the perpetrators and of the victims of transatlantic slavery.

References

Buzinde, C.N, 2007. Representational politics of plantation heritage tourism: The contemporary plantation as a social imaginary. McCarthy, C, Durham, A.S., Engel, L.C, Filmer, A.A., Giardina, M.D., & Malagreca, M.A. (Eds.), *Globalizing Cultural Studies: Ethnographic interventions in theory, method and policy* (pp. 229-251). New York: Peter Lang.

Corkern, W, 2004. Heritage tourism: Where public and history don't always meet. *American Studies International, 42(2-3),* 7-16.

Eichstedt, J. L., & Small, S, 2002. *Representations of slavery: Race and ideology in southern plantation museums.* Washington: Smithsonian Institution Press.

Falk, J.H, 1995. Factors influencing African American leisure time utilization of museums. *Journal of Leisure Research,* 27(1), 41-60.

Falk, J.H, 2009. *Identity and the museum visitor experience.* Walnut Creek, CA.: Left Coast Press.

Gable, E, 1996. Maintaining boundaries, or 'mainstreaming' black history in a white museum. MacDonald, S.J. & Fyfe, G. (eds), *Theorizing museums: Representing identity and diversity in a changing world,* (pp.177-201). Cambridge, Mass.: Blackwell.

Landsberg, A, 2004. *Prosthetic memory: The transformation of American remembrance in the age of mass culture.* New York: Columbia University Press.

McLeod, C, 1996. *Elisabeth Samson: Een vrije zwarte vrouw in het achttiendeeeuwse Suriname.* Schoorl: Conserve.

Smeulders, V, 2009. Exhibiting *The Heritage of Slavery.* Slavery heritage production and consumption in Suriname and Curaçao. Araujo, A. L. (ed.), *Living history: Encountering the memory of the heirs of slavery* (pp. 98-133). Newcastle upon Tyne: Cambridge Scholars Publishing.

Smith, M.K, 2009. *Issues in cultural tourism.* London; New York: Routledge.

St. George, R.B, 1999. Placing race at Monticello. Ben-Amos, D. & Weissberg, L. (eds), *Cultural memory and the construction of identity,* (pp.231-263). Detroit: Wayne State University Press.

Wolf, Eric R, {1982} 1997. *Europe and the People Without History,* California, University of California Press.

Chapter 10

New Museums on the Block:

Creation of Identity in the Post-Independence Caribbean[235]

Kevin Farmer

The independence experiment in the English-speaking Caribbean emerged fully during the 1960s, continued evolving into the 1980s and has apparently reached a plateau as we enter the second decade of the twenty-first century. This experiment has resulted in the creation of independent multi-party democratic states, with varying demographics comprising persons of African, European and Asian descent, with some countries - notably Dominica, St Vincent, Belize and Guyana - nurturing pockets of descendants of the indigenous people of the region. Culturally diverse, the region shares a common pre- and post-colonization history, though nuanced by the peculiar local histories and geographies of the individual countries.

[235] An earlier version of this article has been recently published entitled "Identity Forged: The Museum's Role in the Creation of Identity in the English-Speaking Caribbean", Kevin Farmer and Alissandra Cummins, pp. 375-384 in Basil Reid (ed.) *Caribbean Heritage,* UWI Press, 2012. The present article in this volume addresses the role of museums during the post-independence era in the Caribbean as it relates to the creation of national identity.

Once they had settled down to governing their countries, the emerging Anglophone Caribbean nation-states turned their attention (reluctantly in some cases) to the creation of a national identity that went beyond designing a flag, singing a national anthem and reciting a national pledge. The role of identity creation became the core mandate of cultural institutions, which in many instances were museums and heritage institutions. It is the duality of contested identities between state sanctioned and marginalized groupings that is the focus of this chapter.

Democratizing History, Culture and Space

Following the independence thrust of the post-World War II period in the British Caribbean, initial gradualism gave way to full scale independence in the 1960s for a select few. These pioneer independence movements at the outset sought to grapple with the type of societies they wished to form, and engaged in concrete social engineering through free education, housing programmes and apprenticeship schemes by which they thought to transform their agrarian societies into modern service-oriented and industrial societies. Few of these movements invoked history and heritage as a tool by which to engender national identity, beyond the newly invested symbols of state wrapped in the package of anthem, flag and coat of arms. Nor was the new nation state engaged in an inclusive creation of national identity. Identity engendered by independence rested on the core foundation of repudiating all that was European, replacing this with a nationalist veneer; not by radical change but gradually, clearly a sign that colonialism had embedded a cautious strain when it came to matters of socio-political adventurism. Those states that opted out of the normative social liberal democracy were quickly ostracized or underwent invasion. This occurred in Guyana, prior to independence, when the newly elected Cheddi Jagan government, the first colonially elected legislature, once it voiced its Bolshevik leanings, was quickly routed by the Royal Navy and Army, and replaced with a western-leaning government led by Forbes Burnham. The 'shot across the bow' was given: if one remained within the fold of the Commonwealth one must adhere to the unwritten rule - liberal democracy or else. The irony of the ouster of Jagan was that, once independent, Burnham instituted a Maoist-type revolutionary regime that was to last for many decades. Jagan was simply ahead of his time. Nevertheless, with the painful reminder of what could happen if one strayed away from the liberal democratic path indicated, most English-speaking countries stayed the liberal route with a socialist bent. Culture, regionally, was not seen as pillar of national identity at the outset, though there were some exceptions.

Whether influenced by a radical streak that witnessed the creation of a new religion in the twentieth century in the form of Ras Tafari, or thrown up by the legacy of Pan Africanist Marcus Mosiah Garvey, the earliest form of popular mass museum in the region is seen in the creation of the People's Museum of Craft and Technology (originally called the Folk Museum of Jamaica) in 1961, located in the old capital of Spanish Town, *San Jago de la*

Vega. At the forefront of a revolution taking place in popular culture in Jamaica at the time, the museum was an anti-elitist symbol. Elevating the folk within the space of a museum was an attempt, I believe, to illustrate the worthiness of the downtrodden; whether it was an outcome of such a museum remains unanswered. It is instructive that the museum is situated in a space where former colonial buildings were in a state of disrepair and left as romantic ruins, while its space was rebuilt to house the museum.

Its mandate and purpose were to celebrate the creativity and industry of the now 'emancipated' people as they fashioned a new life for themselves in towns and rural villages across Jamaica. The exhibition offered visitors a truly nostalgic trip down memory lane, back to 'ole time Jamaica' to reminisce and enjoy. In reading its mandate, one is perhaps confronted by its strident call 'to truly appreciate our foreparents' triumph over enormous odds to secure our future in modern Jamaica'. Such naked nationalism was the mantra of museums created during the post-independence phase. In fact in retrospect, across time and space, the museum was a clarion call for the dispossessed and disenfranchised in the region, its siting a clear attempt to reclaim a contested identity from a liminal space. The movement to redress legitimate and perceived marginalization by means of museums had begun.

A later incarnation of this approach was the Saint Lucia Folk Research Centre. Though not a museum *per se* (plans for a museum are ongoing), the Centre is the *de facto* folk museum of the island; it was created in 1973 to combat the 'anglicization' of Saint Lucia. Its aim was to recapture a marginalized past that had been denigrated through British rule of the former French island, which demonized French Creole language and culture.

The objectives of the Centre are as follows: 'The Folk Research Centre (FRC) is a non-governmental organization established in 1973 to preserve and promote the cultural heritage of Saint Lucia and registered as a nonprofit company in 1985. FRC has sought to promote the role of folk arts as a vehicle for change and to illustrate the development potential of cultural heritage, particularly in the field of education and in economic development.'

The Folk Research Centre, like the Museum of Craft and Technology in Jamaica, used forceful language in describing its mission and mandate to champion aspects of the island's traditional culture. Some 40 years after the beginning of the independence movement, such fervent nationalism seems almost a call to arms for the people to defend themselves against unchecked colonialism.

At a national level, these museums sought to distill a national identity that was accessible to all, and increasingly so to the visitor as economic development shifted to tourism. This was now in some countries being joined by the state that acknowledged that the past must be engaged in order for a new type of nationalism to thrive. Social partnerships developed whereby the professional curator, the antiquarian, both amateur and professional historians and others interested in heritage came together to forge or formulate policy for the operation of museums in the region. The museum was therefore evolving from an elitist institution to one that, in addressing populist concerns about representing the 'common man', was now the preserve of an emergent elite middle class. However, it was the role of the state to control the message and the messenger, and in so doing it unintentionally energized a new contested state, apart from the one it was seeking to change.

Identity in the Post-Independence Landscape

The post-independence Caribbean, both ideologically and physically, was determined to discard and distance itself from the colonial past, in some cases going to extremes in dismantling the vestiges of empire, for example, through neglect (and ultimate destruction) of colonial-style buildings. A major catalyst for this ideological shift lay within the developing historiography of the region, disseminated by a new cadre of professionally trained historians returning from the metropole to teach at the newly developed and growing University College of the West Indies (now the University of the West Indies). These Caribbean historians thus had a stage from which they could confront the historiography of the region.

This new cohort of historians - Elsa Goveia, Philip Sherlock, Roy Augier and, later, Bridget Brereton, Woodville Marshall, Keith O. Laurence, Hilary Beckles and Verene Shepherd - sought to interpret the history of the region from a post-colonial, gendered perspective and not that of empire. It was a reversal of the "great man" paradigm of history that had so ingrained the writings and shaded the historiography to date. In so doing, Caribbean historians laid the foundation for a new historiography to emerge that focused on retrieval of the stories/voices of the majority of the population. Their research framed the paradigm through which historical research was carried out in the region. The fruits of such research began to inform, infiltrate and prescribe what and how museums presented and interpreted the history of the society they represented.

This emergent nationalism has also seen the co-option of colonial institutions in the development of the newly independent nation-state, at the same time as new institutions were created to meet the challenges of development. That which was British became West Indian and eventually Caribbean, with some modifications. Alissandra Cummins (1994) notes that colonization was a process of 'deculturalization', and such a process was reflected in the development of museums in the region. Born out of the Victorian desire to explain the world through science and to exhibit its progress, museums in the Caribbean became showcases of technological progress, juxtaposed against all that was primitive. This dichotomy meant that invariably what was presented indicated that all that was European was superior and all that was not (i.e., Amerindian, African and Asian) was inferior. Created by the colonial elite, these often privately funded institutions were governed by a discriminatory mindset which persisted into the post-colonial era.

Existing museums in the region were co-opted by post-colonial governments to become agents of identity creation. This saw existing institutions, such as the Barbados Museum & Historical Society (BMHS), change focus through government intervention to facilitate the creation of a new national identity.

Post-independence West Indian governments, in their developmental thrust, invariably placed culture on the backburner. It was a feature that many governments, until at least the late 1990s, did not see as part of their countries' development, except for Carnival festivals, which were reintroduced as a means by which tourists could be enticed to the islands. Nationalism symbolically manifested itself politically with the election of majority non-white governments. At the national level this meant that the formerly disenfranchised black populace eventually became masters of their fate. However, the result of this has been that, in the experiment of nationalism in the Caribbean, the creation of this image of the region as comprising primarily descendants of Africa has seen the marginalization of certain other ethnic groups.

This has led to a new form of contestation. Sometimes this marginalization has evolved into factionalized political parties, as witnessed in Trinidad and Tobago and Guyana following independence. Independence therefore witnessed the creation of a pro-black nation-state whose institutions and organs were organized to facilitate that shift in the politics of government business. The subsequent response has been an increasing intensity of ethnically oriented cultural activity, not least in the creation in 2006 of the Indian Caribbean Museum in Trinidad and Tobago. This museum is located in the ethnic majority enclave of Chaguanas, and seeks to give voice to the migration experience of this ethnic group in Trinidad, following the end of Emancipation.

While their story has been given some space at the National Museum, it is not exhaustive in its treatment. The attempt to explore in a comprehensive manner, the history and heritage of the Indian migrant and the legacy of their indentureship, has led to the exclusion of any others. There is little attempt to present their story within the fabric of the republic's national narrative. Instead it is an exposition of the legacy and legitimacy of the Indo-Trinidadian experience. In some cases these new museums are not born out of resisting a particular narrative, but of re-informing the present about the past. Such an approach has been undertaken by the new Jewish arrivals in Barbados concerning the Sephardic Jewish presence on the island which predated their presence by some 300 years, having been on the island since the mid seventeenth century. Here were new Ashkenazi migrants, identifying with an earlier presence of Jewish people and taking care to preserve and interpret that past, firstly through restoration of a historic synagogue, eventually creating a Jewish museum on the island. The synagogue and museum are called Nidhe Israel Synagogue and Museum respectively. This reconstruction of a Jewish past in the region is not confined to Barbados as there are similar efforts of various phases of development ongoing in Jamaica, Nevis and Curaçao, whether it's the upkeep of a cemetery or synagogue. For in the twenty-first century, heritage in the region resides within museums, at sites, within historic buildings and in memory.

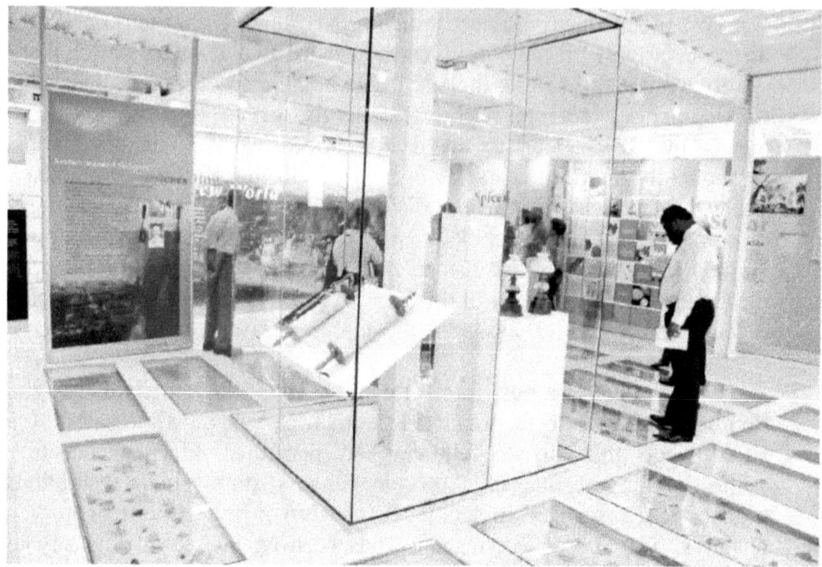

Interior view of Nidhe Israel Museum (Photo Credit: William St. J. Cummins)

Caribbean nationalism, as constructed in the post-independence era, sought to combat the issue of the colonial self as inferior, replacing it with a notion of self as superior and therefore capable of running one's own country. However, there was also a need to face the reality of how to combat 500 years of colonization practised and legitimized by the judicial, political and social machinery of the day. The Caribbean, then and now, can be framed within Lamming's concept of 'Caliban bettering Prospero' (1960). This thesis posits that an emergent Caribbean consciousness, when awakened and rooted in a strong sense of self, is able to overthrow the weight of the colonial stereotype of ineptitude. The emergent Caribbean nation is still grappling with this concept of self-actualization and development of identity, and has turned to its museums to be agents of change. The question is, can they fulfill this role of redefining the national psyche?

The development of Caribbean museums has gone through several phases nuanced by temporal and spatial factors, and as such the region's museums cannot be simply labelled as pre- and post-colonial institutions. One such phase of museum development witnessed the colonial museum, formed in the nineteenth and early twentieth centuries, evolving into a post-colonial institution. This museum has been able to redress its imbalances internally without necessarily resorting to a name change or being shuttered, and has readjusted to reflect the new society in which it now functions - the emerging independent nation-state. Concomitant with this is the development of site- or theme-specific museums, situated at restored plantation houses or historic, industrial or military sites that focus on attracting the tourist, such as Sunbury Plantation in Barbados; Nelson's Dockyard, Antigua; and the Chaguaramus Military History and Aviation Museum in Trinidad and Tobago. Added to these social historic museums are natural history exhibits such as the Soufrière interpretive centre in Saint Lucia and the Montserrat Volcano Observatory (MVO) that explore aspects of the physical landscape and its creation, which are and have become part of the identity of the people. So much so, that the national flag of the independent Saint Lucia utilizes one of the Pitons, a volcanic plug, as a national symbol. Museums in the region have become more selective in what they interpret and exhibit.

The new focus is on thematic museums. Created by energized individuals or groups in the society, they are motivated by creating a space in which their voice can be heard. Such institutions are well intentioned and well-meaning but come with cautionary tales, such as the prehistory museum in St. Vincent and the Grenadines.

The prehistoric archaeology museum founded by the late Dr. Earl Kirby in St. Vincent, sadly now in a state of disrepair, and the Doctor Cecil Cyrus Medical Museum of Caribbean medical specimens and equipment, set up next door - also merit our attention as catalysts for developing small, specialized museums. The former institution's focus disappeared with the demise of Dr. Kirby; while the latter, intent on survival, has found some willing partners but is still in a state of limbo.

Thematic museums also fall within the ambit of 'subaltern' museum spaces, constructed by persons or groups that see themselves as marginalized in society and seek to redress this imbalance through museum creation. Personal or community collections have found fertile ground, inspiring the emergence of 'culture houses' in Belize, *'negga houses'* in Antigua and Barbuda, and Amerindian museums in Dominica, Guyana, Belize and Trinidad. Meanwhile a new thematic museum is that of those concerned with locating the intangible such as the Junkanoo museum in the Bahamas (see Krista Thompson's chapter in this publication). This museum seeks to house objects that traditionally have been destroyed as part of the cycle of their creation. The museum upholds this cultural practice and as such is engaged in safeguarding the intangible through destroying the tangible. Its juxtaposition runs counter to what a museum is, but in fact chronicles an aspect of Caribbean culture that has yet to be fully explored, the inherent destruction of the created object as a form of cultural expression. Perhaps this foreshadows a new movement in Caribbean museology?

These institutions were confronted with similar issues of interpretation, relevance to the communities they served, and the 'democracy' inherent in the creation of exhibits. Cannizzo (1987) states that museums are 'negotiated realities' that reflect the fears and aspirations of those who create them. As elsewhere, museums in the Caribbean rely on their collections to frame the interpretation of history that the viewer will experience. Much of their new direction, however, is designed to lessen reliance on the tangible (where the preserved heritage tends to be largely colonial in origin and focus), and to balance this with intangible memories and historical experiences based on family or community knowledge.

As such, the formulation of Caribbean museums as repositories and showcases of the region's economic and cultural diversity reflects the Enlightenment world view, advanced by the founders of colonial museums and expanded upon by the founders of the post-colonial museum.

But all is not lost. The legacy of Garvey's pan-African movement is reflected in the creation of National Honours in various countries that echo his call to honour self. This in turn has resulted in the establishment of 'national heroes' monuments or galleries, for example, Barbados' Museum of Parliament and National Heroes Gallery. Essentially they are designed to commemorate the lives of persons chosen to be 'heroes' for the national audience. Similarly, the Institute of Jamaica recently created a museum at Liberty Hall in honour of Marcus Garvey during his centenary anniversary. The privately owned Bob Marley Museum in Jamaica, while responding to a more opportunistic imperative, also broadens the base through memory and popular culture in the region.

At the same time, there remains room for the national museum to tell its story. This can be seen in the plans for a national museum complex in Grenada, to allow for the unfolding narrative and heritage of the island for its people. The museum complex allows space for the general history and contemporary art of the island to be seen. While one may argue that such spaces are traditional in their concept, it's left to their interpretation if they will be labeled as Caribbean avant-garde in the future.

Discussion and Conclusion

Caribbean museums are not yet fully democratic, and it is their willingness to combat this lack of democracy and dependency on limited funding that will determine how these museums formulate and develop content, programmes and policies. They must grapple with being spaces for both the tangible and the intangible, being truthful to the communities they serve, and avoid narrow political posturing in their desire to create identity. Museums in the region need to become more reflexive if they are to be dynamic and relevant in the twenty-first century.

This is particularly important in the face of developing globalization and a nascent neo-colonial mentality. The museum must be more than the sum of its collections. Regional museums must construct a hybrid between the traditional 'tangible' orientation of the European model and the intangible modalities of African and Asian museums. They must embrace the oral tradition of storytelling and 'ole talk' and maximize the masquerade festivals and their potential to engage peripheral communities. In this context the Bahamian Junkanoo Expo museum is an exemplar of a new path. Most importantly, regional museums must engage the community.

They must become centres of discourse, willing and able to voice the concerns, fears and aspirations of the multiple voices of the people they represent, without bias or favour. They must reflect the development of the societies they represent and prepare themselves to question - and in some cases help resolve - societal problems through their programmes and heritage interpretation. Both the tangible and intangible components of the society must find equal space within the museum as it strives to give voice to varying constituents in the new century. The museum must not see itself as the singular authority in the construction of national identity but must instead allow itself to be a conduit through which the often multiple voices of the society are heard. The curator is not gate-keeper but custodian by popular decree, not master but servant. The society should be encouraged to shape its national identity within the 'negotiated reality' of the national museum and in association with its 'subaltern' counterparts, though issues of contestation might arise. For in the space between contestation elements of the authentic may be found.

References

Cannizzo, Jeanne, 1987. "How Sweet It Is: Cultural Politics in Barbados". *Muse* 4 (Winter): 22-27.

Cummins, Alissandra, 1994. "The 'Caribbeanization' of the West Indies: The Museum's Role in the Development of National Identity". Kaplan, Flora E.S. (ed.), *Museums and the Making of "Ourselves": The Role of Objects in National Identity,* Leicester: Leicester University Press.

Farmer, Kevin and Cummins, Alissandra, 2012. 'Identity Forged: The Museum's Role in the Creation of Identity in the English-Speaking Caribbean', in Reid, Basil (ed.), *Caribbean Heritage,* UWI Press, p. 375-384

Fanon, Frantz, {1952} 1967. 1st translated edition. *Black Skin, White Masks: The Experiences of a Black Man in a White World.* New York: Grove.

Gathercole , P., ed. 1994. *The Politics of the Past.* London: Routledge.

Karp, Ivan, and Lavine, Steven, eds. 1991. *Exhibiting Cultures: The Poetics and Politics of Museum Display.* Washington, DC, and London: Smithsonian Institution Press.

Lamming, George, 1960. *The Pleasures of Exile.* London: Michael Joseph.

Walsh, Kevin, 1992. *The Representation of the Past.* London: Routledge.

Chapter 11

Framing Identity, Encouraging Diversity:

Recent Museum Developments in Barbados

Roslyn Russell

In an article in *The Observer,* British historian Tristram Hunt dismissed the notion that Barbados stakes its claim to international fame only on its exclusive high-end Platinum Coast resorts, the playground of celebrities and the super-rich. He asserted that

> ...there is another Barbados. This island ... has a remarkable history stretching back, on the one hand, to the Amero-Indians of 4,000 BC and on the other to the apex of British imperialism. And, unlike some former British colonies, it has enough confidence and sense of its own identity to explore this history in a creative and compelling manner. In Barbados you can combine the indulgence of the Platinum Coast with a rewarding account of the past.[236]

This chapter explores the role of museums, galleries and heritage institutions in encouraging an understanding of the nature of national identity in Barbados; the role played by museums and heritage sites in building audiences both within the Barbadian community and among tourists visiting the island; and the ways in which Barbados's museums and heritage sites reflect its rich history and cultural diversity. Barbados has set itself the task of

[236] Tristram Hunt, 'Colonial Riches in Barbados', *The Observer,* 13 November 2011.

demonstrating the pluralistic nature of its society through what Barbados Museum Director Alissandra Cummins has called "a kind of cultural affirmative action, by which people assert their cultural independence or restore a collective heritage".[237]

The recent museums and heritage presentations of Barbados, in addition to celebrating its national history and identity, demonstrate its high degree of connectivity to other places and cultures across its history. Telling the story of Barbadian identity in museums also means exploring the ways in which this has intersected with broader historical themes that have worldwide relevance: slavery and its abolition, of course; but also immigration and emigration; the advances in democratisation of parliamentary institutions around the world; and the rediscovery and restatement of diasporic identities - both African and Jewish. Sport also provides another distinctive example of the connections between Barbados, the rest of the Caribbean, and the wider world.

The role of the government of Barbados in this process has been visible since the 1980s.[238] In the first two decades of the twenty-first century, two circumstances in particular have led to further developments that focus ever more strongly on the role of the island's museums in forging national identity. Firstly, Barbados hosted the Cricket World Cup at Kensington Oval, Bridgetown in 2007. The prospect of this event led to a determination by the government of Barbados to provide, for both visitors and Barbadians alike, new perspectives on the island's history and heritage, and enhanced representations of the nature of its national identity in the island's museums and heritage sites. The second stimulus to further development has occurred (and is continuing) with the inscription of Historic Bridgetown and its Garrison on the UNESCO World Heritage list of properties of Outstanding Universal Value in June 2011.

In December 2006, as part of the preparation for Cricket World Cup, described by the government-sponsored Barbados Tourism Investment Inc. (BTI) as 'the single most important sporting, tourism and business event ever to embrace and showcase Barbados and the Caribbean', BTI announced the restoration of the West Wing of the Parliament building and the establishment of a National Heroes Gallery and Museum of Parliament. These exhibitions were designed to 'tell the history of Barbados, from its founding to

---

[237] Alissandra Cummins, 'The "Caribbeanization" of the West Indies: The Museum's Role in the Creation of National Identity, in Flora E.S. Kaplan (ed.), *Museums and the Making of "Ourselves": The Role of Objects in National Identity,* Leicester University Press, London, 1994, this edition 1996, p. 218.

[238] Cummins describes the process of review of the collections of the Barbados Museum & Historical Society in the early 1980s and the "modification and improvement of the Museum's collections and displays to address an existing focus that did not present a coherent or complete story of Barbados in history". This modification received government funding 'for the museum to become "an instrument of national identity" and an institution "in the service of national development"', ibid., p. 213.

Independence from the viewpoint of the outstanding contributions made by the National Heroes of Barbados. The establishment of this Gallery and the Parliamentary Museum,' said BTI, 'will also go a long way in educating visitors and future generations of Barbadians of our proud tradition of over 350 years of representative government in Barbados.'[239]

This development is one of a number initiated by the government of Barbados since the mid-2000s as part of an overall effort to provide a diverse range of interpretive experiences in museums and heritage sites on the island. Private institutions, with the assistance of BTI, have also developed displays that interpret aspects of Barbados' history, and celebrate its social diversity, highlighting the history and society of Barbados for visitors and locals alike, and asserting the distinctive identity of the island's culture.

Barbados is a small island - 21 miles (33 kilometres) long by fourteen miles (22 kilometres) wide - with a very rich history. The most easterly of the Lesser Antilles, it was originally inhabited by Amerindian Arawak people. When the first English ship arrived in 1625, its crew found the island to be uninhabited. Settlement from Britain began two years later. By the end of the seventeenth century a sugar-based economy had been established; Barbados had its own parliament; and the mass importation of enslaved Africans to work on sugar plantations had begun. At this time Bridgetown, the island's capital, was the second wealthiest city in the British Americas.

English settlers created a tropical facsimile of their homeland on the island, dividing it into eleven parishes, each with a Church of England parish church built of local coralstone in a style that recalls the parish churches of the United Kingdom. Meanwhile, thousands of captured Africans brought to Barbados across the Atlantic via the notorious Middle Passage and sold into slavery were worked to the point of exhaustion, and even to death, to produce the wealth that built the Great Houses of the island's plantocracy and also often created massive fortunes (and structures) in England.

The bicentenary of the abolition of the slave trade in the British Empire was commemorated in 2007 in museums and galleries in the United Kingdom, the Caribbean and Africa. But enslaved people across the Anglophone Caribbean, including Barbados, had had to wait until 1834 to be emancipated; and for several more years before the apprenticeship system that replaced slavery also came to an end in 1838. Freedom did not bring economic prosperity to the formerly enslaved people of Barbados, and life for working-class people was a constant struggle. Over 100 years after Emancipation, the black majority in Barbados achieved political power and representation in Parliament and, with it, the means to make gradual improvements in the lives of Barbadians. In November 1966 Barbados became a sovereign independent nation. All these aspects of Barbados' history are interpreted in its museums and heritage sites.

---

[239] Barbados Tourism Investment Inc., 'Barbados - Going World Class', barbadostourisminvestment.com/news_details.cfm?newsID=io, accessed May 2009.

Africa: Connections and Continuities, Barbados Museum & Historical Society

The Barbados Museum & Historical Society occupies the former military prison at the Garrison Savannah on the outskirts of Bridgetown. Most of its displays interpreting the natural and cultural history of the island date from the period of modification in the 1980s and 1990s mentioned previously. There is, however, a more recent gallery whose content goes to the heart of the celebration of Barbadian identity, cultural diversity and connectivity. *Africa: Connections and Continuities,* opened in 2005, aims to remind the majority of Barbadians of African descent of the cultures from which their ancestors came; and to inform visitors to the island about the diversity and richness of the deep cultural traditions that contribute to Barbadian society and identity. In Barbados, as the Museum's Director Alissandra Cummins has remarked, 'a local culture was created that was derivative of European values (for generations the most dominant force) and bound to African sensibilities'.[240]

The introductory panel to the *Africa* gallery foregrounds its themes of diversity and connectivity: 'Over a period of about 500 years, many Caribbean societies, including ours, were created by the forces of capitalism. We are the amalgam of four continents – Africa, Europe, Asia and the Americas – an archipelago distilled and anew.'[241] The exhibition provides information on the African continent and the antiquity and diversity of cultures within it, and identifies some of the peoples from whom the majority of Barbadians are descended, and which have influenced Barbadian culture. There are displays on traditional and modern housing in Africa, some artefacts displaying the impressive skills of African craftspeople in metal, wood and textiles, and a fascinating display, '*Masquerade*', comparing festival costumes from the Republic of Benin and Barbados.

The *'Masquerade'* display provides a vivid example of cultural transformation in the evolution of a hybrid form from its originating tradition. Two festival costumes are displayed side by side. One is an *Egungun* masquerade costume from the Republic of Benin, worn by members of the all-male *Egungun* society at festivals in south-western Nigeria to commemorate the ancestors. The other is a 'Shaggy Bear' costume created by the descendants of Yoruba people from Nigeria who were brought to Barbados as slaves. The *Egungun* costume uses imported velvet, silk and damask cut into lappets to form multiple layers that flare outwards as the masked dancer moves in a circular fashion, creating a breeze that is believed to be a blessing from the ancestors. The Shaggy Bear costume lacks the formal beauty of the *Egungun* costume, with its rich fabrics and appliqued panels, but its creators, who first

---

240 Cummins, '"Caribbeanization" of the West Indies', p. 192.

241 Interpretive panel, *Africa: Connections and Continuities,* Barbados Museum & Historical Society.

used dried banana leaves to make the costume,[242] then substituted the only fabric that could be obtained by Yoruba descendants in Barbados after Emancipation - 'small strips of different coloured throw-offs begged and borrowed', to create this festival costume that recalls their distant motherland. The Shaggy Bear dance itself maintains the circular motions of the *Egungun,* which in Barbados represent 'the cycle of life'.[243]

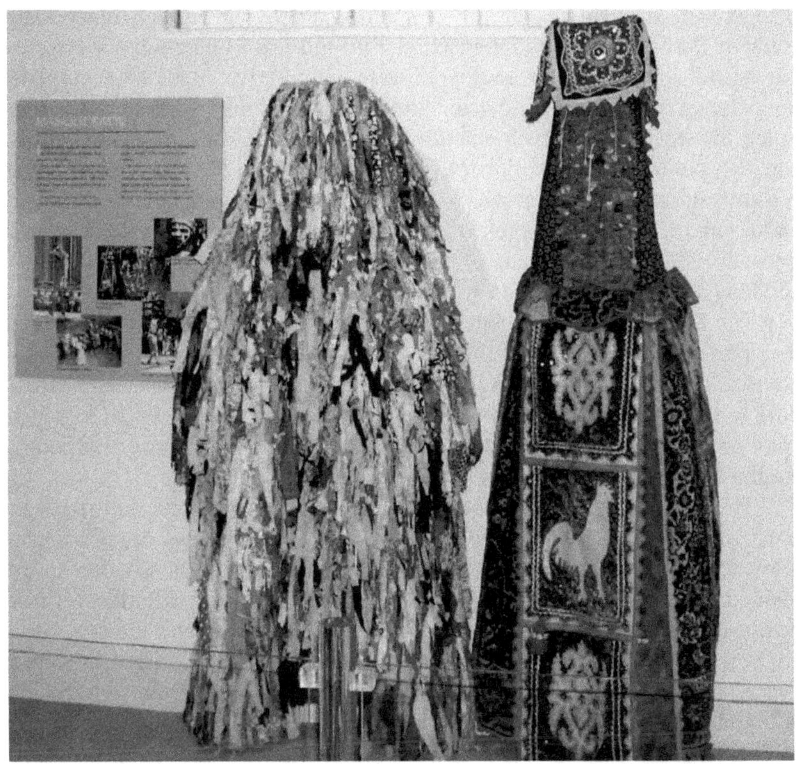

Masquerade display at the Barbados Museum (Photo Credit: Author)

The comparison of the two costumes that the display facilitates is an eloquent testimony to the cultural roots of many Barbadians living on the island today, and the persistence and adaptability of African traditions in a different physical environment.

[242] Marcia Burrowes, 'Losing our Masks: Masquerade and Changing Concepts of Barbadian Identity', Heritage Lecture delivered 14 June 2012, Bridgetown, Barbados, http://www.barbadoscropoverfestival.com/festival-news/522-exploring-the-changes-in-concept..., accessed 9 July 2012.

[243] Interpretive panels for the *'Masquerade'* exhibit, *Africa: Connections and Continuities,* Barbados Museum & Historical Society.

Museum of Parliament and National Heroes Gallery, Parliament Buildings, Bridgetown

The Museum of Parliament, mentioned above as one of the key projects developed ahead of the Cricket World Cup in 2007 to inform both Barbadians and tourists of the rich history of Barbados and the roles played by its National Heroes, is located in the West Wing of the Parliament buildings in Bridgetown. It examines the history and character of parliamentary democracy in Barbados, and its intersection with the rise of black majority rule in the island. The displays employ diverse interpretive media - text panels, sculptures, recreations, audiovisual and interactive multimedia presentations - to tell the story of the development of parliamentary institutions in Barbados, and the political and administrative history of the island. Topics include accounts of episodes of serious rioting by the disadvantaged black majority in 1876 and 1937, the formation of political parties to represent working-class Barbadians, the achievement of representative government and nationhood, and how democracy functions in Barbados today.

The Museum of Parliament thus acts as a reference point for Barbadians seeking to learn more about the history of their nation and the nature of its political and social history and institutions. It also provides an insight to visitors to the island, many of whom are surprised at the antiquity of representative political institutions in Barbados, and that the Parliament of Barbados is the third oldest in the Commonwealth, dating from 1639.

The theme that threads through the Museum of Parliament displays was articulated by the Right Excellent Errol Walton Barrow, the first prime minister of independent Barbados, who at a conference in London in July 1966 declared that 'The strength and durability of our institutions are best demonstrated by the fact that representative government and the rule of law are now administered by people who are different in racial origins from those that established them'.[244] Barrow's words introduce the Museum of Parliament in both audiovisual and text panel formats. This gradual transformation, from the rule of the representatives of the white plantocracy to the representatives of the black majority in Barbados, is conveyed in displays that tell the story from the seventeenth century to the present.

An illustrated timeline on banners wraps around the thick stone interior walls of the museum. There are interactive features that allow visitors to 'leaf through' a handwritten Register of Members of the House of Assembly established in 1639. An electronic timeline, 'Who Could Vote When?', compares the dates when democratic reforms, such as universal suffrage, were achieved in Barbados and when they occurred around the world. The window spaces of the Museum of Parliament hold large banners dealing with two critical uprisings in Barbados - the Confederation riots of 1876; and the 1937 riots sparked by the deportation to Trinidad of labour activist (and now National Hero), Clement Payne, which resulted in over 20 deaths. The names

---

[244] Errol Barrow, 'No Loitering on Colonial Office premises', Address to the Barbados Constitutional Conference, London, July 1966.

of those who lost their lives in the riots are painted on a facsimile of a chattel house wall.

An audiovisual presentation dramatises the words of nineteenth-century novelist Anthony Trollope, who mistakenly wrote in the late 1850s that 'None but white men do vote' in elections for the Barbados House of Assembly. However, very few people of colour at that time could meet the property qualification for voting, so most Barbadians were effectively disenfranchised. The various locations where Parliament met before it moved to its permanent home are also presented in an audiovisual display. The House of Assembly met in taverns and private houses in its early years; and for a while it shared premises in the Old Town Hall with the courts and the prisoners. It moved to the Parliament buildings in Bridgetown in 1874.

Other displays deal with critical moments in the political and social development of Barbados, and the major actors in these stories, including Sir Conrad Reeves, Clement Payne, Sir Grantley Adams, Dr Charles Duncan O'Neal, and Errol Barrow. The final section of the Museum of Parliament illustrates the way in which the Parliament of Barbados operates today, and the conditions under which Barbadians cast their votes.

A linking space between the Museum of Parliament and the National Heroes Gallery deals with slavery and then the emancipation of enslaved people in Barbados. This was the background to social and political developments on the island since its occupation by British settlers in 1627. The lives of all the Heroes, and their actions to overcome discrimination, disadvantage and disenfranchisement for the people of Barbados, arose from the background of slavery. Slavery was abolished in the British Empire in 1834 but the formerly enslaved had to undergo a period of 'apprenticeship' to their former owners until 1838, and poverty and powerlessness for emancipated slaves and their descendants in Barbados persisted for many years thereafter.

Two large murals in the linking space, by Barbadian artists Omowale Stewart and Coral Bernadine, include striking images of oppression and servitude; then rejoicing at Emancipation, and the achievement of eventual political and social reform. Stewart's mural, depicting 'Slavery', traces the pathway to servitude in Barbados from capture in Africa, to the journey in the holds of slave ships across the Middle Passage, then sale, exploitation and frequent punishment in the cane fields, sugar mills and great houses of Barbados. Stewart pays particular attention to the depiction of women working as field slaves, commenting in a video made for the Museum of Parliament and National Heroes Gallery that 'female slaves did a tremendous amount of physical work in Barbados'. The centrepiece of the mural is two large portraits of a male and a female slave, a young man and woman both wearing punishment collars and restraints; 'instruments of torture', says Stewart. The anger in their eyes is palpable.[245]

---

[245] *Concepts of Heroism,* National Heroes Gallery, Barbados, video narrated by Alissandra Cummins and Allison Thompson, Barbados, 2007.

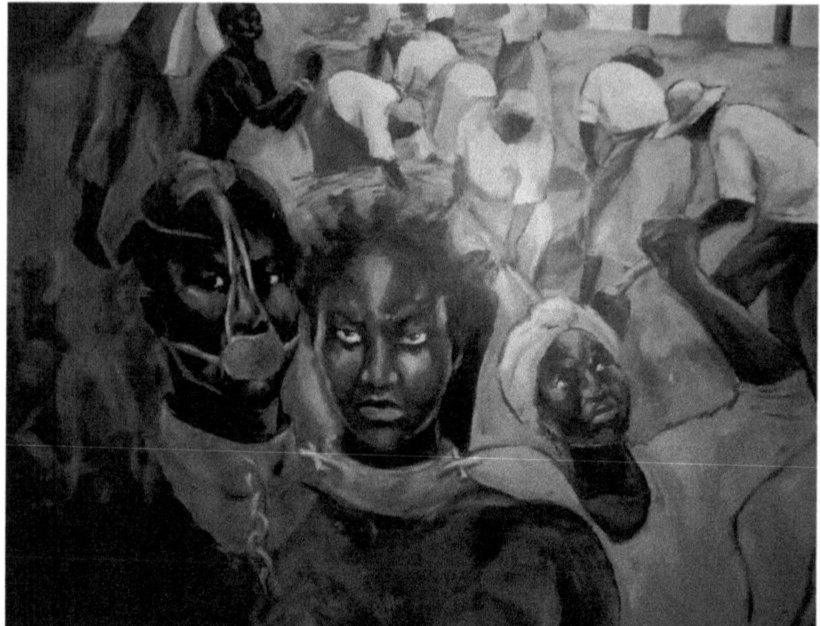

Slavery Mural by Omowale Stewart, National Heroes Gallery and Museum of Parliament (Photo Credit: Author)

Bernadine's 'Emancipation' mural has a centrepiece of a pair of hands in the moment of being unshackled, and images referencing the famous engraving of the moment of Emancipation and the well-known song *"Lick and Lock Up Done Wid"*. Her work also includes images of the key players associated with political progress in Barbados, Sir Grantley Adams and Errol Barrow, and social advances represented by women from a village on a pathway towards higher education and a young man in academic dress heading towards the future.

A National Heroes Gallery had been planned since 1998, when the Order of National Hero of Barbados was instituted. Once the decision had been made to use some of the spaces in the refurbished West Wing of the Public Buildings for this purpose, the question was: how to represent the National Heroes? The island already displays several representational sculptures of the Heroes: the Hero of resistance to slavery, Bussa, is honoured by a prominently displayed sculpture by Karl Broodhagen; Sir Grantley Adams, Sir Frank Walcott, Clement Payne and Sir Garfield Sobers have also been commemorated in portrait sculptures; and recently a large sculpture of Errol Barrow was created by Saint Lucian sculptor, Ricky George, for Independence Square in Bridgetown.[246]

---

[246] The 'Emancipation' statue by Karl Broodhagen (1973) is universally called the 'Bussa statue' in Barbados; the sculptures of Sir Grantley Adams (1997) and Sir

The National Heroes Gallery interpretation took a different direction. Ten artists were commissioned to create iconic representations of each of the Heroes. These would express the qualities of each Hero, the attributes of heroism they represent, or make reference to aspects of their careers, or both. The result is an intriguing collection of sculptures that represent the ten National Heroes of Barbados: Bussa, Sarah Ann Gill, Samuel Jackman Prescod, Clement Payne, Dr. Charles Duncan O'Neal, Sir Grantley Adams, Errol Barrow, Sir Hugh Springer, Sir Frank Walcott and Sir Garfield Sobers, all of whom, as National Heroes of Barbados, are referred to by the title of 'Right Excellent'. The ten sculptural icons embody the qualities and evoke aspects of the lives of each of the Heroes, and the social conditions in which they operated. The Heroes' stories and icons are grouped in themes - Faith and Freedom, Social Justice, Democracy, and Excellence - to indicate the ideals and qualities that motivated the Heroes' actions.

The sculptures display considerable diversity in both their forms and in the materials of which they are composed. Nevertheless, in their various ways they embody what their creators see as the distinctive identity of Barbados and its people, and their passionate identification with the qualities displayed by the National Heroes of Barbados.

A number of the artists who created the sculptural icons for the National Heroes Gallery used material drawn from Barbados' natural and cultural environment. Bill Grace used the coralstone from which the island is formed to create his monolith commemorating Sir Grantley Adams. The sculpted coralstone has coloured glass mosaic pieces representing the islands of the Caribbean embedded in its surface, with blue glass signifying the nations that are part of CARICOM, the successor to the West Indies Federation of which Sir Grantley was the first and only prime minister between 1958 and 1962. The vertical alignment of the monolith means that Barbados appears at the top.

John Burgess, in his representation of 1816 slave rebellion leader Bussa, also used coralstone as the base for his sculpture of severed feet, cane bills, and steel stalks of sugarcane, to represent the geological structure of Barbados. Juliana Inniss and Wayne Cezair combined coralstone with clay, galvanized iron, and purpleheart timber to create a large 'X' to represent Samuel Jackman Prescod and his achievement in bringing the vote to coloured people in Barbados. Their structure incorporates references to the class structure of Barbados, and to the landscape and seascape of the island. Purpleheart timber ties the whole structure together - as an imported timber from other parts of the Caribbean, it links Barbados to its wider context. In *Concepts of Heroism,* a video presentation about the National Heroes Gallery, Juliana Inniss expressed her objective in creating the sculpture for Barbadians

---

Garfield Sobers (2002) are also by Karl and Virgil Broodhagen; the sculpture of Sir Frank Walcott is by Jason Hope, and the portrait bust of Clement Payne is by Arthur Edwards. Ricky George's sculpture of Errol Barrow was unveiled in Independence Square on Errol Barrow Day, 21 January 2007.

and visitors to the island alike: 'I hope they see Barbados - the things about Barbados that they take for granted.'[247]

Other sculptors utilised the beautiful mahogany wood that is plentiful on the island. Goldie Spieler, watercolourist and ceramicist, found a large piece of mahogany on which to mount painted ceramic panels representing the only woman Hero of Barbados, Sarah Ann Gill, who she described as 'full of faith, God's woman'. The mahogany, located in a ship-builder's yard, is said to have come from a tree that was estimated as 250 years old, so would have been growing in Barbados in Sarah Ann Gill's lifetime.[248] Don Small carved an 'open door' of mahogany with a scene in high relief of labour activist Clement Payne addressing the Barbadian masses in 1937, encouraging them to join labour unions. The open door, said Small, symbolises Payne's role in that he 'gave encouragement of what is possible', and 'let them know they have the power to change things'.[249]

Two other sculptors also worked in Barbadian mahogany. Kenneth Blackman carved an immense flame to express the character of Dr Charles Duncan O'Neal, who 'carried the light' and led the movement for democratic reform in Barbados in the early twentieth century. Onkphra Wells wanted to 'show transcendence in the beauty of Barbadian mahogany', and fashioned the wood into a fluid representation of Sir Garfield Sobers batting. For Wells, 'Garfield Sobers is a giant... in lifting himself he has lifted Barbados and the whole Caribbean'.[250]

Found objects also formed the basis for sculptures representing the Heroes. Dr. Lance Bannister created a monumental work from old car parts to represent Errol Barrow, first prime minister of independent Barbados, as a 'man of steel'. For Bannister, Errol Barrow was 'one of the greatest Heroes of Barbados ... a colossus over the political arena'. Ras Akyem chose to interpret labour leader, academic and former Governor-General of Barbados, Sir Hugh Springer, by means of a complex triptych that brings together all the elements of his subject's life and career in an intriguing installation, including a carved wooden suit jacket, shirt and tie. Akyem used a wide range of materials gathered from many contexts around the island - a kitchen table, material from the renovation of the Parliament buildings, chattel house boards - as well as objects to represent Springer's life in education, and the positions he occupied, encapsulating both Barbadian and Caribbean experiences.[251]

It is interesting that the only sculptor to use an overt symbol of Barbadian nationality - in this case the blue and yellow flag of Barbados with its broken trident device - in his depiction of a National Hero was a Saint Lucian, Ricky George. The flag of Barbados is draped around a globe held on high by a pair of hands, and surmounted by a dove, to represent Sir Frank Walcott's role in international organisations, with the hands representing trade union workers.

---

[247] Ibid.
[248] 1779–1866
[249] Ibid.
[250] Ibid.
[251] Ibid.

Audiovisuals in the National Heroes Gallery also feature lively calypsoes about political events and personalities (including one by Mighty Gabby, *'Riots in de Land',* commemorating the deadly riots of July 1937 after the deportation of Clement Payne); and dramatise historic events involving individual Heroes, such as the rebellion led by an enslaved African, Bussa, in 1816.

Nidhe Israel Museum, Bridgetown

Not far from the Parliament buildings, in Synagogue Lane, Bridgetown, is the Nidhe Israel Museum, part of the *Nidhe Israel* ('The Scattered of Israel') Synagogue and burial ground. The Synagogue was rebuilt in 1833 on the ruins of an earlier one destroyed by the hurricane of 1831. Officially opened in the adjacent Synagogue school in January 2008 with a mission to 'foster an understanding of the contribution of the Barbados Jewish community to the history of the island and to provide an environment for research and learning',[252] the museum celebrates the two major phases of the life of the Jewish community in Barbados.

Sephardic Jews from Brazil fleeing the Inquisition arrived in Barbados by 1654. They brought Brazilian methods of harvesting and processing sugar cane and constructing windmills, so were fundamental to the island's prosperity. They were also traders: the museum contains a wall of spices where visitors can sniff the aroma of each of these valuable commodities. The growth and then decline of the Sephardic Jewish community paralleled the fortunes of Barbados as a sugar producer. Many Jewish people began to leave the island in the mid-nineteenth century; by 1925 the community had dwindled to one person, who finally sold the building and closed the doors of the Synagogue.

The Jewish community in Barbados revived when Ashkenazi Jews, fleeing Nazi persecution in Europe, settled there from 1931 onwards. The Synagogue was returned to the Jewish community by Barbados's prime minister, Tom Adams, in 1980, on condition that the building was restored. This task was completed by 1987 through the leadership of the Barbados National Trust, local Jewish businessmen and the committed support of longstanding Jewish visitors to the island. Excavation of the site revealed a large range of artefacts - from ceramics to metal and stone objects - that are now housed in showcases set into the museum's floor. Each rests on a bed of sand, representing the sand floor thought to have been a feature of the first Synagogue, a reference to the sand of the wilderness in which the Children of Israel, led by Moses, wandered for 40 years. One showcase is empty, apart from a footprint embedded in the sand, a symbolic representation of transience, and the diasporic nature of the worldwide Jewish community, represented so effectively in this small but beautifully realised museum.

---

[252] *The Nidhe Israel Museum,* Synagogue Lane, Bridgetown, Barbados, c.2008.

The role of Eustace Maxwell Shilstone - a lawyer and a keen amateur historian and one of the founders of the Barbados Museum & Historical Society - in the preservation of the memory of the Jewish community in Barbados is described in an audiovisual presentation. Shilstone, who was not Jewish but was fascinated by Barbados' past, began the transcription of all the tombstone inscriptions in the Synagogue cemetery in the 1930s. His book, *Monumental Inscriptions in the Jewish Synagogue in Bridgetown,* was published by the Jewish Historical Society of London in 1958, and can still be purchased at the Nidhe Israel Museum.[253] Shilstone's work in capturing the story of the Jewish community in Barbados was the first instance of what has become an ongoing research interest of Barbadian historians, including Warren Alleyne and Dr. Karl Watson, who continue to engage with the history of this minority community that made crucial contributions to the island's economic base, and to its social and cultural diversity.

The Nidhe Israel Museum thus adds another layer to the complex story of Barbadian society as it is represented in the island's museums. Again, it demonstrates the powerful connections between Barbados and other parts of the world, and engages with the themes of emigration and immigration, with Barbados acting as a haven for persecuted Jews in two widely separated periods of history. It also adds another dimension to the story of Barbados' economic development as a sugar producer, which is not a monolithic one involving British planters and enslaved Africans alone, but also includes the role of Jewish innovators and merchants. This museum engages with a variety of audiences, from local Barbadians wishing to understand more about the complex story of their island's development, to visitors from overseas, particularly those of Jewish extraction, who would be fascinated to know the story of this community of the Diaspora.

George Washington House

Another museum in the World Heritage-listed Garrison precinct also features a story with the potential to attract a wide audience, particularly among US citizens and others interested in the connections between what were then colonies in the British Americas. This is the story of the young George Washington's visit to Barbados in 1751.

His visit lasted only two months, but it was the only time that the future first President of the United States of America ever left mainland North America. George Washington accompanied his sick brother Lawrence to Barbados in an (unsuccessful) attempt to cure the latter's tuberculosis. The brothers lived, while in Barbados, in what later became known as Bush Hill House, beside St Ann's Garrison on the outskirts of the island's capital, Bridgetown. Now it has been restored as a house museum, George Washington House, interpreting the period of the Washington brothers' visit, and contextualising their stay in terms of the island's economy and society,

---

[253] Ibid.

and its system of slavery. The restoration of George Washington House, supported by the Government of Barbados, was assisted by American sponsors, designers and by heritage experts at Colonial Williamsburg.

Three crucial things happened to George Washington in Barbados. He contracted smallpox and recovered; and he witnessed at first hand the full extent of the system of plantation slavery in a British colony where its oppressive nature was most vividly demonstrated. Barbados had a reputation as a 'killing field', where slaves were literally worked to death to produce the wealth that created some of the greatest fortunes of Georgian England.[254] Washington also encountered the full might of British military command, and took the opportunity to study the island's defences at James Fort and Charles Fort on Carlisle Bay as well.[255] It is thought that these experiences fuelled his aspirations to military command, so amply fulfilled in the years to come.

The smallpox Washington suffered in Barbados actually stood him in good stead: it gave him lifetime immunity from the dreaded disease which in the eighteenth century regularly killed 400,000 people a year in Europe; and which attacked the troops in the Revolutionary Wars against the British in North America in the mid-1770s. Slavery, though, was a more complicated issue for Washington. As a gentleman of Virginia, he was, as were many of the Founding Fathers of the United States, a slave owner, and he and his family benefited from the labour of enslaved people all their lives.

Nevertheless, he directed that, once his wife Martha had died, 'it is my Will & desire that all the Slaves which I hold in my *own right,* shall receive their freedom'.[256] Washington's attitude to slavery was ambivalent: did the scenes he witnessed as he rode on horseback around the plantations of Barbados plant the seed that led to this act of liberation at the end of his life?

A visit to George Washington House begins with a video presentation on his 1751 visit with Lawrence to Barbados. It shows the brothers sailing to the island, landing, and meeting members of the white plantocracy. In the video Washington is shown riding down alleyways of sugarcane cultivated by enslaved people. Once inside George Washington House, visitors can see the downstairs rooms and the kitchen, fitted up to represent the domestic surroundings the Washington brothers would have experienced during their stay. There is also archaeological material, excavated from a gully behind the House, on display.

---

[254] Henry Wiencek, *An Imperfect God: George Washington, His Slaves and the Creation of America,* Pan Books, London and Basingstoke, 2005, p. 132.
[255] Hunt, 'Colonial Riches in Barbados'.
[256] Quoted in Wiencek, p. 354

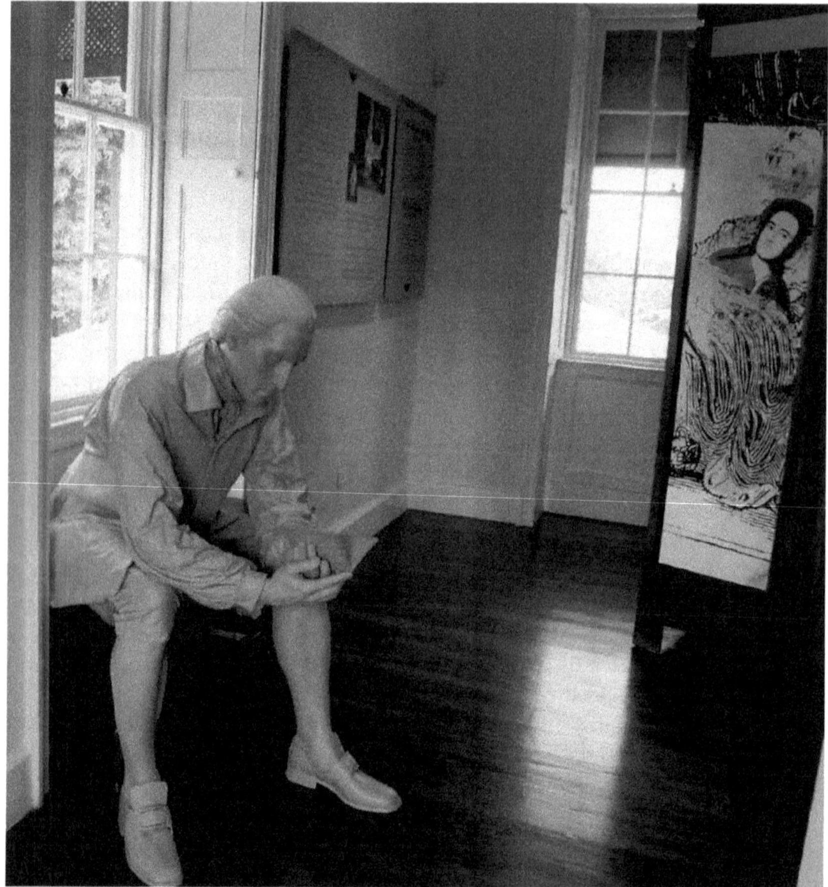

George Washington Reading Letter interpretive display, George Washington House, Barbados (Photo Credit: Author)

The upstairs floor houses interpretive displays on the Washington brothers and their visit, the Barbadian economy and the system of slavery George Washington saw operating in Barbados. The Washington connection with Barbados is only one of many between the island and the North American colonies, and other links are developed here.[257] There was frequent trade between the two when both were part of the colonial network forming the British Americas. There was also migration from over-populated Barbados to North America, where migrants settled on the eastern seaboard, particularly in

[257] Tristram Hunt has asserted that 'The George Washington House Museum overplays its hand when it suggests you cannot understand the American revolution without the Barbados connection. But what this museum does emphasise - in another fine 18th-century domestic setting - is how Barbados and the Thirteen Colonies of America formed part of a broader Atlantic Empire.' Hunt, 'Colonial Riches in Barbados'.

the Carolinas. Texas also boasts Barbadian connections: Austin, Texas was named after a Barbadian; while the Maverick family, whose name has entered the language, is also of Barbadian origin.[258]

Another tourist market segment can be tapped as a result of the work carried out at George Washington House. The House forms part of the historic precinct of the Garrison Savannah, Bridgetown, and enhances the Caribbean Georgian ambience of this area, adding to its potential to attract the many thousands of people worldwide who are interested in recapturing eighteenth-century atmosphere in a tropical environment.

Conclusion

The new museums and heritage displays created in Barbados over the last ten years offer diverse visitor experiences to captivate both local and international audiences, and demonstrate the depth, diversity and drama of the island's history. These museums also represent the highly successful result of public/private partnership, which has been encouraged over the last decade as part of strengthening the social contract within the wider community. They constitute an invaluable resource in educating young Barbadians and those of more mature years in the nature of their history and multiple heritages; and provide a window into the complex identity of this island nation for those visitors who are privileged to discover them.

References

Barbados Museum & Historical Society, *Africa: Connections and Continuities,* interpretive panel.

Barbados Tourism Investment Inc., 'Barbados - Going World Class', http://barbadostourisminvestment.com/news_details.cfmPnews-ID=io, accessed May 2009.

Barrow, Errol 1966. 'No Loitering on Colonial Office premises', Address to the Barbados Constitutional Conference, London, July 1966.

Burrowes, Marcia, 2012. 'Losing our Masks: Masquerade and Changing Concepts of Barbadian Identity', Heritage Lecture delivered 14 June 2012, Bridgetown, Barbados, http://www.barbadoscropoverfestival/ com/festival-news/522-exploring-the-changes-in-concept..., accessed 9 July 2012.

_______ 2013. Losing our Masks: Traditional Masquerade and Changing Constructs of Barbadian Identity, *International Journal of Intangible Heritage*, Vol. 8, pp. 37 – 54.

Cummins, Alissandra, {1994} 1996. 'The "Caribbeanisation" of the West Indies: The Museum's Role in the Development of National Identity', Kaplan, Flora E.S. (ed.), *Museums and the Making of*

[258] Sarah Venable, *From Bush Hill House to George Washington House: The Story of a Restoration,* Bush Hill Tourism Trust Inc., Barbados, 2007, p.21.

"Ourselves": The Role of Objects in National Identity, Leicester University Press, London and New York.

Cummins, Alissandra and Thompson, Allison, 2007. *Concepts of Heroism,* National Heroes Gallery, Barbados, video.

Hunt, Tristram, 2011. 'Colonial Riches in Barbados', *The Observer*, 13 November 2011.

Nidhe Israel Museum, Synagogue Lane, Bridgetown, Barbados, 2008.

Venable, Sarah, 2007. *From Bush Hill House to George Washington House: The Story of a Restoration,* Bush Hill Tourism Trust Inc., Barbados.

Wiencek, Henry, 2005. *An Imperfect God: George Washington, His Slaves and the Creation of America,* Pan Books, London and Basingstoke.

Chapter 12

The Memorial Museum of the Dominican Resistance:

Its Composition and Role in Society

Luisa De Peña Díaz

Exploring Different Types of Museums and Their Collections: Memorial Museums

Introduction

Museums are dynamic organizations in the service of society that reflect the changes and challenges of today's world and contribute to the sustainable development of a nation. The traditional concept of a museum as a place devoted exclusively to the preservation of collections and objects no longer meets the needs of our present-day society that requires new avenues of development.

This new concept of the museum framed the development of the Memorial Museum of Dominican Resistance (MMDR), which adopted guidelines and orientations drafted by international institutions that specialize in memorial museums.

ICOM's International Committee of Memorial Museums for Victims of Crimes Against Humanity describes the objectives of a memorial museum:

> ... to promote responsible memory of history, foster cultural cooperation through education and the use of knowledge at the service of peace, and to pay tribute to victims of ideologically motivated crimes generated by states.
>
> Memorial museums adopt an unambiguous, critical position in regards to ideologies, practices, and concepts of governmental entities that stimulate persecution of persons. These museums commit to memory crimes their own governments perpetrated and they originate as the consequence of a grueling learning process that obliges citizens to ponder how to deal with such crimes, as a matter of public conscience.
>
> Memorial museums also caution the world that the safeguarding of fundamental rights is a vital necessity and call on humanity to oppose all inhumane acts.

From 1930 to 1961, the Dominican Republic endured one of the most oppressive regimes within the Latin American region; thousands of Dominicans lost their lives, were imprisoned and tortured. During this long period of oppression and death, the Trujillo government extended its policy of state terrorism beyond national borders. The involvement of foreign nationals who put their lives on the line for the Dominican cause is an outstanding case of universal fraternity worthy of recognition.

Nearly 40 years after the tyranny came to an end, the Dominican government finally is able to sponsor a programme of restoration of the memory. The study of the Dominican Resistance movement and struggles for democracy, freedom, and respect for human rights is an educational tool that contributes to the creation of a more conscience-based society.

The Museum: Its Characteristics and Societal Role

The MMDR's main location is the *Palacete Vicini,* a nineteenth-century construction in the colonial city of Santo Domingo de Guzman, Dominican Republic.

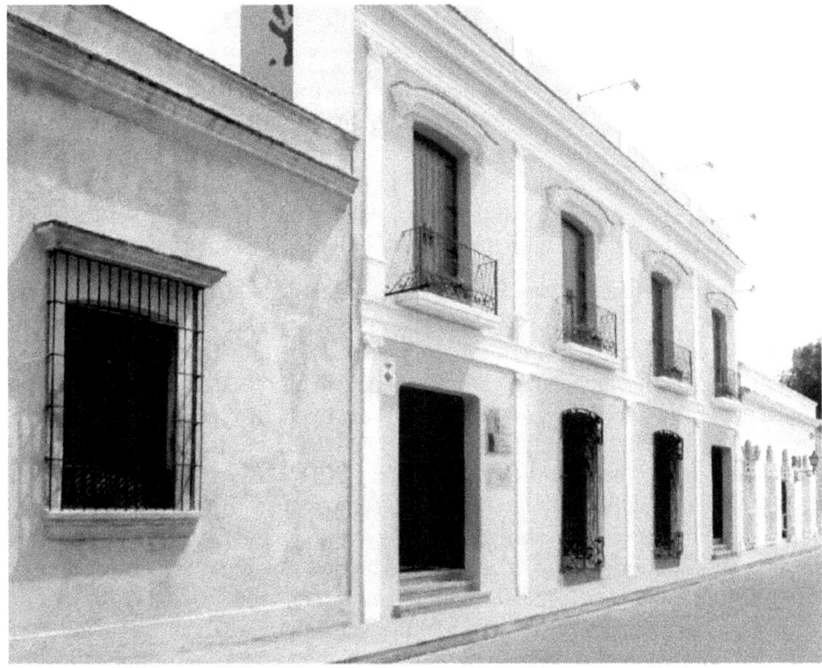

Front Façade, Memorial Museum of the Dominican Resistance
(Photo Credit: Memorial Museum of the Dominican Resistance)

Museum extensions include as a site of conscience the basement of the former *"Prison del 9"*, which operated as the Trujillo dictatorship's principal center of extermination from 1959-1961. Its second extension is the Memorial Hall to Heroes of Constanza, Maimon and Estero Hondo. It also has a cooperative agreement to jointly maintain the *Casa Museo Hermanas Mirabal* (Mirabal Sisters House Museum).

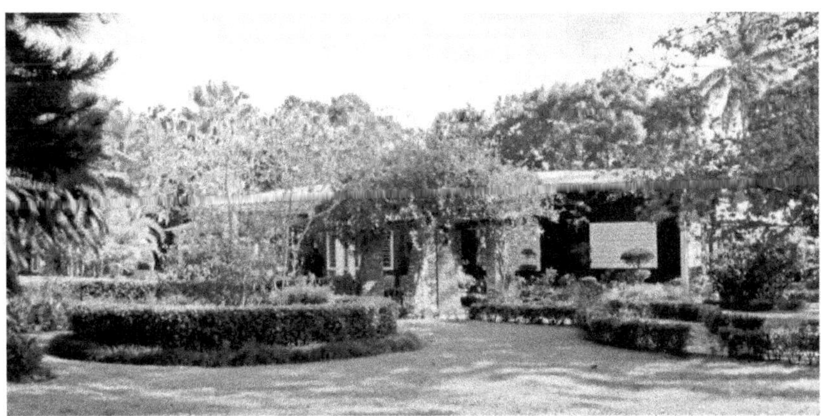

Mirabal Sisters House Museum
(Photo Credit : Memorial Museum of the Dominican Resistance)

Presidential Decrees 282-07 and 404-11 created the museum, defining its mission as follows:

> The Memorial Museum of Dominican Resistance shall be responsible for compiling, organizing, cataloguing, preserving, researching, informing, and exhibiting tangible and intangible national heritage assets related to the struggles of several generations of Dominican men and women during the dictatorship of Rafael L. Trujillo, and shall highlight facts and impact of the same.

The Memorial Museum was founded as a place dedicated to the recovery of the memory of the horrors of terrorism exercised as state policy by the dictatorships of Rafael L. Trujillo Molina and Joaquin Balaguer, while also chronicling the heroic struggles of several generations of Dominican people for democratic freedom. The museum is envisioned as a mechanism to strengthen elements of national identity by contributing to future generations' understanding of the recent national history. The museum is an environment for social and cultural interchange, a setting that fosters the pursuit of knowledge not only of history, but also psychology and pedagogy. Conceived as an institution for a range of research, art, educational, and cultural activities, the MMDR advances critical thinking and reflection. From this point of departure, an array of other programmes and activities can be developed, centring on the integral development of the human being's personal and social dimensions.

Administrative System

A private non-profit corporation, the museum administration draws from innovative management models consisting of a multidisciplinary, open and participatory administrative structure with an operative organization that aims to position itself in society as an agent of change and development.

The following four entities comprise the museum's administrative structure:

1. The *Federación de Fundaciones Patrióticas* (Federation of Patriotic Foundations), consisting of several non-governmental organizations of survivors and victims' family members, is the museum's proprietor.
2. The tripartite Board of Directors is comprised of representatives of the Dominican government, civil society, and survivors, who are permanent Board members.
3. The Museum Advisory Board is the entity vested with upholding the museum's mission.
4. The Friends of the Museum Foundation is a support organization of the Federation that raises funds for the museum's operating budget.

Operating System

Museum operation is the responsibility of a general director appointed by the Federation, an administrative director, and an executive-technical director. In addition, six specialized administrative departments have the three-pronged structure described below:

1. *Centro de Registro Nacional de Victimas, Torturados y Desaparecidos* (National Registry Center for Victims, Torture Survivors and Disappeared Persons)

   The visitor has access to information through computerized lists, biographies and photographs of victims of the dictatorship's state terrorism. If the name of a family member, friend or acquaintance is missing from the roster, the visitor can provide information on a form for verification by the Museum Research Department.

   Our current records indicate that an estimated 50,000 persons endured repression or were forcibly 'disappeared' during the dictatorship period.

   The Registry Center promotes the formulation of state policy for moral, social and material reparation of victims.

2. *Centro de Documentación y Referencia y Archivo de la Resistencia* (Documentation, Resource and Archival Center of Resistance).

   Visitors have access to computerized documentation, photographs, and audiovisual material concerning resistance movements during this period of Dominican history. The archives are open for individual and group research.

   The museum also makes available the Resistance Archives, which serve as a repository for the Patriotic Foundation archives, as well as private archives already entrusted to the museum. There is a safety deposit box in which personal files and objects are protected while maintaining original ownership rights. The Museum has been granted the right to use and publish in conformity with quality control standards for preservation of such heritage material.

3. Permanent exhibit and complementary areas

   In the museum vestibule, a mural by Ramon Oviedo, the great artist whose art portrayed Dominican resistance, greets visitors as they enter.

   The building has an auditorium, three temporary exhibit halls and an educational hall.

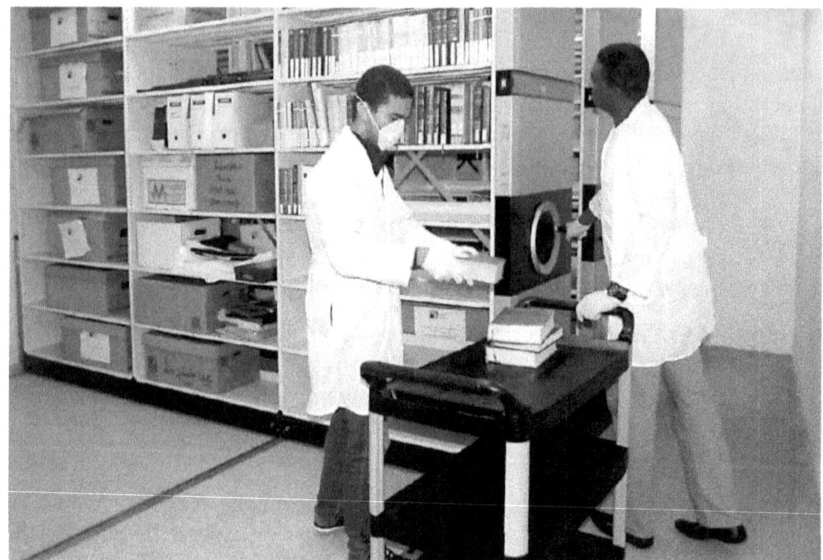

Collections Deposit (Photo Credit: Memorial Museum of the Dominican Resistance)

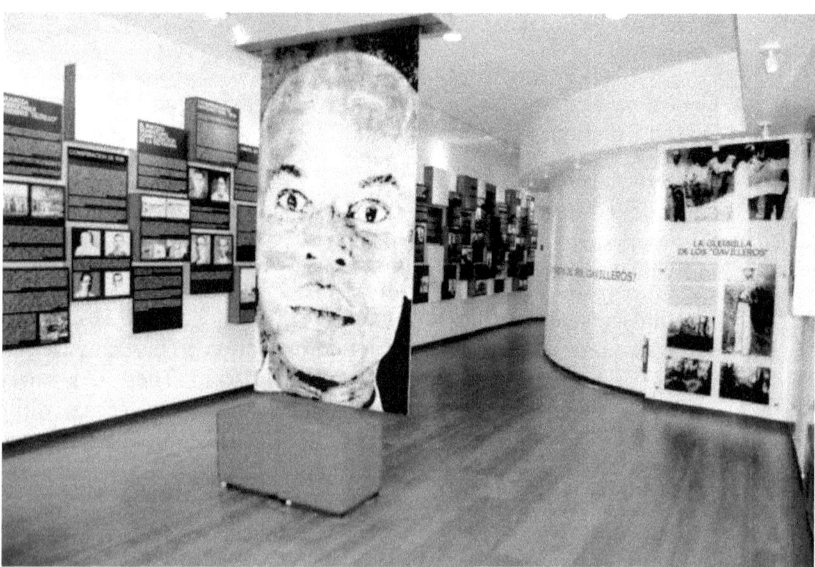

Permanent exhibition (Photo Credit: Memorial Museum of the Dominican Resistance)

The permanent exhibit begins in a hall called *"El Mito de la Era"* (The Myth of an Era), which analyzes the regime's system of propaganda that created various myths such as that of citizen security, economic boom, a corruption-free government and others.

This hall aims to expose the myths of the dictatorship, the effects of whose propaganda machine persist in Dominican society. Even today it is common to hear that peasants had shoes, but no mention is made of the fact that the shoe factory was Trujillo's private property and everyone was compelled to buy them. Or it is claimed that in those days people could sleep with the doors unlocked and wide open, while omitting the fact that the Secret Police (known as the SIM) might abduct you from your home, never to be seen again. Moreover, many Dominicans still refer to the despot with the nickname of *"El Jefe"* (The Boss), reminding us of the plaque citizens were ordered to hang at the entrance to their homes, that read *"En esta casa Trujillo es el Jefe."* (Trujillo is the Boss in this house.)

The next section of the museum takes visitors on a journey through time, back to 1916 when a repressive environment fuelled Trujillo's rise to prominence. Modern audiovisual resources include interactive systems and a hologram of the heroine Minerva Mirabal, resistance leader, who was murdered and hanged, along with her sisters Patria and Maria Teresa, on 25 November 1960. In their honour the United Nations declared this date International Day for the Elimination of Violence Against Women. This horrendous crime portended the dictatorship's own demise, as Minerva prophesied upon learning of the plot against her life: "If he kills me, I will stick out my arms from the grave and will be ever stronger." The men who six months later succeeded in ambushing the tyrant and taking justice into their own hands declared that the crime against the Mirabal sisters was pivotal in their decision.

The museum circuit encompasses the subsequent stages in the fall of the dictatorship, the war of 1965, the dictatorship of Joaquin Balaguer, who was President of the Dominican Republic when Trujillo was executed, ending with the beginning of the process of cleansing Trujillo's influence from the armed forces and the transition to full democracy in 1978.

Our tour concludes in the Contemplation Hall, a setting that encourages the visitor to reflect on the processes and struggles for freedom and basic rights. Here educational facilitators offer visitors the opportunity to consider national and international democratic processes, and to discuss current issues related to these processes.

At this juncture we offer an optional visit to the basement, where the torture chamber of the prison known as *"Cárcel de la 40"* displays torture instruments, the electric chair, and original audiotapes of torture sessions. Only visitors who are at least twelve years of age are allowed to enter this area.

The Collection

The Memorial Museum of Dominican Resistance collection traces events related to the country's history between 1916 and 1978 associated with the struggle for freedom and democracy. Originating from donations, the collection consists of more than 160,000 documents, photographs, films, objects, and books that belonged to individuals who participated in the resistance movement against dictatorship. The collection preserves elements of the

Dominican Republic's recent history and is available to the public through its permanent exhibit in the Documentation Center, where visitors and researchers may access computerized files and images, and the entire historic estate preserved in the collection.

The Dictatorship

The history of the Trujillo dictatorship, accurately described as a tyranny, spanned several decades. Resistance was constant and painful. Repression was systematic, very effective, and continues to have an impact on Dominican society and psyche even today.

The Dominican people learned valuable lessons about the struggle for democratic values; it is our obligation to share these lessons with the country and the world. For this reason, the museum regards education as a prime objective.

We describe that objective in the following terms:

> The MMRD was developed with students, teachers, police officers, Armed Forces personnel and the general public in mind. It is a place for remembering those who fell fighting for democracy, but above all it is an educational institution that will dedicate its mission to engendering consciousness in future generations about the value of life and the fundamental right to freedom, the right to express ideas without fearing the loss of one's family, dignity or life.

Education and Community Outreach Programmes

Education and community outreach programmes were designed to reach diverse audiences.

For our main public, students and teachers, we have educational visits, and a mini-workshop on human rights and democratic values. These are accompanied by guides for teachers to be used prior to the visit, a didactic kit for teachers and an educational CD-ROM for the use in the classroom after the visit. To these resources we add four workshops per year, aimed at teachers, on how to teach human rights in the classroom and on the importance of the rescue of historic memory. Finally twice a year we also offer open doors to teachers, when over a full day the museum education team conducts exchanges with teachers on our educational resources.

For the public made up of survivors and relatives we have three primary activities: the Tertulia of Resistance; Pillars of Heroism; and the piece of the month. Through these activities participants have the opportunity to discuss a specific topic; they can leave their testimony and especially start a catharsis, which involves dealing with the crimes and recognizing themselves as victims. The first is an open exchange where, after a formal presentation, a discussion begins among the attendees; the second is an interview recorded on their memories and experiences; and the piece of the month involves choosing a character and inviting family and friends to an exchange through a temporary exhibition.

We have also designed programmes to link both generations through the testimonial visit and family workshops. A testimonial visit is simply an exchange with a survivor and a group of students. The family workshops involve parents and children, grandparents and grandchildren in a dynamic of exchange where past experiences are compared with current situations.

Of course we have activities for a open public, unrelated directly to the museum and who we want to attract - the movie night, the sunsets in circulation of books, the nights of music in the courtyard - these activities open our doors to visitors who for various reasons do not know the museum. These programmes with the community are a first step to introducing them to our other educational programmes.

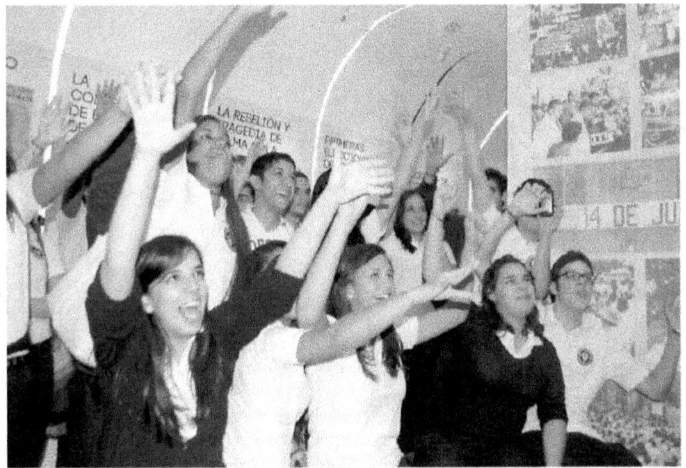

Students inside the permanent exhibition during a discussion (Photo Credit: Memorial Museum of the Dominican Resistance)

The Museum Today

The decree that created the museum introduced mandatory visits as part of the Dominican secondary school curriculum, as well as police and military academy programmes - an outstanding achievement for the institution.

The Memorial Museum of Dominican Resistance was accepted as an institutional member of the International Coalition of Museums of Historical Sites of Conscience. It is also a member of the International Council of Museums (ICOM), the Museums Association of the Caribbean (MAC) and the American Association of Museums (AAM).

In 2006 the United States Ambassador's Cultural Preservation Fund provided a grant to computerize the photographic and audiovisual collection for its preservation.

In 2007 Spain's Ministry of Culture awarded the museum a scholarship for the recovery of archives of repression.

At present the files of repression maintained in the Attorney General's office - until now off limits to the public - are in the process of computerization and classification.

The Museum's collection was inscribed on UNESCO's Memory of the World International Register in 2009.

The museum serves as an educational tool, imparting the legacy of the Dominican people to present and future generations of the world, to foster a society founded on a culture of peace, tolerance, no discrimination, truth, justice and respect for human rights.

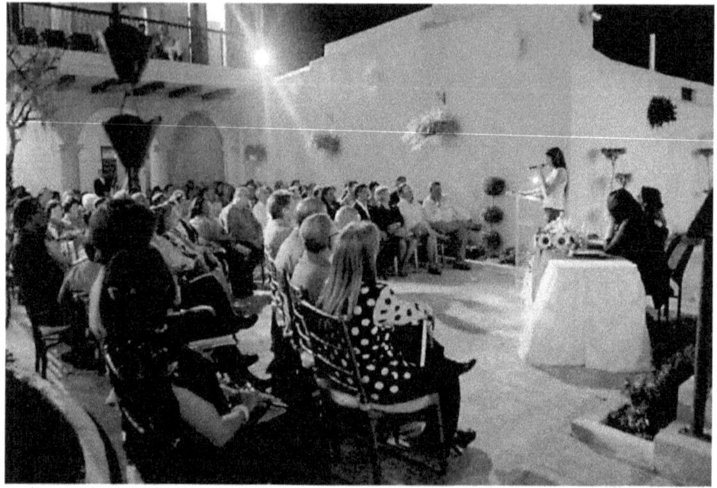

Open discussion with Victoria Donda, one of the children kidnapped by Argentina's dictatorship (Photo Credit: Memorial Museum of the Dominican Resistance)

Chapter 13

'Children Get Your Culture':

Museums, Individualism, and Nationalism in Jamaica

Rebecca Tortello

Children Get Your Culture: Jamaican Children and Their Museum Experiences

Introduction

The title of this chapter is inspired by the lyrics to the 1973 Bob Marley song, "Natty Dreadlocks" (Island Records): *"Children get your culture and don't stand there and gesture."* The word 'get' is critical, meaning both the need for young Jamaicans to:

i. be proactive and seize their culture;
ii. and better understand individual and national connections to their culture.

Marley's message still rings true in Jamaica today, speaking to a need that is arguably even greater given the rise of globalization and increase in movement of people, ideas and images; the global 'flows' so well described by Arjun Appadurai in his 1995 book *Culture and Modernity.*

Museum education programming has existed in Jamaica for over a century and the island now has close to 30 different museums. Yet although many of them have specific education programmes, the role of museums as educational institutions in Jamaica has not received the attention it has been accorded in developed countries. The small number of visitor studies conducted in Jamaica stands as a case in point. The rationale behind this research, conducted between 2001-2002, therefore included: (i) to consider whether the open, child-centred trend in museum exhibition development witnessed in many countries post-1960 was occurring in Jamaica; (ii) how museums interacted with schools; and (iii) what were the results of these interactions?

Brief Background on Jamaica and Museum Development on the Island

Jamaica is the third largest island in the Caribbean and the largest English-speaking island in the region. With a population of close to 2.7 million, the island experienced a steady rate of increasing emigration overall within the first decade of the twenty-first century (jumping from some 18,698 persons in 2000 to some 28,808 persons in 2007). It is important to note that the highest percentage of those leaving Jamaica consistently fall within the under eighteen-years-old range (JSLC, 2007, pp. 20.5-20.6). The Jamaican economy is fragile, with an excess of imports over exports, and a heavy internal debt. Education attracts the highest government expenditure next to debt repayment (on average fifteen per cent of the annual budget with debt servicing). Significant inequity remains, however, as is indicated by the amount spent on students in different socioeconomic levels (i.e. by consumption group, the wealthiest quintile spent more than twice that of the poorest quintile on education-related items (JSLC, p. 4.13-4). This is a basic reflection of the inequity that plagues the country itself, where the consumption rates of the highest socio-economic levels are more than six times that of the lowest (JD$355,084 vs. JD$53,960) (JSLC, 2007, p. 2.3).

Yet literacy rates are said to be close to the 85 percentile for both men and women, and Jamaica can boast universal primary enrollment, but not attendance (MOE Briefing, 2008). The average teacher-student ratio is 1-35 and some classes can have as many as 45-50 students (Task Force Report on Education, 2002). It is challenging to make those loud, crowded spaces, often divided by blackboards, into dynamic ones open to individual explorations and learning. The tendency is to use 'chalk and talk'/orderly rote teaching methodology.

Historically, Caribbean islands were alternately pawns of war over territory and sugar-producing components that oiled the wheels of British mercantilism (Cummins, 1994). Today experiences include the strong effect of American media, business practice and development standards. The very existence of museums in the region parallels the development of colonialism and post colonialism, as museums were first established by colonial governments largely for the entertainment of the upper classes as well as to showcase the countries' natural resources, promote a better understanding of the culture of the Mother Country, and hopefully foster investment. Their exhibition formats reflected the didactic models of education identified with that time period.

Jamaica's museums include both government and privately run institutions, ranging from the Institute of Jamaica (IOJ) founded in 1879 (government) to the Bob Marley Museum (private), to installations at historic houses and heritage sites (government). Although visitor statistics are not readily available for most Jamaican museums/heritage sites because the data is simply not routinely collected, surveys of museum reports at the Institute of Jamaica indicate that most of its museums see less than 15,000 visitors annually, with the exception of the small museum located inside Port Royal's Fort Charles, which is a family and tourist venue and sees approximately 20,000 visitors. It is important to note that the privately run Bob Marley museum sees close to 30,000 visitors (Museum Board minutes, 2011). This is likely due to the fact that the museum is based at the home of the late reggae superstar and as such is a popular tourist stop despite the fact that Kingston is not considered to be one of the more popular Jamaican tourist destinations. The low visitation at the Institute of Jamaica is partly because of weak marketing on the part of the government's museum network, and also because sustainable partnerships with tour companies to bring visitors to these sites have yet to be firmly established. Of those Jamaicans who do visit government-run museums, reviews of the visitor statistics collected and referred to in museum reports indicate that the majority tend to be schoolchildren, especially in June - the last month of the school year - when schools traditionally take trips, and October, which is recognised as national heritage month.

The Educational Value of Museums

Museums can allow the visitor to make his/her own meaning of what he/she sees and can therefore encourage greater open-endedness, critical choice and thought. Learning in museums is individual, intellectual, emotional and physical, as well as both planned and unplanned (Falk and Dierking, 2000, Hein 1998). The ability to be presented with an array of information, to distill it and choose that component deemed most interesting/relevant is a vital skill in an increasingly global world where messages and technology abound (Falk and Dierking, 2000, Halpin, 1997, Hooper-Greenhill, 1992 and 1994, Karp and Lavine, 1991, and Hein 1998).

Museums, if seen as accessible in every sense of the word, can present educational opportunities that provide a degree of self-directed identity development - certainly an important component of individual development, and therefore of any educational system and of national development.

Museum collections and exhibits can remind us that teaching and learning are lifelong endeavours that do not only occur in school. This connection between museums and the holistic, pedagogical philosophy of learning for life is well expressed by Alberta Sebolt-George in her chapter, 'Critical Issues for Museums in our Expanding Role':

> In the education of a nation, however, as with that of an individual, the greater part of learning occurs outside the school or formal setting. We learn what we live. While the classroom offers a special kind of learning, our communities and the rich resources of museums have an important role to play. To educate for life - not merely for living - is the real mandate ... (Pittman-Gelles, 1999, p. 38).

Research Design

A collective, qualitative, exploratory and largely descriptive case study, this research compares the museum experiences of twelve groups of urban and rural Jamaican primary school students, including in-school and after school visits. In total 215 students ranging in age from six to thirteen-years-old were interviewed. The sample represented groups of museum visitors from three different parishes (districts) - one urban, one semi-urban and one rural. It included nine school groups (three from private schools and six from public schools), and three after-school groups. One child from each group visiting a museum was observed in detail and also interviewed individually; along with 44 others drawn from larger focus groups into smaller interview groups of four to six students each.

The four museums chosen for this study represented a cross section of subject matter, size and location. All have collections and missions in keeping with the International Council of Museums' (ICOM) definition of a museum as a socially responsible institution dedicated to serving the public.

Data analysis included a review of available annual museum reports and newspaper articles, as well as academic writing on museum development within the region. Coding was based on themes that emerged during the research, and conclusions were made based on triangulation of all the data.

The Children's Voices

Before presenting the children's general reactions to their museum experiences it is important to understand the context in which their museum visits occurred. Overall, the museum visits were arranged for, and not by, the children. They went because they had to go as part of their regular school day, or as part of a pre-organized after-school activity. Yet all except a few children said they would visit the museum again. Those few who said they did not want to return gave no reason for this position other than "because I just don't want to go back." All, however, indicated a desire to visit new museums.

Museum experience was taken to mean the time spent, and activities participated in, during a museum visit, be it in school or after school. Museum experiences were considered from emotional, sensual, and intellectual levels (Hudson, 1999, p. 377). They involved multiple senses and physical, personal, and sociocultural perspectives - echoing Falk and Dierking's (2000) Contextual Model of Learning (p. 10). These experiences were seen to have revolved around individual connections; therefore, so did the children's reactions and reasons. Many were also object based, whether they were allowed to touch the object or not.

The following experiences of five children represent a cross-section of ages, socioeconomic levels, locations and museum experiences. Each one exemplifies one of the five major themes that emerged during the research.

First Theme—Tara—Experience within an Experience

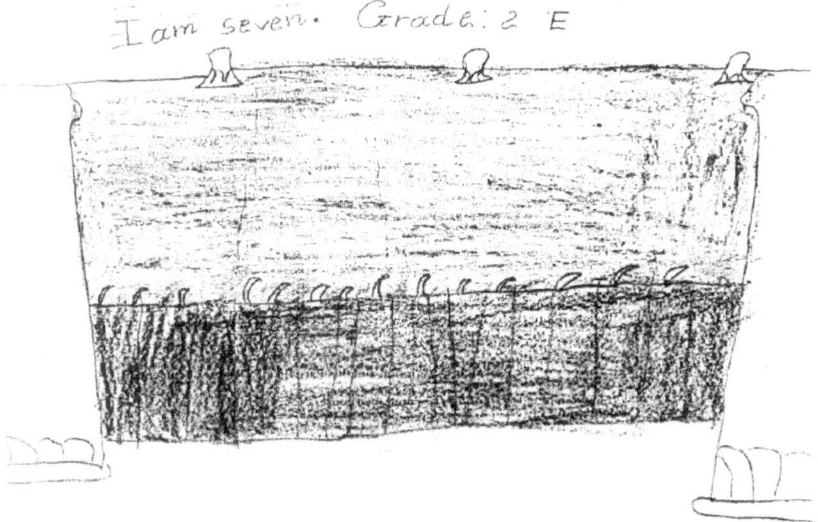

Tara - Experience within the Experience (Photo Credit: Author)

Seven-year-old Tara was from a middle socioeconomic neighbourhood and in second grade at a private school in a semi-rural area, located near to the IOJ's People's Museum of Craft and Technology in Spanish Town (a semi-urban area). During an interview a few days after her visit, she drew the verandah of Old King's House, the nineteenth-century Governor-General's residence, with bold, dramatic black strokes. Tara said she liked this part of her museum experience best because she remembered having seen a picture of it in the museum before being able to actually go and stand in the very same spot shown in the picture. "It was," she said, pointing to the centre of the verandah, (and echoing information shared with the students by the tour guide when they visited the site) "where the governor stood and said that all the slaves were free." Both her drawing and her statement that when she walked around the verandah, touched the railing and stood in the spot she drew she could "feel the history" indicate a merging of passive and active educative styles grounded in reflection. Tara explained that the spot she drew was important to her because her ancestors were slaves. By singling it out in her memory she may have been attempting to explore her own connection to the legacy of slavery in Jamaica. Perhaps in choosing to draw a place where she had stood and touched, a place she knew was connected to a significant period of Jamaican history, Tara was recording a feeling of individual and national significance that she felt when she stood there. Perhaps she was trying to indicate a feeling of awe. Either way, it is no surprise that she drew it large enough to cover the width of her piece of paper. In addition, the drawing, in its use of a single colour and its large size, also reflects Tara's ability to be contemplative and absorb the individual and national meaning of the space.

Second Theme—John—Seeing New Things

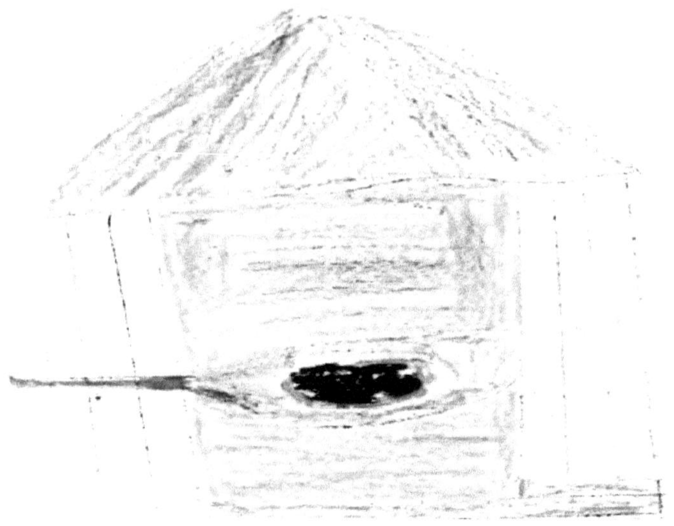

John – Seeing New Things (Photo Credit: Author)

Unlike Tara, eleven-year-old John was from a low socioeconomic neighbourhood and attended an inner-city public school. He also visited the IOJ's People's Museum and had the same tour guide as Tara, but his visit took place over six months prior to his being interviewed. John's favourite part was the experience he had when entering the blacksmith's hut located inside the museum. This indicates how individualistic museum reactions can be to tours given by the same person and involving the same objects. John drew the blacksmith's hut with coal being burned in preparation for shoeing. His active educative style was reflected in his use of multiple colours, and his explanation of how he liked being able to go into the hut and touch the tools because he could pretend to be a blacksmith putting on a horse's shoes. John's memory of his class visit was strong. He explained that he was interested in the blacksmith's hut because he liked horses. John also admitted that before visiting the museum he had never heard of a blacksmith or a blacksmith's hut and that he never knew horses wore shoes. Having had this experience within an experience, he said he now knew what horseshoes looked like, who made them, why and how. He did say that he had noticed that horses wore "things on their feet, but I did never know where they did come from."

Third Theme—Bianca—Seeing Old Things Differently

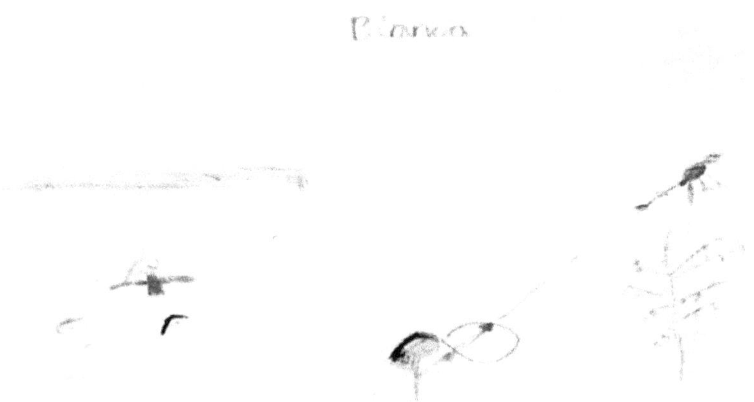

Bianca – Seeing Old Things Differently (Photo Credit: Author)

Unlike Tara and John, seven-year-old Bianca was from a high socioeconomic neighbourhood and attended a rural private school. Bianca visited the small Hanover Museum and drew herself in her picture, remembering a museum trip from over a year ago. She drew herself shooting at a bird with a bow and arrow. Bianca explained that she was "a Taino Indian hunting her 'prey' so she could 'eat' it". Bianca explained that although she had seen bows and arrows before in books, it was the first time she had ever shot one herself, after having been shown how by the tour guide and given the chance to take a turn using the child-sized bow and arrow at the museum site. It was also the first time she said that she had ever thought of birds as a type of food eaten by people. By putting herself in the centre of her drawing, having all eyes on her, having all action stem from her, and having that action be successful, Bianca made the experience positive, and also tried to make the experience her own by representing herself in action as one of the subjects on display. She may have been indicating the strength of the individual connection she felt with this experience within a museum experience. Her use of bright colours simply reinforced her excitement, energy, enthusiasm, and eagerness.

Fourth Theme—Arthur—Access to Quiet Space

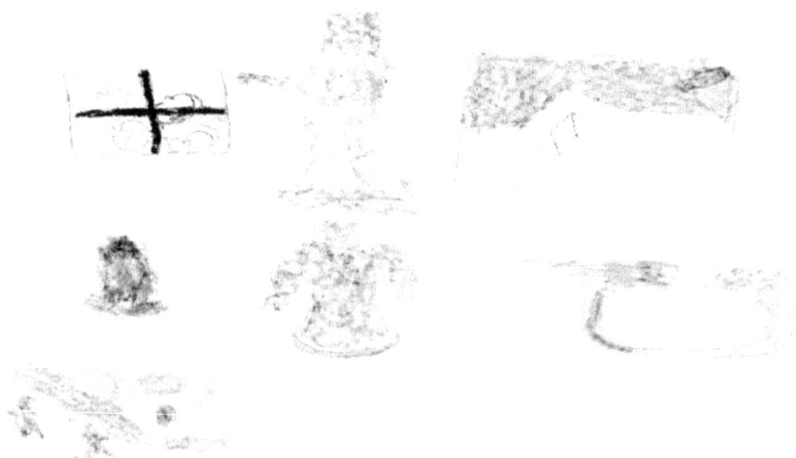

Arthur – Access to Quiet Space (Photo Credit: Author)

Arthur, a twelve-year-old inner-city student, visited the National Gallery of Jamaica located in downtown Kingston. He said that what was important to him was the quietness of the space, the mood he felt in the museum; the time it gave him to think on his own with no expectations. Arthur explained that it is not often very quiet living in inner-city Kingston and being a part of a crowded classroom, so he appreciated the chance to think in quietness. Although he did not include it in his drawing, Arthur's favorite part of the tour was the *East Meets West* sculpture because, "when you look at it and even when you are just in the gallery, you feel as if you in a mood - far away, in a place where time is still and you justa watch things go by. Is hope you hope you coulda be in there forever." Arthur drew a variety of images, reflecting the range of impressions this experience evoked for him.

Fifth Theme—Tina—Our Place

This theme was seen most at the Hanover Museum, the smallest, and due to the very personal involvement of the executive director, the most intimate. In many ways, the museum served as a community centre for these children. They managed to forge a relationship with the museum that was based not primarily on their reactions to the museum's collections, but on their sustained relationship with a person, the executive director, whom they all cited as the reason for their regular visits. These children spoke of how she welcomed them and remained interested in them as individuals. Tina, a thirteen-year-old, from a middle-to-low socioeconomic background, said that she liked to come to the museum simply because she could sit and think and chat with the executive director. Although she did not put her thoughts into images, the power of her words resonates:

> This place is our place. We can come here and no one troubles us. We can go wherever we want and look at what we want, when we want for as long as we want.

A few years after this research was conducted, the Hanover Museum became part of the Institute of Jamaica's national network of history museums, joining the People's Museum and four other museums operating in different locations island-wide.[259] However, the director has since retired and the museum was closed for repairs for a lengthy period. It was reopened in 2011 showcasing new exhibits including one that explains the history of the parish of Hanover. Notably, this exhibit features interactive flip charts and multimedia installations to be more inclusive and also attract young audiences.

As examples of personal meaning maintained over lengthy pieces of time, these children's reactions to their museum experiences indicate that Jamaican museums can present equal, open-ended educational opportunities that might result in a degree of self-directed identity development which is certainly an important component of any national educational system. As the transmission of ideas, goods, money, services, and people across national boundaries continues to grow, it is also one that is increasingly worthy of study.

Conclusion

Regardless of how the rationale for the museum trips was perceived, and notwithstanding the fact that this study did not aim to analyze differences by gender, age, socioeconomic status, geography, or time elapsed between museum experience and interviews, no great differences emerged in these categories in terms of reactions to the museum experiences themselves. The reactions were overwhelmingly positive.[260] This speaks to the need for individual connections to be made in the formation of a national identity, and for a new approach to teaching and learning that maximizes informal education and the use of institutions such as museums in the regular curriculum, so that the goals are aimed at learning "for life and not merely for living".

The implementation of stronger museum-school connections will not be easy for reasons that are primarily psychological, administrative, and financial.

---

[259] The five museums in the Institute of Jamaica's national network of history museums are: The Fort Charles Museum at Port Royal, the People's Museum of Craft and Technology in Spanish Town, St. Catherine, the Museums' Division's Exhibition Gallery and additional exhibition space at the Institute of Jamaica in Kingston, the Museum of St. James in Montego Bay, the Hanover Museum in Lucea and the Taino Museum at White Marl, St. Catherine. The latter was closed in 2010 for repairs and due to high incidences of violence. The artefacts were returned to the national collection for safe-keeping and a more viable museum location is still to be confirmed.

[260] All could serve as the basis for future studies on the roles of museums in developing countries.

Psychologically, many who have not experienced the benefit of the type of open-ended experiential learning to be found in museums may be inherently skeptical. Similarly, many schooled in the more traditional didactic method of teaching may not be open to including new methods of teaching and learning, and may question the usefulness of new methods in meeting the national standards on which school and teacher performance tend to be based. In addition, the benefits of facilitating self-driven learning (the type of pedagogy this study advocates as present in Jamaican museums) are harder to prove because this type of learning is aimed at long-term rather than short-term gain. It can also be hard to assess quantitatively and show returns for money expended, an increasingly common condition of grant funding. The incorporation of museums into the formal curriculum is a delicate matter because, if it is overdone, the spontaneity that leads to memorable museum moments, the magic that can be found from individual connections made with things seen and done on a museum visit, can be threatened.

Lastly, to heighten their role in the informal education system, Jamaican museums have to overcome numerous obstacles, including dispelling perceptions of elitism, presenting themselves as an attractive, fun leisure-time option for people across all socioeconomic levels, and competing with concerts, football games, the movies, the beach, and so on. Currently, many museums are not open for the entire weekend, or even on Saturdays, when much leisure time activity occurs. This, of course, requires increased programming, more active exhibition schedules, and standards in some cases, which in turn require more funding, staffing, and training.

Administratively, the Jamaican education system is mired in bureaucracy and although that is changing as it evolves into more of a central policy-based ministry, many of its members may not readily respond to the need to establish new partnerships and systems. In addition, any type of classroom methodology that places the individual at the centre, and focuses on emphasizing dialogue over didacticism may be seen as threatening to teachers who count on maintaining control in their classrooms. In Jamaica where classrooms tend to be overcrowded and teachers tend to be short on teaching materials and general classroom space, the maintenance of order can become paramount.

Financially, the Ministry of Culture is under-funded. It somehow does not seem to have come 'into its own', so to speak, whether partnered with education as it has been in the past, or with other ministries such as its current pairing with youth. Commitments such as the need to improve school infrastructure and access to school feeding programmes and so on take precedence, especially given that policy change and implementation take time.

The above challenges do not represent an exhaustive list. Others may probably surface before this study's findings can be realized, and, indeed, even before they could be seriously considered at the policy level. Yet policy change and funding can overcome many of these issues. The government can create policies that would increase the mandate for museums and their partnerships with schools and teachers' colleges, which in turn might increase family attendance, as more individuals would be exposed to, and potentially reflect on and discuss, museum experiences. Museums might also increasingly become seen as sites of individual and national pride. Yet for international and local funding to be found, widespread belief in the cause of learning for life and the educational value of the museum must first be established. For this to happen, more research considering Jamaican museums as offering a new and valid pedagogical approach needs to be conducted. The good news is that since this research was conducted, more focused and frequent lobbying has begun, which seems to have resulted in a change in perception and practice that is beginning in relevant ministries.

Although I played a role in the beginning of this change, serving as an advisor to the Minister of Education from 2007-2011 and as chair of the Museums Board from 2008-2011, the idea of strengthening links between museums and the formal education system, as well as the need to recognize and act on the importance of experiential, play-based learning in general, have found broader support at the Senior Policy level within the Ministry of Education and within the Institute of Jamaica. Play is a critical component of the recently developed national early childhood curriculum and former Education Minister Andrew Holness spoke repeatedly about the value of play and child-centred learning. It is therefore not surprising that during his tenure, a draft Play Policy was developed by the Ministry of Education. It is slated to go to consultation in 2012 and will then move through the process to be eventually tabled in Parliament. This movement has also been bolstered by the Governor-General's declaration in 2011 of the last Friday in May as a National Play Day in Schools. In addition, the Bureau of Standards has established a Technical Sub-Committee to develop standards for playground equipment which are due to be finalized later in 2012.

Similarly, in the Jamaican museum world, increased child-centred programming for children is occurring, having found support at the board and administrative levels, all of which is grounded in the concept of experiential play. As a result, new, visitor-friendly, constructivist approaches to exhibition design and programming, focusing on younger audiences as well as family audiences, are increasingly apparent throughout the Institute of Jamaica's national network of history museums. The IOJ's Museums Division has opened its Kingston location on some Saturdays and also developed supporting family activities. In addition, in November 2010, when it opened an exhibit entitled *War to Windrush/War... Lest We Forget,* in partnership with London's Imperial War Museum featuring the travelling version of their successful *War to Windrush* exhibit, the *War...Lest We Forget* section curated by the Museums Division included a definitive children's area. Inside it, children were invited to tackle interactive exhibits that explicated different aspects of Jamaica's war history. These included: large, velcroed puzzles of naval destroyers on one wall, tyres laid out as a pretend training course, a life-sized dress up 'paper dolls' area on a velcroed backboard facing a full length mirror with the faces cut out so that children could stand behind them and pretend to be dressed as soldiers, large three-dimensional, pyramid shaped puzzles with images of soldiers and medals and a map with clues that carried you from country to country in order of World War II's major battles. According to informal discussions with the Deputy Director of the Institute of Jamaica and the exhibit tour guides, this has proven to be one of the most popular exhibits in recent years. Informal surveys recently conducted with schoolchildren by the tour guides support the essence of this study's findings, even though it was conducted a decade earlier. The majority of the children from the four schools (a mix of rural and urban) surveyed had never visited museums before, liked the interactive displays best, and said the experience was different from learning in school because they could move around, touch things and play. The children overwhelmingly said they wanted to return, primarily with their parents to show them how much fun the museum visit can be.

Importantly, the IOJ's Museum's Division has also developed "discovery cards" to encourage family tours, and "exhibit walks" that include games and activities for most of its current exhibits island-wide. These are now being web-enabled to augment the Museums Division's section of the Institute of Jamaica's website. In addition, it is also important to note the intent stated in a review of the minutes of the Museums Division's board meetings (2008-2011), that when a national museum of the Jamaican people is finally constructed (and plans are in place to have this become a reality by within the next decade), there will be a designated children's section interpreting Jamaican history to a young audience and the museum itself will open on weekends. These minutes also referenced the need for stronger connections to the Ministry of Education, including a more vibrant school outreach programme which is linked directly to the curriculum, and to the Ministry of Education's regular teacher workshops as well as its soon-to-be established teacher-licensing system. This relationship is already being strengthened as Museums Division staff members have met with senior policy members of the Ministry of Education and presented to principals from schools island-wide at annual conferences.

Educational reform can occur both in the formal and the informal systems, and both are equally deserving of concern at the levels of policy and practice. Museums, as they exist in Jamaica and, by extension, in other developing countries, whether geared towards child audiences or not, can provide unique opportunities for the growth of progressive education and the stimulation of critical thinking, creativity, and the appreciation of self and others. These opportunities will only be realized, however, if those responsible for education policy and those who manage its transfer into practice, rather than seeing museums as old, dead structures and administering them as such, recognize their importance to a young audience that seems eager to embrace their relevance. In the end, then, perception holds the key to this type of educational re-imagining. Without the will to move towards such an understanding, the realization of an approach to teaching and learning that focuses on facilitating individualism, whether in the informal or formal education system, no matter how much funding is available, will remain elusive.

This study, although conducted a decade ago, is still relevant in the Jamaican context today. It no doubt raises as many questions as it answers, not the least of which has to do with whether policy drives practice or vice versa. Other questions relate to the concept of education at its most elemental. The children's reactions to their museum experiences suggest that the power to imagine, to create, and to reflect are magical elements of learning that can, in turn, be the basis for the development of flexible, innovative, independent, and individual thinkers. Curiosity sparks creativity, and both can lead to individual growth - but only if children are given the space and opportunities to explore their interaction. Perhaps other researchers will be stimulated to begin their own investigations in different regions of the developing world, so that the knowledge base on informal education, as well as the roles of culture and community and learning in museums, can expand to include a more international perspective.

References

Appadurai, A, 1995. Culture and modernity. Breckenridge, C. (ed.). *Consuming modernity: Public culture in a South Asian world,* (pp. 23-48). Minneapolis, MN: University of Minnesota Press.

Bettleheim, B, 1980. Children, curiosity and museums. *Children Today, 9* (1), 16, 22-23.

Bitgood, S., Serrell, B. and Thompson, D, 1994. The impact of informal education on visitors to museums. Crane, V. et al. (eds.). *Informal Science Learning*, Dedham Mass: Research Communications.

Bourdieu, P, 1984. *Distinction: A social critique of the judgment of taste.* (R. Nice, Trans). Cambridge, MA: Harvard University Press.

Bourdieu, P. et al, 1993. *The weight of the world.* (P. Ferguson, Trans.). Stanford: Stanford University Press.

Bruner, J, 1990. *Acts of meaning.* Cambridge, MA: Harvard University Press.

Claxton, M, 1994. Culture and development: A symbiotic relationship. *Culture Plus* 12-13,13-16.

Csikszentminhalyi, M, 1975. *Flow: The psychology of optimal experience.* New York: Harper Collins.

Csikszentminhalyi, M. and Hermanson, K, 1995, May-June. Intrinsic Motivation in museums: What makes visitors want to learn? *Museum News 74* (3), 34-37,59-61.

Cummins, A, 1994. The "Caribbeanization" of the West Indies: The museum's role in the development of national identity. Kaplan, Flora E.S. (ed). *Museums and the making of "Ourselves": The Role of Objects in National Identity* (pp. 192-220). Leicester University Press, London and New York.

Dewey, J, 1933. *How we think: A restatement of the relation of reflexive thinking to the educative process.* Boston: D.C. Heath and Co.

Dewey, J, {1938} 1963. *Experience and education.* New York: Collier Books.

Duckworth, E, 1987. *The having of wonderful ideas.* New York: Teachers College Press.

Falk, J.H. & and Dierking, L. D, 1992. *The museum experience.* Washington DC: Whalesback Books.

Falk, J.H. & and Dierking, L. D, 2000. *Learning from museums: Visitor experiences and the making of meaning.* Walnut Creek, CA: Altamira Press.

Freire, P, 1970. *Pedagogy of the Oppressed.* New York: Continuum Publishing Co.

Gardner, H, 1985. *Frames of mind.* New York: Basic Books Inc.

Geertz, C, 1973. *The interpretation of cultures.* New York: Basic Books Inc.

Goffman, E, 1963. *Behavior in public places.* New York: The Free Press.

_______, 1974. *Frame analysis.* New York: Harper and Row

Graburn, N, 1977, Fall. The Museum and visitor experience. Nichols, S. K., Alexander, M. and Yellis, K. (eds.). *Museum education anthology 1973-1983: Perspectives on informal learning - A decade of Roundtable Reports* (pp. 177-182). Washington DC: American Association of Museums.

Halpin, M. M, 1997. Play it again, Sam: Reflections on a new museology. *Museum International, 49* (194), issue 2,52-56.

Hein, G, 1998. *Learning in the museum.* London: Routledge.

Hirzy, E.C. (ed.). 1992. *Excellence and equity: Education and the public dimension of museums.* Washington, DC: American Association of Museums.

Hooper-Greenhill, E, 1992. *Museums and the shaping of knowledge.* London: Routledge.

_______, 1994. *The educational role of the museum.* London: Routledge

Hudson, K, 1999. Attempts to define 'Museum'. Boswell, D. and Evans, J. (eds.). *Representing the nation: A Reader - Histories, heritage and museums,* (pp. 371-379). London and New York: Routledge.

Jamaican early childhood national curriculum. Online at www.ecc.gov.jm

Jamaican Ministry of Education and Culture, 1997. *Consultative guidelines for use in defining a national cultural policy.* Kingston, Jamaica: Jamaica Information Service (JIS).

_______, 1999. *Cultural policy.* (Draft). Online, available at www.educateja.edu

_______, 2001. *Education, the way upwards: A plan for Jamaica's education at the start of the new millennium.* Kingston, Jamaica: Author.

Jamaican Ministry of Education, Youth and Culture, 2004. *Task Force Report on Education Reform.* Kingston, Jamaica: Author.

_______, 2008. Media Briefing on Literacy Initiatives. Kingston, Jamaica.

Jensen, H, 1994. Children's Perceptions of their museum experiences: A contextual perspective. *Children's Environments, 11* (4) 300-324.

Karp, Ivan, and Lavine, Steven, eds. 1991. *Exhibiting Cultures: The Poetics and Politics of Museum Display.* Washington, DC, and London: Smithsonian Institution Press.

Karp, Ivan, Mullen Kraemer, Christine and Lavine, Steven, eds. 1992. *Museums and Communities: The Politics of Public Culture.* Washington DC: Smithsonian Institution Press.

Leichter, H.J, 1973. The concept of educative style. *Teachers College Record,* 75(2X239-250.

Marley, B. 1973, Natty Dreadlocks. Island Records.

Museums Division of History and Ethnography. *Annual Report 1996-97.* Kingston, Jamaica; Institute of Jamaica (IOJ). Unpublished material.

_______. *Annual Report 1997-98.* Kingston, Jamaica; Institute of Jamaica (IOJ). Unpublished material.

_______. *Annual Report 1998-99.* Kingston, Jamaica; Institute of Jamaica (IOJ). Unpublished material.

_______. *Annual Report 1999-2000.* Kingston, Jamaica; Institute of Jamaica (IOJ). Unpublished material.

_______. *Annual Report 2000-2001.* Kingston, Jamaica; Institute of Jamaica (IOJ). Unpublished material.

_______. *Annual Report 2007-2008.* Kingston, Jamaica; Institute of Jamaica (IOJ). Unpublished material.

_______. *Annual Report 2008-2009.* Kingston, Jamaica; Institute of Jamaica (IOJ). Unpublished material.

_______. *Annual Report 2009-2010.* Kingston, Jamaica; Institute of Jamaica (IOJ). Unpublished material.

Museums Division of History and Ethnography. *Board Minutes 2008-2011.* Kingston, Jamaica; Institute of Jamaica (IOJ). Unpublished material.

_______. *Informal visitor surveys, 2011.* Kingston, Jamaica; Institute of Jamaica (IOJ). Unpublished material.

Nettleford, R. 1979. *Caribbean cultural identity: The case of Jamaica.* Los Angeles: The Centre for Afro-American Studies at the UCLA Latin American Centre Publications.

Planning Institute of Jamaica (PIOJ) April, 2008. *The Economic and Social Survey of Jamaica* (ESSJ) 2007. Kingston: Jamaica: Authors.

Planning Institute of Jamaica (PIOJ) and the Statistical Institute of Jamaica (STATIN) 2000. *The Jamaica Survey of Living Conditions* (JSLC 1999). Kingston: Jamaica: Authors.

_______. Nov. 2008. *The Jamaica Survey of Living Conditions* (JSLC) 2007. Kingston: Jamaica: Authors

Sebolt-George, A.P. 1980. Learning in museums. *Roundtable reports,* 5 (3), 9-12.

_______. 1999. Critical issues for museums in our expanding role. B. Pittman-Gelles (ed.). *Presence of mind: Museums and the spirit of learning, (p. 37-45).* Washington, DC; American Association of Museums.

Spock, M. 2000 Spring-Summer. Tales of alonetime and owntime in museums. *Journal of Museum Education,* 25, (1 & 2), 15-19.

Chapter 14

Outreach or Out of Reach? Seeking New Audiences:

The Turks and Caicos National Museum Children's Club

Nigel Sadler

Introduction

The diverse nature of the countries in the Caribbean, especially the small island nations, means there is a wide range of legislation that affects the care for children throughout the region. However, there is nothing to compare to the laws that exist in the USA and in Britain. The *No Child Left Behind Act* of 2001 was enacted in January 2002 in the USA and was "an act to close the achievement gap with accountability, flexibility, and choice, so that no child is left behind". Similar legislation entitled *'Every Child Matters'* came into operation in Britain in 2004, stating that every child should be healthy, stay safe, enjoy and achieve, make a positive contribution and achieve economic well-being.

Museums in Britain and the USA were quick to adopt programmes so that they met the objectives of this legislation. In many ways the new laws made it easier to implement these programmes - staff had to accept the changes, as they were encompassed in meeting legal requirements. More importantly, grants and training schemes were also made available to enable museum staff to meet these goals.

Without such strong political and legal guidance, museums in the Caribbean need to set their own targets and agendas. Is it possible for Caribbean museums to provide similar or better programmes?

The Beginnings of the Children's Club

Before 2000 there seemed to have been an informal policy by the Turks and Caicos National Museum staff of locking the front door at 2.30pm, the time the local schools turned out. This meant visitors had to ring the doorbell to be allowed in. The claim was that the children came into the museum to be a nuisance and negatively affected the experience of paying visitors. In 2000 the new Director instructed the staff that this policy was to end immediately, and if children entered the building it was the responsibility of the staff to engage them and encourage their learning. This was the first step towards the introduction of a more formal policy of engaging positively with children.

The Children's Club was not an immediate development but evolved out of the introduction of two other programmes. The first began in November 2000 and was the reintroduction of Museum Day. Soon after the museum had been opened to the public in November 1991 an annual event was introduced to mark its date of opening, but this had only lasted for a few years. The reintroduction was a means of commemorating the museum's founder, who had died in 2000, and as a way of utilising the Museum Garden for performances. The first year was very successful, especially as it brought in local schoolchildren to be the main performers (Sadler, 2001).

Over the next few months children told staff members that they wanted more activities like Museum Day. The museum did not have the finances or staff to be able to organise more than one big event annually, so a different, cheaper way was needed to involve the children. This led to the second development, the introduction of Children's Workshops; the first one was held in May 2002 (Sadler 2002a). David Bowen, the Cultural Officer at the Tourist Board, offered to run a workshop making musical instruments, including how to turn conch shells into horns. At the end of the workshop the newly created instruments were played by this impromptu band. One of the museum assistants was made available to Bowen, as this was seen as a formal way of providing them with training in dealing with children. The event was a great success and was oversubscribed - there were nearly twice as many children who wanted to attend as the 25 places available. To meet this interest, the museum put out a request to find others like Bowen, willing to use their time and skills to provide free workshops for children.

The Museum Club Begins

The Children's Club was launched during Museum Day, November 2002. It was part of the museum's move towards becoming a community-minded organisation and growing local participation. This had seen the removal of admission charges for Belongers (the name that the locals give themselves) and residents, the encouragement of schools to visit, and the Museum Day itself. The launch of the Children's Club coincided with the appointment of a new Museum Manager in November 2002, who was given the task of overseeing the Children's Club. This action clearly indicated that work with the children was now a core function of the museum.

The Children's Club formalised the activities already being undertaken to encourage children's participation, and placed them all under one umbrella. The plan for the Children's Club was not only to provide an alternative to the ubiquitous internet and satellite television available to the young, but also had a long-term objective. The children who would become members will be the next generation of school teachers, business leaders and politicians who may not personally wish to revisit the museum as adults, but will remember the good times they had and the value of the museum. This may lead to them encouraging school visits, sponsorship, and also the involvement of the museum within policy-making decisions of the government.

To keep numbers more manageable membership was restricted to seven to thirteen-year-olds. However, it was clear that during school holidays some children were tasked with looking after their brothers or sisters. This meant that some children who wanted to attend could not do so because they had to look after their younger siblings, whilst other children who wanted to attend were under the care of an older sibling. It was hard for the museum to stop children attending if they had such responsibilities. Flexibility was introduced so that even though membership was limited to seven to thirteen-year-olds, the museum had events where the age range covered ages six to fifteen to cater for this care issue. However, activities had to be limited to 15-25 children, depending on the type of workshop, the space needed, and the level of interaction required by the activity leader.

Activities

To keep the children's interest in the club, the museum had to hold a wide variety of activities. For inspiration the museum looked at traditional toy or game making, cultural and heritage legacies, present environmental issues and museum research projects. The planning of activities for the Children's Club also inspired research into the life of children in the Turks and Caicos Islands in the past, the games they played and how they spent their spare time (Mulligan, 2005).

Each activity had to have an underlying educational goal, but only if it could be done in a fun way and in a manner that the children would probably not encounter in a formal educational setting. One of the first Children's Club activities was getting members together to take part in the annual Department of Environment and Coastal Resources *Beach Clean Up* Day. However, this was to be different, taking a more innovative approach. This included cleaning up a beach that was generally not utilised by tourists but by local residents and fishermen, and that had not had any formal cleaning for many years. During the beach clean up the rubbish collected was divided, and museum staff took the material that couldn't be used in an art project to the Island's landfill site. All other material was taken to the museum, where staff cleaned it. Three days later the children involved in the beach clean-up came to the museum to take part in a *Beach Art Project,* converting this 'rubbish' into art - a form of recycling.

Other Children's Club activities included Christmas card and decoration making, mask making using recycled water bottles, natural history walks on Grand Turk, kite making, film shows, and a sleepover in the museum. In 2003 members were invited to meet international free diver Tanya Streeter when she visited the museum to donate some of her equipment used during her recent record-breaking dives in the country (Sadler, 2003a).

In one of the more detailed workshops a story teller recounted a traditional *b'bookie* and *b'rabbie* story. Following the story he broke it down into its elements, especially the story's moral and the role of each character, and then with the children created a modern story including the museum, schools, library, lighthouse, and the Governor's house as the settings.

The most popular activity was the visit to Gibbs Cay, a small uninhabited island near to Grand Turk where tourists visit to swim with stingrays. The first Children's Club visit there was in the spring of 2003 (Sadler 2003b). Two boats and crew were provided free by Oasis Divers, who carried 20 children and three members of museum staff to the island. Out of these 20 children, seventeen had never been off Grand Turk before, and nineteen had never been in the water with stingrays. The aim of the trip was to encourage the children to have a healthy respect rather than fear of the stingrays, and to value the environment. For the third Gibbs Cay trip, the children and museum staff were joined by the Governor's wife and her youngest child. The children were excited immediately, as just after the boats left the beach they were joined by a pod of dolphins that played around the boats for about ten minutes, again a first for most of the children.

All activities that took place outside the museum premises required permission slips from the children's parents or guardian. This often proved to be difficult, as children forgot to get their permission slips signed and were unhappy when the museum would not let them participate; or in some cases the parents or guardians could not speak English and were not clear about what they were signing for.

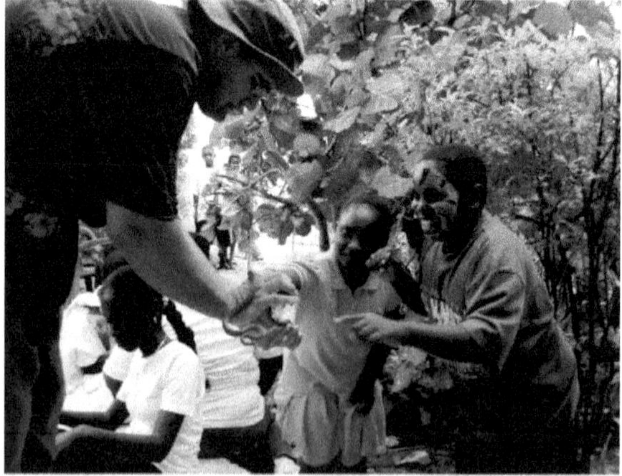

Children's Club activities on Museum Day (Photo Credit: Author)

Museum Day

The annual Museum Day became one of the highlights for the Children's Club, whose members organised their own performances aided by one of the museum assistants. This required planning and maintaining the children's interest during the rehearsals, a time when the children were to bond and work together, and when they learnt songs and created their own dance routines to be performed. Their show during Museum Day created a tangible product for parents and other community members to see the benefits of the Children's Club, and in some cases gave acceptance for some of the children who were marginalised at school.

One of the limitations of Museum Day was that it was generally more popular with girls. Boys may have wanted to participate but seemed less able to commit to a rehearsal schedule; and boys also seemed to be more concerned about how their peers who were not in the Children's Club would judge their attendance at rehearsal, and their participation in the performance on Museum Day.

During the Museum Day in 2005 Children's Club members were invited to enter a competition, and the ten winners all received a limited edition Museum Club t-shirt. The aim was to give the winners a sense of uniqueness, but also to promote the Children's Club to other children on the island. All museum staff were given a shirt to be worn during Museum Day, and at future Children's Club activities. The image on the back of the shirt was the flag of the local pirate, *Calico Jack.* The limited issue t-shirt was very popular with the children and the museum staff, and had the desired effect of bringing in more members for the club. It had been intended to produce a 'pirate flag' that would be flown from the museum's flag mast to indicate when a Children's Club activity was being held at the museum. Unfortunately, a local flag maker couldn't be found, and the idea was dropped.

Newsletter

From the start of the club a monthly newsletter was produced to keep children informed of what was happening at the museum. The single-sheet newsletter was produced in-house, and contained a quiz that was historical or environmental in nature and was often based on the museum's collection, a word search, a story/article related to a recent museum research project or related to a museum item, and the latest news from the museum which included advertising forthcoming children's events. It also named the winner of the previous newsletter's quiz.

The newsletter had to be collected from the museum by members, not only to save postal costs, but also so that the children could be informed in person about changes or projects that might be relevant to them, and encourage them to sign up for forthcoming workshops and events. It was also an ideal way for staff to learn who was in the Children's Club and to interact with them outside of scheduled events.

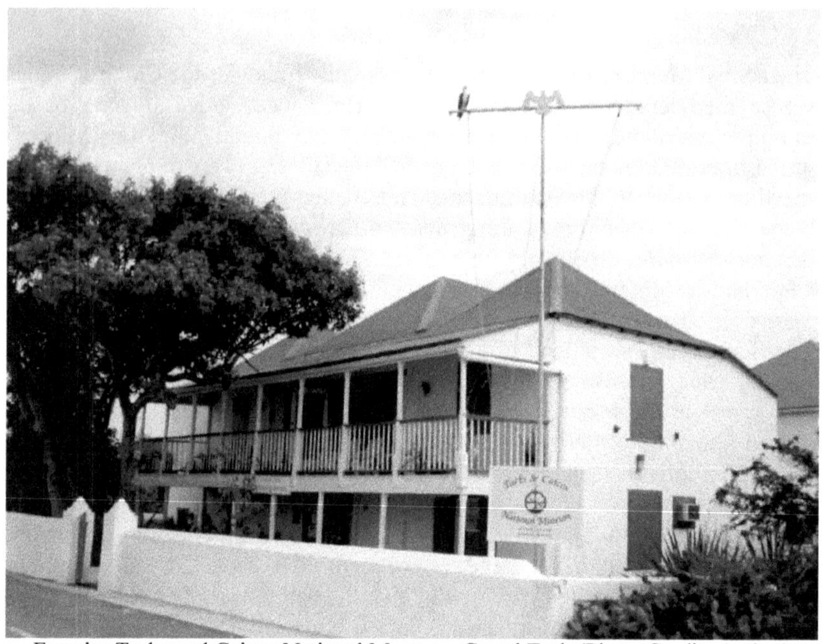

Exterior Turks and Caicos National Museum, Grand Turk (Photo Credit: Author)

Limitations

The Children's Club suffered from the same limitations that faced many of the other museum activities. The museum is on Grand Turk, the political capital of the country, and when the Children's Club started the island had a population of just less than 6000. However there are seven other inhabited islands in the country (with a total population at the start of the Children's Club of around 15,000), so providing any services on these islands was limited by staff and financial resources. Limiting the Children's Club to Grand Turk made it more manageable: the monthly newsletter was collected from the museum, and activities needing a room could take place for free at the museum. Fortunately, on several of the other islands where the museum was not able to provide a service to the country's children, the National Trust had its own children's activities. This meant that probably 75 per cent of the country's children had access to either museum or National Trust activities.

Membership was free - just the child signing up to the newsletter - so that the museum could create a database of children interested in participating in activities. The first sign-up list had 80 names on it, but it soon became apparent that there was a small core of children who wanted to be involved in everything, whilst others were only members because they wanted to be involved in the key events such as the Gibbs Cay trip.

Not all staff had the same enthusiasm for working with children's activities. Its success was reliant on a few staff; and leading this were part-time staff who were also studying at the community college. In 2000 the one full-time museum assistant post was adapted so that four community college students could be employed part time. This was ideal for the Children's Club development, as these students had different skills and interests, several of the staff wanted to be teachers, and most had younger siblings who wanted to be involved in the museum Children's Club. When one student left, another was hired, and in this process the museum made sure that at least two staff members were interested in managing the Children's Club activities.

Funding

Initially there was no dedicated funding for the Children's Club and costs were hidden in other budgets (for example, the production of the monthly newsletter was covered in the stationery budget). However, the museum was fortunate that, as the Children's Club grew, it gained the support of the community that saw free soft drinks for events being supplied by local retailers, a local restaurant funding a breakfast, Oasis Divers providing two boats and crew each year to carry the children to Gibbs Cay, and one individual donation of $1000 to cover the purchase of material for activities, whilst others provided supplies for the art workshops including crayons, paints, brushes and paper. The museum Director also sacrificed his moustache which he had grown for eighteen years on Museum Day in 2003, having it shaved off to raise $500 for the Children's Club.

Funding for the Children's Club became more formalised in 2008, mainly thanks to the release of Donna Seim and Susan Spellman's book *Where is Simon, Sandy,* the story of a donkey on Grand Turk. Profits from the publication are dedicated to the Children's Club (Hitch 2008).

Spin-offs from the Children's Club

The children began to use the museum informally as an after-school meeting venue where they could do their homework in an air-conditioned and safe environment. The children were aware that if visitors entered the museum they would have to move, however there were many occasions when visitors had commented on how nice it was to see children in the museum, and on some occasions the children supported a museum assistant in giving a guided tour.

The museum staff learnt how to deal with and encourage children through trial and error. In 2005 the museum Director attended a meeting in Barbados organised by the Commonwealth Association of Museums to discuss child-friendly policies for museums (Irvine, 2005). At this meeting museums were able to exchange best practices and lessons learnt from projects with children, and several new ideas were taken on board by the museum; this included the development of the Children's Gallery.

One reason why the museum had not been a regular haunt for children prior to 2000 was that there were few interactive displays, and those that existed were noisy, so regular use 'upset' the staff. With a limited budget there was not much that could be done initially to create child-friendly displays. Eventually though, members of the Children's Club were consulted on the development of a small gallery in an unused storage room. The limitations of the room size and budget meant that everything had to be produced in house, including the construction of a new display case which contained the traditional display behind Plexiglas, but also an interactive area where children could either put their hands into concealed boxes to touch items for identification, or to pick up objects (mostly seeds and plants) for smelling.

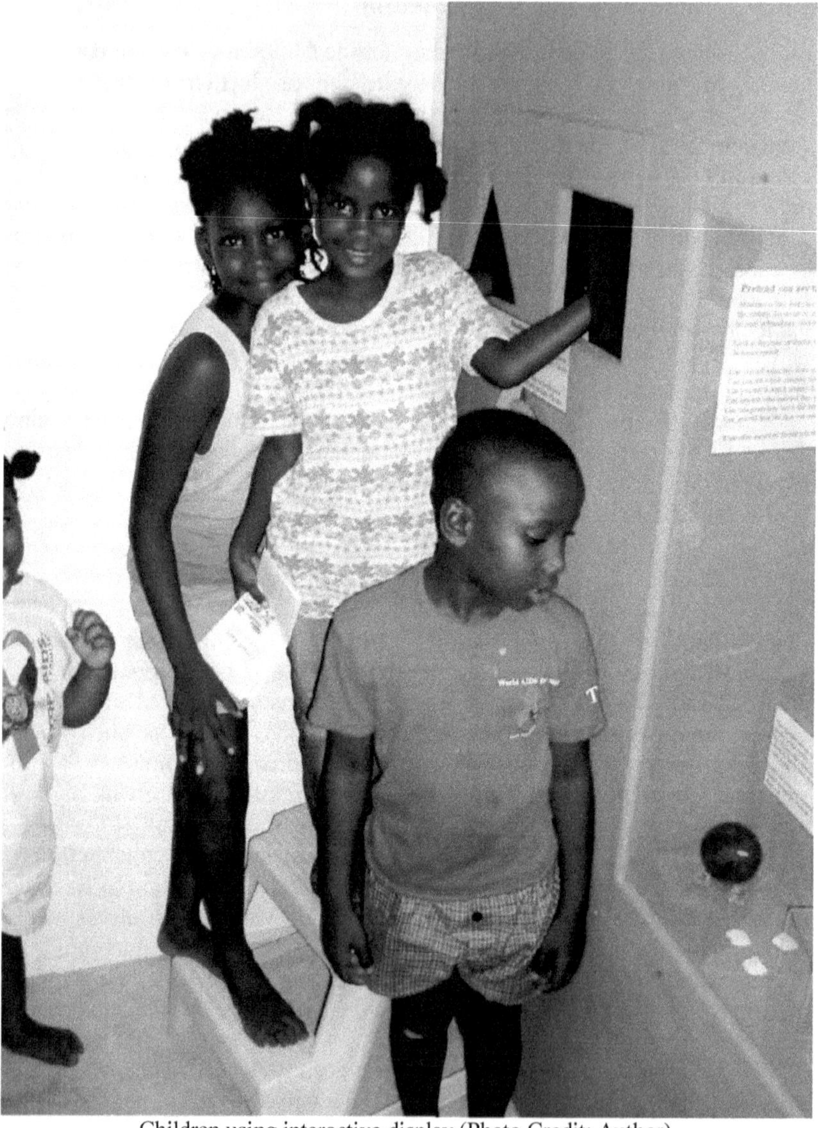

Children using interactive display (Photo Credit: Author)

One wall of the gallery had objects placed in clear plastic boxes at different heights more suitable for children, either being at their eye level or higher up, so that a child could stand underneath and then see the bottom of the object. All items in the gallery were selected to help children navigate around the rest of the museum, and the gallery was designed so that the objects could easily be changed.

Events and Launches

Soon after the Children's Club was set up it was decided that some of its members would be selected to attend the more formal museum functions. This was done either through creating competitions and then the winners being invited to attend a museum event, or in some cases children were chosen as a reward for their help with the Children's Club, or because they had shown an interest in the project that was being launched. Not only did this introduce children to the more formal part of the museum work, but it provided access to the museum's Trustees and supporters. This not only created a means for the children to develop social skills, but also allowed the museum to promote its work with the young citizens. Several of the Children's Club members were invited to attend a book launch at the museum. At the end of the evening a museum Trustee commented on how surprised and delighted he had been with the way that one of the smartly dressed children had given him a tour of the museum, with this man's position in the museum unbeknown to the child. The Trustees had been impressed that the Children's Club had generated such enthusiasm, and it had opened their eyes to the benefits of this aspect of the museum's work.

On one occasion two Children's Club members (one boy and one girl) were selected to accompany the museum Director to an event at the Governor's office. This gave them an insight into something that they had only heard or read about, and their attendance gave them access to the Governor and his family as well as the political and business leaders of the country. The invitations had come because the Governor's wife had attended some of the Children's Club events with her youngest child and had been impressed when she had talked to the children and museum staff.

Conclusion

Usually children perceive that museums are boring, dusty places and their only interaction with museum staff and collections is during an obligatory school trip. However, to grow a museum must encourage community support, and the future of any organisation and indeed any country, lies in the hands of its children. They will grow up to become the next business people, developers, government ministers, community representatives and teachers. Children need to be inspired to become better citizens. They should be seen as a major resource to be nurtured and allowed to develop with the proper guidance. This guidance is clearly in the hands of their parents and of the formal education system. However everyone in the community, be it an individual or organisation, must take some responsibility for the general education of the country's children.

Museums can clearly play an active part in attracting and encouraging children to participate. Not only do they learn history and environmental issues, but more importantly they learn to work together, to make friends with people they might not meet at school, and to gain confidence in a non-school environment.

The Turks and Caicos National Museum's Children's Club had similar objectives to the Children's Acts in the USA and Britain but pre-empted the UK Act by a year and began a few years after the USA legislation, of which the museum staff were unaware. The museum would like to believe that its staff were ahead of their times and were leaders in the field, but this was not so. It was because the museum staff saw the need and identified a way to engage the young residents on Grand Turk, regardless of good practices from elsewhere. Then again it wasn't rocket science. There was an audience that the museum wasn't engaging effectively, and an exciting way had to be found to encourage the young residents to become involved with the museum.

When the museum Director who had started the Children's Club left in December 2006 he recalled that 'One of my greatest senses of achievement was the inclusion of children into the museum and its activities, highlighted by two major developments - the Children's Club and the annual Museum Day. There is nothing more satisfying than watching children's eyes light up as they learn or have fun and seeing them push their own limits and succeed where they thought they would fail.' (Sadler 2007 p 90)

References

Legislation

Department for Education and Science, 2004. Every Child Matters: Change for Children. Department for Education and Skills (DfES).

No Child Left Behind Act of 2001, http://www.gpo.gov/fdsys/pkg/ PLAW-107publno/content-detail.html

Children's Club

Hitch, Neal 2008. Where is Simon, Sandy. Astrolabe. *Times of the Island Magazine,* Spring 2008 p. 119.

Irvine, Lois 2005. Children and Museums. Child-Friendly Policies for a child-friendly future. Astrolabe. *Times of the Island Magazine,* Fall 2005 p. 96-98.

Jennings, Nikki 2011. Clubbin' in Grand Turk. Astrolabe. *Times of the Island Magazine,* Winter 2011/2012, p. 54-56.

Mulligan, Jackie 2007. A Nation at Play: Childhood in the Turks and Caicos Islands. Astrolabe. *Times of the Island Magazine,* Fall 2005 p. 87-95.

Sadler, Nigel 2001. Turks and Caicos National Museum Day 2000, Astrolabe. *Times of the Island Magazine,* Spring 2001 p. 58.

_______, 2002a. Children's Workshop at the National Museum, Astrolabe. *Times of the Island Magazine,* Fall 2002 p. 70.

_______, 2002b. Tenth Anniversary Celebration, Astrolabe. *Times of the Island Magazine,* Spring 2002 p. 83.

_______, 2003a. Keeping Up With The Kids, Astrolabe. *Times of the Island Magazine,* Winter 2003/2004, p. 85.

_______, 2003b. Museum Children's Club Outing, Astrolabe. *Times of the Island Magazine,* Summer 2003 p. 85.

_______, 2003c. The Children's Club, Astrolabe. *Times of the Island Magazine,* Spring 2003, p. 80.

_______, 2007. So Long and Thanks for all the Fish, Astrolabe. *Times of the Island Magazine,* Spring 2007 p. 89-97.

Chapter 15

Museums and the Challenge for Heritage Organizations in Saint Lucia

Winston F. Phulgence

The island nation of Saint Lucia has a very rich history and is endowed with a long and interesting heritage. Evidence of this history litters the landscape: recent archaeological excavations are bringing even more of this history to the surface. Saint Lucia's history runs from the contributions of the first settlers centuries ago to those of the present post-colonial generation. The history and heritage of a country are very important components in the creation of a unique national identity which reflects the people of that country. Museums play a pivotal role in the creation of this identity by preserving and displaying the physical manifestations of that heritage.

Three decades after independence in 1979, Saint Lucia does not have a national museum. In this chapter I will highlight the importance of museums in helping to shape national identities, and explore the reasons for the lack of a national museum in Saint Lucia. The role of heritage organizations will be discussed, along with the challenges which these face in setting up museums.

The Role of Museums

In his seminal work, *The Past is a Foreign Country,* David Lowenthal instructs us that "The past is integral to our sense of identity; 'the sureness of I was is a necessary component of the sureness of I am'." (Lowenthal 1985) The history of the people in the nation must inform the identity of that nation, and museums are poised to help shape that identity. When people are able to identify with their past it gives meaning and purpose to their being.

There is much historical data from the period of written history that can be used to inform the creation of an identity which is Saint Lucian. From the time of the arrival of Europeans in the seventeenth century much data is available on the interactions of the many races, nationalities and even ethnicities that have occupied - and occupy - the islands. Much of this history is "ruptured" and fragmented; museums can help reconstruct this past through the objects and artefacts chosen for display (Cummins 2004).

In the process of identity creation, museums also have the responsibility of dealing with the many silences which exist in the history of places. These silences are created by the power relations that have existed throughout the history in that place. (Trouillot 1995) The legacy of colonialism is such that those who control the reins of power ensure the creation of a history that reflects the power relations existing in the society. If the history of the nation is to inform the identity creation process in which museums play a pivotal role (Cummins 1996), then museums must ensure that they do not replicate the inequities pervading the society (O'Neil 2006).

These inequities pervade much of our knowledge of who the first settlers of the Caribbean islands were. The historical narrative in this situation also has many silences. Much of what is known of the first inhabitants perpetuates the European world view in the fifteenth century. The story that Saint Lucia has inherited is that these first settlers were savages who reveled in the barbarity that is cannibalism. Much of the data presented by archaeologists and anthropologists working in the Caribbean today disputes this version of history (Keegan 1996, Allaire 1996), but little of this alternative version is reflected in the historical narrative.

While this new information has still not had an effect on the teaching of history in Saint Lucia's schools, a national museum displaying the material culture of the first settlers would certainly have an impact. Museums can, through the use of artefacts and material culture that now forms a large part of the archaeological heritage of the nation, correct the historical record.

In the Post-Independence era the museum can be used, not only to create a national identity, but also to influence the general public's world view. In a time when globalization threatens to create a homogenous world view, museums must play a role in celebrating distinctive national qualities. When these institutions display that which is perceived to be "national", it can lead to the expression of that which is seen as unique to the society (MacDonald 2003). This is especially true in the area of Fine Arts, where small island states often have to devote scarce finances to sectors deemed to have more tangible returns.

The History of Museums in Saint Lucia

Any discussion of museums in Saint Lucia must mention the efforts of the heritage organizations that have worked assiduously to preserve the natural and cultural heritage of the country. These include the Saint Lucia Archaeological and Historical Society (A&H) and the Saint Lucia National Trust.

The Saint Lucia Archaeological and Historical Society, established in 1954, is one of the oldest heritage societies in the English-speaking Caribbean. For decades it has been fighting to preserve the archaeological heritage of the nation. The diligent work of the Society has meant that it now holds in trust the island's largest archaeological collection.

The National Trust grew out of the A&H, and was set up in 1975 by an Act of Parliament. This organization is a statutory body that oversees the protection of natural heritage and cultural heritage through its management of the nation's national parks and nature reserves. The responsibility for national parks has also placed many historical sites under the supervision of the National Trust.

Between them, these organizations have responsibility for much of the nation's natural and cultural heritage. They are without clearly defined roles, and there is much overlap in their responsibilities. Most attempts at setting up museums on the island have been made by one or other of these two organizations.

The first public display of artefacts by the Saint Lucia Archaeological and Historical Society took place in 1964. This was a small display housed in a restored eighteenth-century military barracks building on Morne Fortune. This mini-museum arrangement lasted for almost a decade, until the rent-free space was required for the Ministry of Education for the setting up of the Organization of Eastern Caribbean States secretariat. The Society's inability to acquire its own building meant that the collection that had been on display went into storage.

In 1979 the Saint Lucia National Trust opened its own interpretative display of Amerindian artefacts at the Pigeon Island National Park, a historic park containing many eighteenth-century military buildings. It was closed in 1985 after vandals broke into the building and removed some of the artefacts.

During this time, however, the Trust had opened another interpretation centre in the south of the island as part of the Maria Island Nature Reserve. The display included Amerindian artefacts and exhibits of natural history relevant to the Reserve. The centrepiece was a species of reptiles which are endemic to Saint Lucia.

In 1994 an interpretative display of Pigeon Island's history was opened by the National Trust at Pigeon Island. This was an elaborate display tracing the history of the islands from the time of the first Amerindian settlers to the eighteenth-century Battle of the Saints. Funding for this project came from the Canadian Small Projects Implementation Facility.

In 1999 the Governor-General of Saint Lucia set up a small museum, called *Pavillion Royale,* at Government House, the official residence of the

Governor-General. The display included many artefacts depicting life within this historic residence and in Saint Lucia generally.

Clearly these attempts at displaying artefacts and interpreting history do not meet professional standards for museums. However they bear witness to the fact that since the island set up its first heritage organization in 1954 there has been interest in a national museum. Even after independence in 1979, interpretation centres were the only places displaying any of Saint Lucia's heritage.

It must be noted that, since 1954, several archaeological excavations have taken place in the island that have yielded many artefacts from different time periods. Many have been taken out of the island, but a large number remain in storage in Saint Lucia. Clearly the lack of a museum is not caused by lack of a large national collection. The number of attempts to set up museums also illustrates a desire for such an institution.

Call for Action

At the end of the 1990s attempts were made to set up a national museum. Investments were made in human resources when sponsorship was sought by the National Trust and the Archaeological and Historical Society to have two Saint Lucians trained in museology. This led to attempts to secure government support for the acquisition of a building to house a national museum. However, these moves proved futile. By the year 2000 Saint Lucia was the only island in the Eastern Caribbean without a national museum.

In the twenty-first century, new impetus was given to the movement to develop a national museum. The Saint Lucia National Trust spearheaded a project to develop museums. This was a new approach, because the project goal was a system of museums and not one national museum. With funding from the Inter-governmental Agency for Francophonie, committees were created to lay the foundation for this new system. This project included a number of other organizations and not just the National Trust and the A&H. This time the Folk Research Centre and the National Archives were also involved in the process.

A series of meetings and seminars was held with assistance and guidance from experts in the field of museology. Assessments were made of the capacity of the heritage organizations to develop museums in their respective sectors of heritage. A lamentable feature of this period is that funding opportunities were missed, as bureaucratic bottlenecks and an apparent lack of political will on the part of the directorate blocked progress on the formation of a national museum (or system of museums) for the island.

In 2012 Saint Lucia still does not have a national museum or a system of museums. The National Trust still runs the interpretation centre at the Pigeon Island National Landmark and is redeveloping the one at Maria Island Nature Reserve. The Archaeological and Historical Society exhibits some artefacts on occasions of national significance such as Independence anniversaries. Much of the collection however remains in storage.

Issues

For much of the last 30 years the Saint Lucia Archaeological and Historical Society and the Saint Lucia National Trust have been the recognized custodians of the cultural patrimony of Saint Lucia. As a result, these organizations are poised to lead any movement towards the development of a national museum or a system of museums.

The difficulty with these organizations, however, is that their roles are not clearly defined. There is no legislation on the statute books of Saint Lucia governing the Archaeological and Historical Society in its function as a heritage management organization. To all intents and purposes it functions as a Non-Governmental Organization (NGO). It does, however, receive a small subvention from the government.

The National Trust, on the other hand, is a statutory body created by legislation. Even then the responsibilities of the organization are not very clear. A cursory glance at its objectives on its website suggests that it is the protector of all things "heritage" on Saint Lucia. This puts the Trust very often in conflict with the A&H in the area of cultural heritage management.

For more than 50 years the A&H has held the largest collection of archaeological heritage on Saint Lucia. Any such artefacts held by the Trust are on loan from the A&H. Thus any attempt at setting up a museum requires the co-operation of the two organizations, necessitating the clarification of the role of each in the management of the cultural patrimony of the nation.

The setting up of a national museum requires the development of human resources and expertise in the field of museology. Although steps were taken in the 1990s to train people, their skills were never used. There was no museum to utilize the human resources that had been developed.

Another major issue hindering the setting up of a national museum is the lack of will on the part of government to support and fund the project. Governments must be convinced that a national museum is a wise investment of the scarce resources of the nation.

Conclusions

Heritage organizations in Saint Lucia have shown that there is a desire to set up a national museum or a system of museums for Saint Lucia. However, a great deal more than desire is required. Several challenges have to be overcome before a museum can be established.

The first of these is the clarification of the role and status of the two largest heritage organizations. Unless this is done, and proper legislation is put in place giving clear mandates to both organizations, and implemented, turf battles will continue. This will hinder any attempt to set up a museum. The one undisputed and indisputable fact is that the A&H has the collection.

When the idea of a national museum was being pursued in the late 1990s, the respective roles of the Saint Lucia Archaeological and Historical Society and the Saint Lucia National Trust as heritage organizations were at the forefront. Even today any discussion on museums must include these two organizations. However, they should be given clearly defined roles, as suggested above, and a separate museum authority should be set up to spearhead a national museum initiative. If the A&H and the Trust are relieved of that responsibility, moving forward might be less difficult.

If any attempt at setting up a national museum in Saint Lucia is to succeed, the people of the nation must be allowed to take ownership of their cultural and national heritage. When the nation claims this heritage, the government will see the need to facilitate and ultimately finance a national museum. As long as this process remains in the hands of a few with vested interests a national museum to serve the needs of identity creation, education and heritage preservation will remain elusive in Saint Lucia.

References

Allaire, Louis, 1996. 'Visions of Cannibals: Distant Islands and Distant Lands in Taino World Image', Paquette, Robert and Stanley L. Engerman (eds), *The Lesser Antilles in the Age of European Expansion,* University of Florida Press, Gainesville.

Barrow-Whatley, Lesley, 2000. Saint Lucia National Museum Development Project Two Day Workshop and Site Visits, Saint Lucia National Trust.

Cummins, Alissandra, 1996. 'Making Histories of African Caribbeans', Kavanagh, G. (ed), *Making Histories in Museums,* Routledge, Leicester.

Cummins, Alissandra, 2004. 'Caribbean Museums and National Identity', *History Workshop Journal* (58):224-245.

Duncan, C, 1991. 'Art Museum and the Ritual of Citizenship', Karp, Ivan and Lavine, Steven D. (eds) *Exhibiting Cultures: The Poetics and Politics of Museum Display,* Smithsonian, Washington D.C

Fyfe, Gordon, 2004. 'Reproductions, cultural capital and museums: aspects of the culture of copies', *Museum and Society* 2(1) 47-67.

Keegan, W. F, 1996. 'Columbus Was a Cannibal: Myth and the First Encounters', Paquette, Robert and Engerman, Stanley L. (eds), *The Lesser Antilles in the Age of European Expansion,* University of Florida Press, Gainesville, pp. 17-32

Louis, Michael, 2000. *A Museum System for St. Lucia: A Review of the Literature and the Way Forward,* St. Lucia National Trust.

Lowenthal, David, 1985. *The Past is a Foreign Country,* Cambridge University Press, Cambridge.

Lowenthal, David, 2006. *The Heritage Crusade and the Spoils of History,* Cambridge University Press, Cambridge.

MacDonald, Sharon J, 2003. 'Museums, National, Postnational and Transcultural Identities', *Museum and Society* 1 (1): 1-16

McLean, Fiona, 2005. 'Museums and National Identity', *Museum and Society* 3(1):1-4.

McLean, Fiona, 2006. 'Heritage and Identity', *International Journal of Heritage Studies* 12(1).

Newman, Andrew, McLean, Fiona and Urquhart, Gordon, 2005. 'Museums and the Active Citizen: Tackling the Problems of Social Exclusion', *Citizenship Studies* 9(1):41-57.

Newman, Andrew and McLean, Fiona, 2006. 'The Impact of Museums upon Identity', *International Journal of Heritage Studies* 12(1):49-68.

O'Neil, M, 2006. 'Museums and Identity in Glasgow', *International Journal of Heritage Studies* 12(1):29-48.

Rounds, Jay, 2006. Doing Identity Work in Museums, *CURATOR* 49(2):133-150.

Trouillot, Michel-Rolph. 1995. *Silencing the Past: Power and the Production of History*, Beacon Press, Boston. p. 25.

Chapter 16

Destroying while Preserving Junkanoo:

The Junkanoo Museum in the Bahamas[261]

Krista Thompson

As New Year's Day breaks in Nassau, capital of the Bahamas, the sun rises to find the main street littered with abandoned Junkanoo costumes, vacant shells left over from the biannual parade which filled the streets in the dark hours of the morning.

The tradition of costuming in Junkanoo (or John Canoe) has been a part of Christmas celebrations in the Bahamas (and other parts of the Anglophone Caribbean) since at least the mid-nineteenth century, when black Bahamians clothed in ribbons and others on stilts poured into the streets on Boxing Day morning. Since the early twentieth century, participants have used a variety of materials to create Junkanoo costumes including wire-mesh masks, sponges, newspapers, and, more recently, colourful fringed crepe-paper, glitter, and feathers. Between the hours of 12 a.m. through the early morning on Boxing Day and New Year's mornings, Junkanoo participants transform the main

[261] This chapter by Krista A. Thompson, "Destroying While Preserving Junkanoo: The Junkanoo Museum in the Bahamas," in *Museum Frictions: Public Cultures/Global Transformations*, Ivan Karp, Corinne Kratz, Lynn Szwaja, Tomas Ybarra-Frausto (eds.), pp. 500-503.

streets of the capital through a brilliant display and energetic performance of their costumes, against the musical backdrop of a pulsating drumbeat.

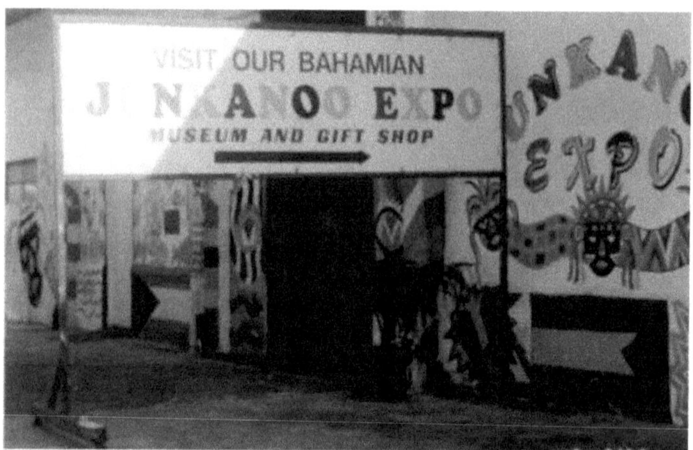

Junkanoo Expo Entrance, 1997. (Photo Credit: Author)

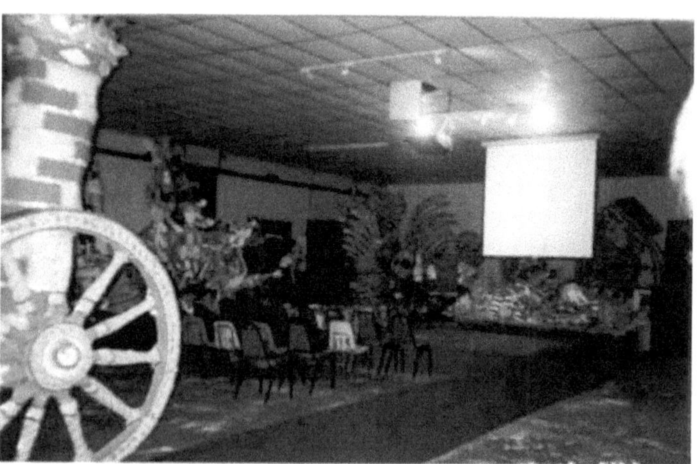
Junkanoo Expo Interior, 1997. (Photo Credit: Author)

For decades many Junkanooers abandoned their handmade costumes immediately after the festivities, despite the months of preparation that went into pasting the elaborate and sometimes costly crepe-papered creations. Some participants explain that this practice stems from their belief that the costumes are no longer meaningful outside of their communal creation and public performance. The abandonment and immediate destruction of the costumes became a part of the cycle of Junkanoo or 'junk-a-new', as some Junkanooers describe the artistic process of destruction and recreation.

In 1992, a museum, the Junkanoo Expo, opened in Nassau, saving some of the costumes from their ritual abandonment. The museum collected and exhibited many of the larger pieces used in the street parade, especially those that had been awarded prizes in the judging competition. The museum provided the first public exhibition context for costumes outside of the performance frame of the parade. But was the museum, in its efforts to display costumes that were typically discarded after the festivities, interceding in the cycle of costume creation and destruction? Was the museum inherently unsuitable for the display of the traditionally ephemeral arts of Junkanoo?

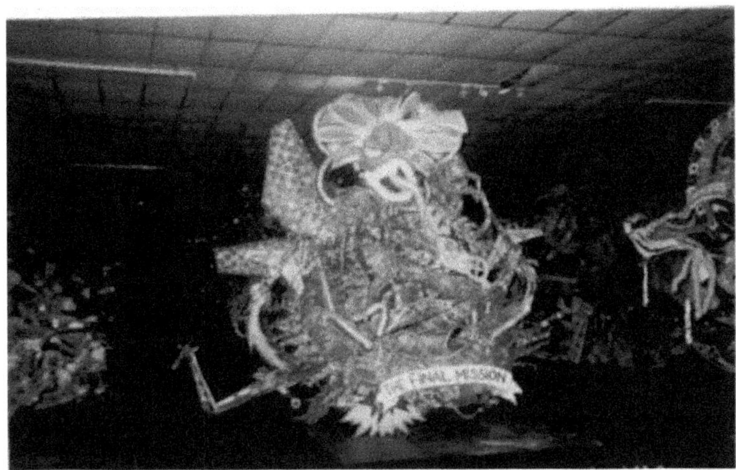

Junkanoo Costume, The Final Mission, as displayed at Junkanoo Expo, 1997. Costume was created by John Beadle and Jackson Burnside III (designers and builders), pasted and decorated by Jonathan Adderley, Derek St. Claude, Edgar Tucker and Gary St. Louis. (Photo Credit: Author)

Significantly, the Junkanoo Museum started to reproduce some of the cyclical practices inherent in Junkanoo. On a yearly basis the museum's staff would destroy the majority of the costumes on exhibition to make room for the newest ones. In this way the museum interceded in, yet reproduced, the cycle of renewal and destruction evident in Junkanoo. Indeed, parts of the costumes removed from the museum could reappear in upcoming parades. As a museum that destroys, the Junkanoo Expo's collection and annual active deaccession policies reflect some of the long-standing local practices that have surrounded the temporary use and display of Junkanoo costumes in Bahamian society.

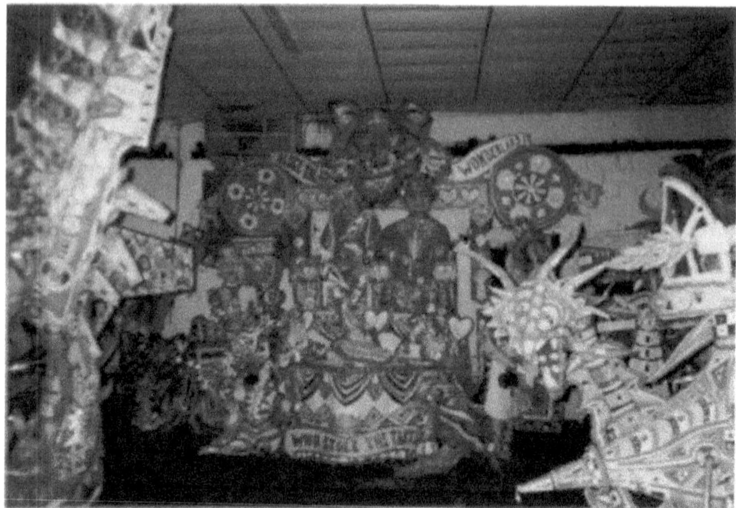

Junkanoo Costume, Who Stole the Tarts, 1997 (Photo Credit: Author)

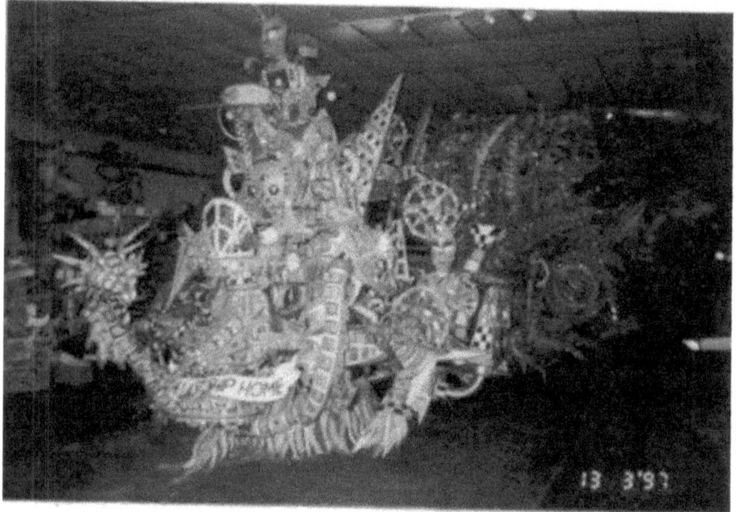

Junkanoo Costume, Last Ship Home, 1997 (Photo Credit: Author)

Author Biographies

Christine Chivallon is an anthropologist and geographer, and director of research, employed by the CNRS (National Center of Scientific Research) in France. Her studies are focused on space and identity, mainly in Caribbean societies and through Caribbean migration in Europe, including research on memory of slavery. Among her major recent works are *The Black Diaspora of the Americas. Experiences and Theories out of the Caribbean,* Kingston, Ian Randle Publishers, 2011; "On the Registers of Caribbean Memory of Slavery", *Cultural Studies,* Vol. 22 (6) pp. 870-891, 2008. Her latest book is *L'esclavage, du souvenir á la mémoire. Contribution á une anthropologic de la Caraibe* (Paris, Karthala, 2012).

See: http://www.lam.sci-encespobordeaux.fr/pageperso/chivallon.htm

Alissandra Cummins, GCM, BA (Hons), MA, FMA, is the Director of the Barbados Museum & Historical Society. She is a recognized authority on Caribbean heritage, museum development and art, and has lectured in Heritage Studies, Caribbean Art and Museums at the University of the West Indies for almost two decades. Her research interests include Caribbean art history, museum history and theory, heritage studies and heritage resource management. She was awarded Barbados' Gold Crown of Merit (GCM) in 2005.

Ms. Cummins was instrumental in establishing the Museums Association of the Caribbean, serving as its founding President, and is a Fellow of the

Museums Association (FMA, UK). She was elected President of the International Council of Museums (ICOM), the first woman and first to serve from the region from 2004 until 2010. She was also President of the International Association for Caribbean Archaeology (IACA). Ms. Cummins has also served variously as: Chairperson of UNESCO's Intergovernmental Committee for Promoting the Return of Cultural Property to its Country of Origin or its Restitution in Case of Illicit Appropriation (ICPRCP), 2003-2005; Chairperson of the International Advisory Committee of UNESCO's Memory of the World Programme, 2007-2009. Ms. Cummins also served as Vice President and Rapporteur of UNESCO's prestigious World Heritage Committee between 2008-2011. In November 2011, she was elected Chairperson of the Executive Board of UNESCO until 2013.

Ms. Cummins was recently appointed Editor in Chief of the *International Journal of Intangible Heritage.* She has co-edited *Curating in the Caribbean* (2012) with David Bailey, Allison Thompson and Axel Lapp. She has also contributed to various publications including *Art and Cultural Heritage: Law, Policy and Practice,* and *History Workshop Journal.* More recently she has contributed to a number of heritage publications including M L Stefano, P Davis, and G Corsane, G (eds) (2012), *Touching the Intangible: Safeguarding Intangible Cultural Heritage* and Basil Reid (ed), *Caribbean Heritage* (2012); as well as B-T Albert, R Bernecker, and B Rudolff (eds), *Understanding Heritage: Paradigms in Heritage Studies* (2013) and *The Encyclopaedia of Caribbean Archaeology* (forthcoming 2013).

Luisa De Peña Díaz holds a Bachelor of Arts Degree in Interior Design with a Master's degree in Museology and Museography specializing in Management, Economy and Financing of Museums, as well as in recovery of repression archive. She is Director/CEO of the Memorial Museum of Dominican Resistance

She is former Chairperson of ICOM Dominican Republic (2007-2010), Board Member of ICMEMO (2007-2010), Caribbean Region Coordinator and liaison with MAC for ICOMLAC (2007-2010), Legal Affairs Standing Committee of ICOM (2008-2011) and Member of the National Programme Committee of AAM (2008-2009), and ICOM Executive Council member (2010-2013).

Ms. De Peña has conducted many national and international conferences and has received several international awards and published her research over more than 20 years. Her recent interventions include: *Museums as Agents of Social Change,* Florianopolis University, Brazil (2008); *Management of Museums and the Social Reality of the Americas,* Catholic University of Ecuador (2008); *The Memorial Museum of Dominican Resistance,* University of Salamanca, Spain (2008); *History of the Dictatorial Regimes in Latin America: Their Development and Mutual Comparison,* Terezin, Czech Republic, 2009; *Historical Memory: Importance Worldwide,* Guatemala, 2009; *The Digitilización Collections and the Internet: Case of the Memorial*

Museum of Dominican Resistance and Recovery of Memory, AAM Meeting, Los Angeles, among others.

Kevin Farmer, MA, is the Deputy Director of the Barbados Museum & Historical Society (BMHS). He holds a Master's Degree in Heritage Studies from the University of the West Indies, Cave Hill, Barbados, and is currently pursuing doctoral studies in archaeology at the University of Sussex in the United Kingdom.

Formerly curator at the BMHS, from 2010 to 2011 he was Assistant Lecturer in Archaeology in the Department of History at the University of the West Indies, St. Augustine, Trinidad and currently delivers the Caribbean History and Heritage, and Landscapes of the Eastern Caribbean courses for the MA in Heritage Studies at the University of the West Indies, Cave Hill, Barbados.

Mr. Farmer was the principal researcher on the Barbados Museum's nomination to the UNESCO Memory of the World Register, examining the location and condition of extant documents relating to slavery and the slave trade in the Caribbean which resulted in the successful inscription of the Slave Trade archives housed at the Barbados Museum on the Memory of the World Register. He serves as an active member of the Barbados World Heritage Committee and is the Vice President of ICOMOS' Barbados Chapter.

Mr. Farmer is a contributing author for *Caribbean Heritage* (2012), *Protecting Heritage in the Caribbean* (2011) and *The Encyclopaedia of Caribbean Archaeology* (forthcoming 2013). Mr. Farmer also authored the chapter entitled "Forward Planning: the Utilization of GIS in the Management of Archaeological Resources in Barbados", in *Archaeology and Geoinformatics: Case Studies from the Caribbean* (2008). His research interests include the creation of cultural identity in post-colonial states, the role of museums in national development and the management and curation of archaeological resources.

Professor Amareswar Galla, an alumnus of the Jawaharlal Nehru University, New Delhi, is Professor and Executive Director, International Institute for the Inclusive Museum, Copenhagen (www. inclusivemu-seum.org). He was formerly Professor of Museum Studies, University of Queensland, Brisbane and Professor and Director of Sustainable Heritage Development Programs, Australian National University, Canberra. Between 1994 and 1999 he was the International Technical Adviser for the transformation of Arts Councils, National Museums and the South African National Parks Board in post-apartheid South Africa.

His work, listed as best practice in the 2009 World Culture Report by UNESCO, includes the establishment of World Heritage Areas as culture in poverty alleviation projects - Ha Long Bay and Hoi An, Vietnam and Darjeeling Himalayan Railway, India. His latest book *World Heritage: Benefits Beyond Borders,* Cambridge University Press & UNESCO Publishing, 2012, is the flagship project of the 40th Anniversary of the 1972

UNESCO World Heritage Convention. He is the Editor of *International Journal of the Inclusive Museum* and *International Journal on Environmental, Cultural, Economic and Social Sustainability* and former Editor-in-Chief of the *International Journal of Intangible Heritage.*

A champion of cultural democracy and UN Millennium Development Goals, Amar has been honoured internationally on several occasions including Outstanding Conservationist of the Year Award by the Vietnamese government in 2002; the European Best in Heritage Award in 2008; and the ICOM Australia 2012 Individual Achievement Award for Excellence for extensive and ongoing commitment to museums, sustainable development and poverty alleviation through culture.

Edward Cecil Harris, MBE, JP, PhD, FSA, is a native Bermudian and an archaeologist, and has directed the National Museum of Bermuda since late 1980. He is internationally known for his invention of the 'Harris Matrix' and its publication in 1979 in the seminal work, *Principles of Archaeological Stratigraphy,* a small book that has revolutionized methods of interpreting and recording on archaeological sites: the volume is available for free downloading at www.harrismatrix.com. Dr. Harris is the author of the fifteen-year study, *Bermuda Forts, 1612-1957,* and since early 2005 has published some 350 weekly articles in the local newspaper, under a column entitled 'Heritage Matters', which expound upon the history and heritage of the island and are much read and appreciated throughout the community. He lives with two black cats, and occasional friends, above one of the finest harbour and sea views in Bermuda, looking towards the setting sun and America.

José Linares Ferrera is a Cuban architect who graduated from Havana University in 1964 and also from the Architecture School of the Fine Arts Academy at the Charles University in Prague in 1967. In 2008 he was awarded a PhD in Sciences of Arts at the Higher Institute of Arts (ISA) in Cuba.

He has dedicated all his professional life to museology, museography and architectural interventions on buildings with patrimonial values. Linares has developed outstanding work on training personnel. He has also played a significant role in more than 80 projects for museums' adaptation, and the organization and assemblage of the Cuban network of museums, as well as leading technical assistance programmes for Latin American, Caribbean and African countries. From 1962 to 2001 he worked at the National Council for Cultural Heritage in the Cuban Ministry of Culture. Since 2001 he has worked for the Havana City Historian's Office as an architect and adviser.

Among his most important projects in recent decades are the renewal and museographic installation of the *José Marti Memorial* in the basement of the *José Marti Monument* at the Revolution Plaza in Havana (1994); *National Fine Arts Museum Complex* in Havana (1996-2001); venue of the *San Gerónimo de La Habana University School* in Old Havana (1999-2006); and restoration of the Napoleonic Museum in Havana (2011-2012).

Dr. Linares has been the Cuban representative to numerous symposia, seminars and expert meetings both in Cuba and abroad. In 1967 he joined the Cuban National Committee of ICOM and is currently the Executive Secretary of this organization. Since 2010 he has also been a member of the ICOMOS Cuban Committee. For his long-term dedication, expertise and transcendental contribution to the Cuban culture and to other nations, José Linares has often received awards. His latest award has been the National Prize from the National Committee on Landmarks in 2012 for the restoration of the Napoleonic Museum of Havana.

Hilde Neus-van der Putten was born in the Netherlands. After teaching in Tanzania she moved to Suriname in 1991. She majored in 'Dutch Language and Culture' at the University of Amsterdam in 2003. She has taught the subjects Dutch Language and Arts and Culture at high school. Since 2000 she has been working as the Education Officer for the Suriname Museum Foundation where she develops school programmes and builds exhibitions. Neus writes regular book reviews for the daily newspaper *de Ware Tijd* and articles on the museum in *Museumstof.* Since December 2009 she has taught at the Advanced Teacher Training College (IOL) on Colonial and Modern Literature and is now head of the Dutch Language department.

She published *Susanna du Plessis. Portret van een slavenmeesteres, a study of a cruel slave mistress* (KIT 2003). In 2007 she edited *Diversity is Power,* an anthology to commemorate the 5th International Literature Festival Suriname. She co-authored *Gerrit Schouten. Met meesterhand vervaardigd* (Libri Musei Surinamensis 4, 2008) with Laddy van Putten. A number of articles concerning her interests - Literature and History, have been published elsewhere.

Winston F Phulgence, BA, MA, is a lecturer in History at the Sir Arthur Lewis Community College in Saint Lucia. He received a BA in History from the University of the West Indies, St Augustine Trinidad and an MA in Anthropology from the University of Florida. His research interests include Caribbean prehistory and archaeology and cultural heritage management in the Caribbean. He recently co-authored "Patrimony or Patricide" with Dr. William F. Keegan in the book titled *Protecting Heritage in the Caribbean* (2011) edited by Peter E Siegel and Elizabeth Righter.

Veerle Poupeye is a Belgium-born, Jamaica-based art historian and curator specialized in the art and visual culture of the Caribbean and its Diaspora. She holds a Master's degree in Art History from the Universiteit Gent in Belgium and a PhD in Art History and Cultural Studies from Graduate Institute of the Liberal Arts of Emory University. She is currently Executive Director of the National Gallery of Jamaica and sits on the Board of Directors of the National Gallery of Jamaica and the Editorial Board of the Edna Manley College of the Visual and Performing Arts.

Veerle Poupeye's publications include *Caribbean Art* (1998), which was published in Thames and Hudson's World of Art series, and *Modern Jamaican Art* (1998), which she co-authored with David Boxer, and many journal articles and exhibition catalogue essays on Jamaican and Caribbean art and culture. She has previously worked as a Curator at the National Gallery of Jamaica, as Coordinator of the Visual Arts programme of the MultiCare Foundation and, most recently, at the Edna Manley College, where she served as Research Fellow and the Curator of the College's CAG[e] gallery and final year exhibitions. She has also taught Art History, Visual Studies and Curatorial Studies at the Edna Manley College of the Visual and Performing Arts in Kingston, Emory University in Atlanta and New York University.

Roslyn Russell, BA (Hons), MA (Hons), PhD, is a historian, editor and museum consultant who lives in Australia. Her doctoral dissertation dealt with 'Travel writers, museums and reflections of empire, 1770-1901', and she has written a number of books and articles on Australian history and literature. She is the co-author, with Kylie Winkworth, of two guides for assessing the significance of cultural heritage objects and collections, *Significance* (2001) and *Significance 2.0* (2009), and has conducted workshops on significance assessment in Australia and Barbados.

She was Managing Editor of *Museums Australia Magazine* from 2000 to 2009; and the *Friends of the National Museum of Australia Magazine* from 2004 to 2011, and has been Editor of the *Friends Review* of the Australian Federation of Friends of Museums since 2009. She chaired the International Advisory Committee of the UNESCO Memory of the World Programme from 2009 to 2013, and its Register Sub-Committee from 2007-2009, and has conducted workshops for the Programme in Australia, Barbados, Saint Lucia, South Korea, Iran and Indonesia. Dr Russell's consultancy practice, Roslyn Russell Museum Services, has developed content for exhibitions of Barbados and Caribbean history and art since the mid-2000s, beginning with the Museum of Parliament and National Heroes Gallery in the Parliament Buildings in Bridgetown, Barbados. Her illustrated e-book on Barbados' history and heritage, *Barbados: More Than A Beach,* was published in 2011. She continues to work on museum exhibition projects in Barbados.

Mike G. Rutherford, BSc (Hons), MAppSc, graduated with a Bachelor's Degree in Zoology from the University of Glasgow, Scotland in 1998, and completed a Master's degree in Conservation Biology at James Cook University, Townsville, Australia. He then worked as a zookeeper at Newquay Zoo in Cornwall, England, then for Glasgow Museums, based at the Kelvingrove Museum. Commencing work there as a research assistant in Natural History, he soon became Curator of Non-Insect Invertebrates. A big refurbishment project was underway at Kelvingrove Museum and he was responsible for the development of several major displays, including *Nature's Record Breakers, Wildlife in Danger, The Last Pearl Fishers, Animal Armouries* and *Animal Speak.*

After working there for seven years he moved to Trinidad to take up the brand new post of Zoology Curator for the University of the West Indies Zoology Museum. Since then he has been cataloguing the collections, and helping students, staff and foreign researchers to use the collection. He recently began a PhD on a biological recording system for Trinidad and Tobago with a focus on land snails. He is an active member of the Museums Association of the Caribbean and was on the Board for 2012. He also serves on the committees of the Trinidad and Tobago Field Naturalists' Club and The Asa Wright Nature Centre, and is Deputy Chair of the UWI St. Augustine Campus Museum Committee.

Nigel Sadler graduated from Manchester University in 1986 with a degree in Geography and Archaeology. After spending two years in the Middle East and two years in Britain as a field archaeologist, Nigel moved into Museum Management. After working in London for eight years he moved to become Director of the Turks and Caicos National Museum in 2000, a post he held for seven years. In the Turks and Caicos Islands Nigel began to research the slave history of the country, especially the legacy of the slave ship *Trouvadore* which was wrecked in 1841. His aim was also to make the museum more inclusive for the local population, highlighted by his introduction of the Museum's Children's Club and the annual Museum Day.

He returned to Britain in 2007 to set up Sands of Time Consultancy to work on projects to commemorate the Bicentenary of the end of the British slave trade and to work on projects in the Caribbean to make museums more inclusive. In 2009 and 2010 Nigel worked as a Museum Development Officer in London, but still carried out small projects with his company Sands of Time Consultancy, and at the end of 2010 returned to full-time self-employment. Since 2000 Nigel has been an active member of the Museums Association of the Caribbean (President 2003-2006, Vice President 2008-2011) and since 2004 has been active in ICOM, joining the board of ICOM UK in 2011 and was nominated to ICOM Disaster Relief Task Force in 2011.

Valika Smeulders, PhD, studied Languages and Cultures of Latin America at the University of Leiden. As a freelance journalist and researcher she specializes in diversity in the Netherlands, focusing on the position of the Dutch Antillean community in Dutch society. She is especially interested in the heritage of colonial slavery and the way this is dealt with nowadays in different countries. She is co-author of *Op zoek naar de Stilte: Sporen van het slavernijverleden in Nederland* (KITLV, 2007), a book on heritage institutions and slavery heritage in the Netherlands. In "Exhibiting The Heritage of Slavery", published in *Living History: Encountering the Memory of the Heirs of Slavery* edited by A.L. Araujo (Cambridge Scholars Publishing, 2009) she compares the organization and reception of a traveling slavery exhibition in Suriname and Curaçao.

For her PhD thesis at Erasmus University Rotterdam, she travelled to Ghana and South Africa as well. Thus she explores the roles of locality and globalization on both sides of the Atlantic in presentations of the slavery past and their audiences in her dissertation, *Slavernij in perspectief. Mondialisering en erfgoed in Suriname, Ghana, Zuid-Afrika en Curaçao. (Slavery in perspective. Globalization and heritage in Suriname, Ghana, South Africa and Curaçao).*

Krista Thompson, PhD, born in Nassau, Bahamas, is Associate Professor of Art History at Northwestern University and the author of *An Eye for the Tropics* (2006). She has written articles in *Art Bulletin, Art Journal, American Art, Representations, The Drama Review,* and *Small Axe,* and curated several exhibitions, including the *National Exhibition (NE3)* (2006) and *Developing Blackness: Studio Photographs of "Over the Hill" Nassau in the Independence Era* (2008) at the National Art Gallery of the Bahamas.

A J. Paul Getty Foundation postdoctoral fellowship recipient (2008), Thompson was awarded the David C. Driskell Prize from the High Museum of Art in Atlanta, Georgia in 2009, which recognizes "original and important contributions to the field of African-American art or art history." Thompson is currently the recipient of a fellowship from the American Council of Learned Societies (ACLS) and is completing the manuscript *The Visual Economy of Light in African Diasporic Practice* on the intersections among black vernacular forms of photography, performance practices, and contemporary art in the Caribbean and the United States (forthcoming, Duke University Press). She is also working on a transnational exhibition on contemporary performance art in the Caribbean with co-curator Claire Tancons.

Rebecca Tortello holds a PhD in Comparative Education and Sociology from Columbia University, a Master's degree from the Harvard Graduate School of Education, a Bachelor's Degree with Honours in History and Literature from Harvard University and a Certificate in Museum Studies, also from Harvard University.

Before returning home to Jamaica Dr. Tortello was an Assistant Professor of Education at New York's Adelphi University where, among other general education courses, she developed and taught the university's first course in museum education. Since 2005 Dr. Tortello has lectured in the Department of Education at the University of the West Indies, Mona. She is the author of a number of articles on education as well as the popular history book, *"Pieces of the Past.'"* Dr. Tortello has also produced material for two Caribbean early childhood series, and has authored a number of children's books.

From 2007-2011, Dr. Tortello was a Senior Advisor to Jamaica's Minister of Education. She has also served on the boards of early childhood institutions, the National Council on Education, the Early Childhood Commission, the Jamaica Library Service, the Council of the Institute of Jamaica (IOJ) and the Jamaica National Commission for UNESCO, where she was appointed Jamaica's representative to International Bureau of Education. In addition, while Chairman of the (IOJ) Board of Museums of History and Ethnography, Dr. Tortello strengthened educational and family programming and was instrumental in establishing a foundation focused on creating a national museum of the Jamaican people, in which she remains actively involved.

Marie-Lucie Vendryes holds a degree in Art History, a Masters and a D.E.A. in Museology from the Université du Québec in Montréal and the Université de Bourgogne in Dijon. She has worked in Haiti as an adviser to several institutions and organisations in the establishment of museum projects, most notably the Numismatic Museum of the Bank of the Republic of Haiti, *La Route de I'Esclave,* and the City Hall of Pétion-Ville. In 2004 she was appointed Director-General of the Musée du Panthéon National Haïtien. In 2010 she participated in the project of the Haiti Cultural Recovery Center, overseeing the restoration of the private collection of paintings of the Centre d' Art, which had been rescued from under the rubble. She has also worked on the important collection of ethnographical objects from the Lehmann collection.

She has taught museum studies for the Master's program Histoire, Mémoire et Patrimoine of the Université d'État d'Haiti. She is the author of several articles on museums in Haiti, and has presented many communications on cultural objects. She is a board member of the Fondation Culture Creation, and is a founding member of *Fragments et traces d'Haiti* and of *Muséofil,* both for the preservation and the valorization of Haitian cultural heritage. She now lives in Montréal, Québec where she works freelance.

Index

A

C

D

E

F

G

H

J

K

L

M

N

O

P

Q

R

S

T

U

V

W

Z

www.ingramcontent.com/pod-product-compliance
Lightning Source LLC
LaVergne TN
LVHW020506100826
845148LV00003B/711

9781612290737